Terra Australis reports the results of archaeological research, in the main of staff and students of the Department of Prehistory, Research School of Pacific Studies, The Australian National University.

Its region is the lands south and east of Asia, though mainly Australia, New Guinea and Island Melanesia, that were *terra australis incognita* to generations of European prehistorians today.

Its subject is the settlement of the diverse environments in this isolated quarter of the globe by peoples who have maintained their discrete and traditional ways of life into the recent recorded or remembered past and at times into the observable present.

Terra Australis

2

OL TUMBUNA

Archaeological excavations in the Eastern Central Highlands, Papua New Guinea

J. Peter White

Department of Prehistory, Research School of Pacific Studies

The Australian National University   Canberra

1972

Printed and manufactured in Australia by Canberra Publishing & Printing Co. Pty. Ltd.

Registered in Australia for transmission by post as a book

National Library of Australia card no. and ISBN 0 909846 01 4

FOREWORD

Situated between Indonesia, Oceania and Australia, the huge island of New Guinea straddles the cultural geography of an entire region and is strategically placed to encompass its culture history.   Its myriad small scale societies have long made it a classic region for ethnographic research and the names associated with it, Miklukho-Maklai, Haddon, Seligmann, Thurnwald, Malinowski, Fortune, Bateson, Mead, read like a history of anthropology itself.   The slowness of European penetration of the interior has meant the continuing discovery into our own generation of untouched stone-using horticultural communities and the consequent development of the region as a focus for ethnographic attention of the most varied kind.

Yet, while the cultural and linguistic complexity of the traditional societies of New Guinea, and their artistic vitality and variety, have encouraged culture-historical speculation on an extensive scale, it is barely a decade since serious archaeological work began there.   Also, though the region offers unique opportunities for pursuing archaeological research in an ethnographic context, the number of archaeological projects is still small.

The present volume, which reports some of the results of one of these, is therefore a welcome and substantial addition to a small and insubstantial literature.   It presents reports on excavations carried out by Dr J. Peter White in the course of archaeological and ethno-archaeological fieldwork as one of the first research scholars in prehistory at the Australian National University and the first such scholar to work in New Guinea.   His was the second serious archaeological project to be carried out there, following Susan Bulmer's pioneering work in the Western Highlands in 1959-60.   In every sense then the present volume is a basic document in a new and important field.

Born in 1937, Dr White read History Honours at the University of Melbourne and after graduation tutored in the Department of History there.   In 1961 he was awarded a Commonwealth Scholarship for two years to read prehistoric archaeology in the Faculty of Archaeology and Anthropology at the University of Cambridge.   On the successful completion of his Cambridge studies he was awarded a post-graduate scholarship at ANU which he held from 1963 to 1967.   From 1967 to 1970 he was Assistant Curator of Anthropology at The Australian Museum, Sydney, from where he moved to his present position as lecturer in the Department of Anthropology at the University of Sydney.   He has continued to be active in New Guinea archaeological studies, concentrating particularly on the record and investigation of stone-tool manufacture and use amongst late contacted populations in the far Western Highlands District of the New Guinea interior.   He spent 1970 as a Harkness Fellow doing research on ethnographic stone-tool manufacture and use with Professor J.D. Clark at the Department of Anthropology of the University of California at Berkeley.   His publications include a number of general articles discussing some of the exciting perspectives in New Guinea prehistory that the limited archaeological explorations of the past decade or so have opened up.

Jack Golson

PREFACE

The excavations reported here were carried out in 1964-5 when I was a Research Scholar in the prehistory section of the Department of Anthropology and Sociology, The Australian National University. They were presented, with other material, as a PhD dissertation in 1967. For reasons of economy some of the more detailed descriptions of artifacts and minutiae of excavation and analytical procedures have been omitted from this report, but I have tried to give sufficient information to allow other workers to reanalyse the material if desired. There are some minor differences between the data presented here and those given in the thesis and published elsewhere. They arise from a thorough rechecking of all notes and calculations prior to publication, so that this should be the most accurate account of the excavation available. Errors doubtless remain, for which I alone am responsible. All the material is now housed in The Australian Museum, Sydney.

J. Peter White
March 1972

CONTENTS

FIGURES

PLATES

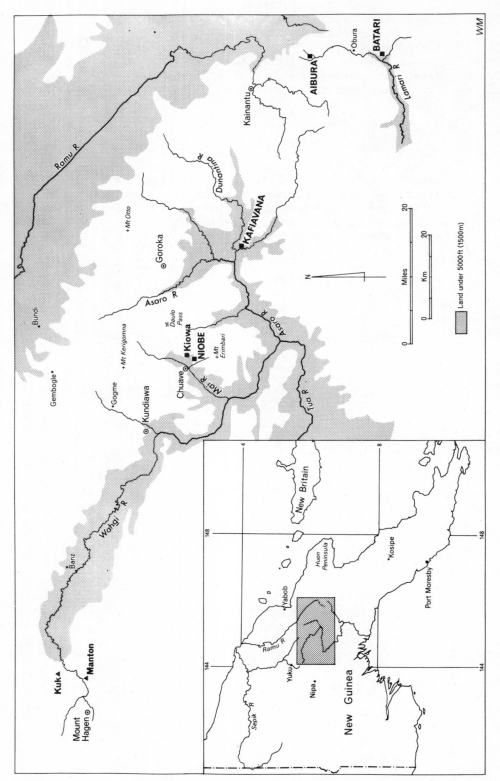

Fig.1 Locality map

I INTRODUCTION

THE PROBLEM

Synchronic data apart, the prehistory of the Central Highlands of Papua-New Guinea was unknown until 1959-60 when S. Bulmer surveyed the area from Mt Hagen to Chuave, finding rockshelters, house depressions, burials, buried ditches, salt and axe-stone sources and rock paintings. She subsequently excavated at the rockshelters of Kiowa (Chuave) and Yuku (Baiyer River) (S. Bulmer n.d., 1964a, 1964b, 1966a, 1966b; S. and R. Bulmer 1964). Later fieldworkers have concentrated primarily on open village and agricultural sites (Golson *et al.* 1967; Lampert 1967; D. Cole pers. comm.), rockshelters (White 1965a, 1965b, 1967, 1969; Kobayashi pers. comm.) and axe-stone sources (Chappell 1966).

The primary problem when this study began in 1963 seemed to be the need for spatial and temporal frameworks. How typical and widespread was the industrial tradition discovered by Bulmer? For example, did it extend eastwards from the Mt Hagen-Chuave area into the Asaro valley-Kainantu region which anthropologists (Read 1954), linguists (Wurm 1961) and physical anthropologists (Macintosh *et al.* 1958) had seen as different in many ways? What was the time-depth of this tradition? What ecological and economic information could be recovered, especially in relation to the presumed 'neolithic revolution' in Highlands prehistory?

A second, more methodological problem was the extent to which ethnographic studies of present-day agriculturalists, especially their technology, could be used directly to assist in the interpretation of the archaeological record. This work has been reported elsewhere (White 1967, 1968a).

The following chapters therefore set out the archaeological data related to the primary problem. The archaeological material comes from caves and rockshelters which were chosen as likely to provide a record of a longer continuous sequence of events than open sites. They should thus provide a time scale for and a general picture of changing technology and economy in the Highlands.

THE AREA

Only a brief and general account can be given of the geology, climate, flora and fauna of the area, since few detailed data are available.

In the Eastern Highlands the terrain is dominated by massive ranges aligned WNW-ESE. Between these, and about 5-7000 ft (1550-2150 m) below them, lie valleys with floors at 4-6000 ft (1250-1850 m) asl. In the main valleys at least, original stands of forest are rare and grassland or secondary growth predominates. In the Kainantu area the country is more undulating than further west and the grasslands are more noticeable. Over most of the area the rainfall is 40-80 in. (100-200 mm) annually, with a drier season in May-August (Brookfield and Hart 1966).

The marsupial fauna is considerable. Much of it is restricted to forested areas, where the largest mammal is the tree kangaroo (*Dendrolagus*), which weighs less than 20 lb, and the largest bird is the cassowary (*Casuarius*), which may weigh up to 100 lb.

Nearly all the present human population lives in the valleys at altitudes of less than 8000 ft (2500 m). The very high population densities in some areas show that the region is generally capable of intensive agricultural exploitation (Brookfield 1964:25-9).

The sites reported here all lie on the floors or lower slopes of the valley systems (fig.1). Batari and Aibura are both on the upper Lamari

River, within the river-cut gorge (Dow and Plane 1965) which is grassed up to 6500 ft (2000 m) or more.   Kafiavana lies at almost the lowest point in the Asaro valley, near the junction of the Asaro, Dunantina and Fayantina Rivers, and is surrounded by grassland for a considerable distance (Haantjens 1970). Niobe lies on the eastern edge of the Chimbu-Wahgi system, on the backslope of Mt Erimbari, in a widespread area of gardens and secondary bush.

   All sites are thus well within the altitudinal zone of modern occupation (Brookfield 1964:20-4) and probably lie within the zone of earlier occupation, which is normally assumed to be below about 6000 ft (1850 m) (S. and R. Bulmer 1964:51).   The sites may therefore be taken to represent, to some extent, the use of caves and rockshelters throughout the prehistoric period.

II FIELD METHODS AND ANALYTICAL PROCEDURES

All excavations and the analyses of material from them have been carried out according to the same basic principles, definitions and procedures which are described in this chapter. Modifications required by particular problems are described in the appropriate site chapter.

EXCAVATIONS

The excavation techniques were designed to produce the following data, limited only by time, money and available manpower:

1. stratified dated sequences of artifactual material;

2. the position of implements in sufficient detail to allow for the discovery of horizontal and vertical distribution patterns (Matthews 1964);

3. all possible floral, faunal and other environmental data;

4. information about the material in the deposit and the way this was built up.

A base line was laid out and a datum point fixed, usually by hammering a nail into the cave wall. The site was then gridded into excavation units of 1 m square, which were lettered in one direction and numbered in the other. Deposit was mostly removed with triangular-headed paint scrapers, brushes and ash shovels. The excavation units were 5 or 10 cm spits, depending on conditions at that point in the deposit. At all times the trend of the visible stratigraphy was followed as closely as possible, with spit depths being adjusted accordingly. The depth below datum at the base of each spit was measured at nine points with a tape and line level. Except at Aibura, all excavation was done by the author or C. White.

The position of all artifacts recognised *in situ* was recorded three dimensionally by relating the artifact to two designated sides of its metre square and by recording its depth below datum. All artifacts so recorded were numbered sequentially within each square and both square and number were written on the artifact. A record was made of the spit from which each artifact came. The rest of the deposit was then screened through $\frac{1}{4}$" mesh plastic sieves by local labourers, usually 12-16 year old youths. From the retained fraction they removed all bone, shell, worked stone and other foreign material. I inspected all sieves before any remaining material was dumped. Later the retained material was washed and I roughly sorted it in the field.

Samples for radiocarbon dating were taken wherever a hearth or congregation of charcoal lumps was found. Owing to the small amount of macroscopic carbon in most sites, and a misunderstanding on my part as to the total amount of carbon required for dating purposes (see Polach and Golson 1966:24-6), I took fewer good samples than I would now like to have done. The position, nature and environment of each sample were recorded.

Samples of all characteristic soils were taken from each site. In three sites a vertical column sample, consisting of a bag of soil, was taken from each alternate 10 cm. The position of all samples was recorded.

FAUNAL ANALYSIS

A wide range of faunal remains was found at all sites. Mammals, both wild and domesticated or feral, predominated, while birds, reptiles, mollusca and fish also occurred.

Ideally, faunal collections from archaeological sites should be analysed to provide maximum information about the 'cultural filter' through which they have passed (Reed 1963). For example, the range of animal types represented, when contrasted with the total faunal picture of the area today, will give some idea of hunting specialisation, environmental and cultural changes in past times, and also the environments exploited by prehistoric men. The relative numbers of different bones of a particular species may also provide information about prehistoric butchering techniques. The amount of meat represented by the bones has sometimes been used as a basis for inferring human population size (Heizer 1960).

The use of only mandibles and maxillae in discussing faunal collections is not normally recommended. While they may be useful in discussing some specialised questions (e.g. Higgs and White 1963), some features of the fauna may be overlooked. For example, if some heads are removed at the kill spot, there will appear to be fewer animals at the campsite than there really are. In the present collections, mandibles and maxillae represent 5%-25% of the total number of identifiable bones. The standard for archaeological collections seems to be 15% or less (King 1962; Coon 1951). Even this is considerably higher than any theoretical expectation (1%-2%) and must be attributed to overrepresentation of the more robust bones of animals due to some material being eaten by scavengers, burned or overlooked by the excavator. The reasons for the very large numbers of mandibles in some Highlands sites will be discussed later.

There are two main reasons why the Highlands present a difficult problem to the prehistorian interested in faunal questions:

1. Knowledge of the local fauna is very fragmentary. The current taxonomy is based almost entirely on skull (especially dentition) and skin forms (Tate 1948; Laurie and Hill 1954:115-16; Zeigler and Lidicker 1968). It has been common zoological practice not to preserve post-cranial skeletons, so that, in Australia, there were no collections of these available for comparative study by the archaeologist. While many excavated post-cranial bones could probably be identified by a specialist, the few experts are unable to find time for such a laborious task. Consequently none of the excavated post-cranial bone was identified.

2. The habitats and sizes of local animals are too badly known to allow many deductions about the meaning of faunal assemblages to be made. Some data of this kind were obtained from H.M. Van Deusen and are given in Appendix 1. He points out (pers. comm.) that until animals are clearly identified to specific level, many environmental inferences are of doubtful validity. He stresses that although the exact habitat of individual animals is known in thousands of cases, it is at present rather dangerous to generalise about any species of mammal in New Guinea as there are so many variables involved. Nevertheless, he is optimistic that the occurrence of different mammal species at different altitudes in the Highlands will eventually be put to good use in assessing the altitudinal zones in which prehistoric hunting occurred. One obvious difficulty in applying this idea, however, comes from the fact that today many Highlanders hunt over a wide altitudinal range. Therefore, any prehistoric alteration in the altitudinal zonation of a species, however caused, may not be detected, since the hunters may simply catch the animal downhill from the camp site rather than uphill.

In spite of the uncertainties of the present situation, and using only mandibles and maxillae, I have made some inferences about the fauna, assuming that the ecology and ethology of each species have remained largely unchanged during the Holocene. The relative proportions of animals hunted are deduced by assuming that prehistoric practices are similar to modern ones and that a random selection of animals is brought back to the site for butchering. Change in the proportions of animals present at different times has allowed some environmental inferences to be drawn, though these are gross since habitat information is so limited. Some suggestions are made concerning the age and importance of domestic animals in the Highlands. All these inferences are limited, but they are more than is normally done with Australian-type fauna from archaeological sites (McCarthy 1964; Wakefield 1964; cf. Jones 1966). The limitations will remain until some systematic well identified collections of post-cranial bones are available for comparative study and more detailed studies of the ecology of a number of Highlands mammals have been published (cf. Van Deusen and Keith 1966).

As is the case with most archaeological faunas, nearly all mandibles were broken at the symphysis and are technically half-mandibles. I follow common usage, however, in calling them mandibles. All mandibles and maxillae found in the sites were identified to order level, most to generic level, and some to species level. All mammal identifications (except rodents from Aibura) were made by the author or J.H. Calaby. Collections of skulls in The Australian Museum, in the Division of Wildlife Research, Commonwealth Scientific and Industrial Research Organisation, and the author's possession were used as the basis for classification. B.J. Marlow and J.H. Calaby advised on nomenclature.

The large collection of rodent mandibles and maxillae from Aibura site was identified by J.A. Mahoney. He points out (pers. comm.) that the current taxonomy of Highlands rodents is extremely confused and needs thorough revision using the large collections in the British Museum (Natural History) and the American Museum of Natural History. His identifications were used as a basis for work on other site collections. Mahoney also provided some information about the habitats of various rodent species.

All mandibles and maxillae were separately listed, sorted into left and right side and, with some animals, adult and juvenile. Within-spit fragments have been summed to make whole sides. From these counts, minimum numbers of animals can be calculated either for the site as a whole or for any part of it. In all cases, the largest number in one of the four units - left or right, mandibles or maxillae - is the minimum number of animals.

All mollusca were identified by D.F. McMichael, who also provided some information about habitats and advice about the uses to which certain genera are put by man.

Some birds, and all human remains, reptiles and fish were identified by specialists, whose reports are given in the respective site chapters.

ARTIFACT JOINS

Whenever any stone material was handled, an attempt was made to see whether broken implements could be joined together, flakes replaced onto their cores and so on. In many cases, of course, tools or flakes which were broken in antiquity remain close together, but in some cases they migrate both horizontally and vertically. Some causes of vertical migration of artifacts within a deposit have been discussed recently by Matthews (1965), who illustrates a possible instance of this but does not document the extent and percentage occurrence of migration. I suggest that this may be measured by joining artifacts together. It is clear that the amount of migration will vary greatly according to the site, the character of its soil, intensity of occupation and so on. Given thousands of waste flakes - and only these or potsherds provide a large enough sample - the physical problems are daunting, yet this method seems to hold most promise for a numerical assessment of the problem.

In these sites I have been able to join very few pieces and, since analysis was done by vertically rather than horizontally adjacent units, it may appear that there was relatively rather more vertical movement than actually occurred. In spite of these limitations one or two points of interest have emerged which will be discussed in relation to particular sites.

STONE TOOL ANALYSIS

S. Bulmer (n.d., 1964a, 1966a) has defined many of the formal tool types which occur in the Highlands industries, such as axe-adzes, waisted blades, and pebble tools. Some comments on her classes and my use of them are given below. These groups, however, make up only a small proportion of the stone tools found in the excavations. The majority are small, morphologically heterogenous, flaked tools which present major analytical problems. These have been discussed in detail elsewhere (White 1969) and will only be outlined in this section.

Axe-adzes

Like S. and R. Bulmer (1964:53) I define all pieces of ground stone which resemble those hafted and used as axes or adzes in recent times as 'axe-adze' or 'axe'. In the absence of the haft there is no way of distinguishing blades hafted as axes from those hafted as adzes (S. Bulmer 1964a:247-8). It should be noted that native informants are also often unable to make this distinction (Strathern 1965:185).

The terms used in the description of these tools follow closely the definitions given by Davidson (1961) for Polynesian adzes, with two modifications:

1. With symmetrical Highlands axes it is immaterial which face of the tool is towards the observer, since no distinction can be made between faces.

2. The cross-sections recorded by Davidson were amplified by S. Bulmer (1964a) who used the term 'planilateral' to refer to axes which are basically lenticular but have flat sides. I have adopted this term.

The two most important features of Highlands axes are usually taken to be the presence of grinding and the shape of the cross-section, which is claimed to have pan-Melanesian cultural and chronological significance (e.g. Riesenfeld 1950). S. Bulmer (1964a) has already pointed out that an axe blade with two sides and two faces is not necessarily 'quadrangular'. It should also be noted that there has been no study of any collection of Highlands axes to show that a particular type of cross-section can be consistently defined and metrically separated from its neighbours. This could be demonstrated by a cross-section index, perhaps the ratio between thickness at the centre and at the side of an axe (cf. Roe 1964). The graphic picture of the cross-sections could be compared between areas, thus avoiding subjective judgements. Only then will one be able to test, for example, the claim that 'planilateral' and 'oval-lenticular' sectioned axes are characteristic of the Western and Eastern Highlands respectively (S. Bulmer 1964a). Inspection of collections in The Australian Museum and the Department of Prehistory, The Australian National University, suggests that there *is* an increase in 'flat-sidedness' from east to west, but exactly how this is expressed and what it means have not been determined.

The same general criticisms may be applied to statements about the temporal priority of lenticular axes (S. Bulmer 1964a, 1966a; S. and R. Bulmer 1964), with the additional point that the numbers involved are statistically insignificant (S. Bulmer 1966a:108a,129a).

Waisted Blades

These axe-like implements have a pronounced indentation flaked on each side (S. Bulmer 1964a:267). The indentations occur either as a pair of notches ('waisted') or as a reduction in width of the butt part ('shouldered'). The flaking is similar to that on axes and some implements are wholly or partly ground.

S. Bulmer has also included within this definition unground or slightly ground blades which are markedly widest at the cutting edge with 'a slight reduction in their sides, giving a concave appearance' (1964a:252). This definition may include some axe-adzes and the presence of these specimens underlines the difficulties of separating axes and waisted blades into two absolute categories. One useful method of distinguishing the groups may be the construction of length and breadth indices.

Pebble Tools

S. Bulmer (1966a:87) defines pebble tools as implements made by steep flaking to produce a working edge on a water-worn pebble or a thick flake from a water-worn stone. The dimensions of the finished tool are nearly those of the original pebble, with water-worn cortex generally being visible on more than one side.   The primary flaking, other than the working edge, which is present on a minority of these implements, seems to serve to flatten the pebble.   Elsewhere (S. Bulmer 1964a:262) she implies that pebble tools are distinctly larger than the normal run of flaked implements and also points out that the unifacial working is restricted to one end or side or two sides converging to a wide point (S. and R. Bulmer 1964:59) although 10% are 'aberrant' (S. Bulmer 1964a:263).

There are four problems apparent in this definition:

1.   Many Highlands artifacts not regarded as pebble tools by Bulmer are made on river pebbles, so that the name is an inexact one, although it serves to imply that these artifacts are similar to 'pebble tools' from Africa and Asia (Mason 1962; Cole 1964; Movius 1954-5; Walker and Sieveking 1962).

2.   It is not shown that the metrical limits of the class serve to distinguish this group from other tools made on pebbles (S. Bulmer 1964a:262-4, 1966a:112), a problem recognised by Movius in a different context (1954-5:261).

3.   The step-flaking which commonly occurs on these artifacts, although in widely varying amounts, is characteristic of a majority of artifacts within Highlands industries.   This feature then cannot be used to differentiate this group.

4.   The majority of flaked artifacts is unifacially worked and this feature is not one exclusive to pebble tools.

However, a group of 'pebble tools' may be subjectively selected from the industries at Kafiavana and Niobe and are clearly absent from Aibura and Batari.   These tools tend to be larger than normal flake tools, although the division is not an absolute one.   For example, of twenty-one 'pebble tools' at Kafiavana the smallest weighs 114 gm and there are nine 'non-pebble tools' heavier than this.   Pebble tools are commonly made in light-coloured non-greasy chert or coarser-grained rocks, whereas other flaked tools are commonly made of fine-grained darker, greasy cherts.   Further, they generally have a 'chunky' appearance, reminiscent of the Australian 'horsehoof' core (McCarthy 1967:18), although the amount of retouch may be inconsiderable. Pebble cortex frequently provides the unretouched side of a retouched edge, an uncommon feature on other flaked tools.

Although none of these attributes, even when taken in combination, serves to distinguish absolutely 'pebble tools' from other, smaller, flaked tools, it seems worthwhile admitting that this group may exist pending fuller definition, since its occurrence does appear to be geographically and temporally variable. The group is, therefore, distinguished in the 'intuitive' typology but included with other artifacts in the 'edge analysis'.

Large Flake Tools

This type includes both utilised flakes and worked flakes with a markedly thick side opposite the utilisation (S. Bulmer 1966a:88).   Of the fifteen examples at Yuku seven are utilised and eight retouched and all are metrically 'clearly separated' from other flake tools.   (Note that S. Bulmer (1966a:129a) wrongly gives the totals as 5 and 10 and appears to have reversed the stratigraphic position of the sub-groups (1966a:118-28)).   At Kiowa this group forms a continuous size series with smaller flake tools (S. Bulmer 1966a:88).   In all sites reported here this type could not be separated on the basis of size and is therefore not accepted.

Other Types

S. Bulmer records eight bifaces at Kiowa and Yuku (1966a:108a,129a) and five burins at Kiowa (1966a:108a).   Neither of these types was recognised in my material.

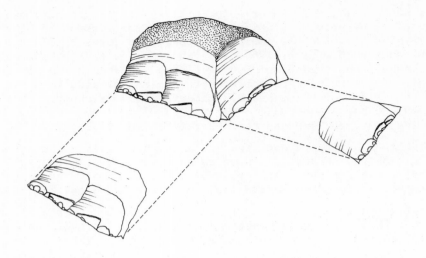

Fig.2   Method of drawing flaked implements

Flaked Implements

More than 90% of all retouched implements in the Eastern Highlands
industries would normally be called 'miscellaneous scrapers' (cf. Mulvaney
and Joyce 1965:182).   All collections of these implements show a very high
degree of similarity since they are largely composed of small, chunky,
morphologically unpatterned tools with a high incidence of step-flaking:
the method of drawing these artifacts is shown in fig.2.   Some tools are
utilised but not retouched; these are usually treated cursorily (Mulvaney
and Joyce 1965:175; Clark 1954:114) but are so characteristic of the Eastern
Highlands industries that they have been included in the detailed analyses.
        The typological methods used to analyse these implements have been
elaborated elsewhere (White 1967,1969).   Briefly, two typologies are used.
The first is an 'intuitive' one, similar in kind to those common in the
literature (e.g. McCarthy 1967; Bordes 1961; S. Bulmer 1966a).   The classes
used differ from S. Bulmer's in that they are based primarily on the position
of retouch in relation to the long axis of the tool.
        The other classification is an attribute analysis of retouched and used
edges.   The theoretical justification of this typology rests on ethnographic
observations which suggest that Highlanders use a piece of stone for a
particular task if it has features suitable for the work in hand, rather than
regarding a stone tool as a functional whole (White 1967,1968a; Strathern 1969).
An implement is not regarded primarily as a 'type' but simply as a piece of
stone with edges appropriately shaped for one or more particular functions.
This analysis, therefore, takes as its basic unit the 'altered edges' of
implements and considers other features of the implement only in relation to
each edge.   The term 'altered edge' is neutral with respect to purpose and
also allows both retouched and unretouched but used edges to be included in
the definition.   An 'altered edge' is defined as 'a length along the
intersection of two surfaces (planes) of stone, one or both of which surfaces
bear retouch or use-wear'.
        The code used to record the attributes of all retouched and used edges
and of the implements on which they occur took account of the following:

1.   location of the implement within the excavation;

2.   type of stone;

3.   size and shape of implement;

4.   nature of base and preparatory flaking;

5.   type, shape, size and angle of retouched edges;

6. type, shape, size and angle of use-wear on retouched and unretouched edges.

The IBM cards, data sheets and output for each site have been deposited with the Department of Prehistory, The Australian National University.

It must be stressed that, since the typology is based on individual edges, all observations were made in relation to these. No attempt was made, for example, to record the sequence in which altered edges were made or used on an implement, or the position of one altered edge in relation to another on the same implement. To include such data would have been difficult in practice. It would also have over-ridden the basic assumption which was that, within a fairly broad range, the makers of these implements were concerned with an individual edge for a specific function rather than with the implement as a whole.

Trimming Flakes

This name has been given to flakes whose dorsal surfaces carry considerable portions of retouch. The retouch normally occurs on the dorsal edge of the striking platform, but it may also run in a 'keel' down the dorsal surface or, occasionally, in other directions. It is usually truncated by the edges of the flake.

Trimming flakes can nearly always be distinguished from flakes which carry on their dorsal surfaces the record of several previous attempts to remove them from their cores. There is more retouch on a trimming flake and the retouch is longer than a few mm; in addition, this retouch is normally step-flaking and not the rather amorphous, deeply concave shattering that appears on ill-struck flakes. The flakes under discussion result from striking a large flake from an 'altered edge', normally using the base of this edge as a platform. The most likely interpretation of them is that they result from the premeditated removal of a heavily retouched and used edge so as to resharpen it. Some, of course, may result from the accidental removal of flakes during a retouching process and this is particularly likely to be true of those with a very small striking platform. In the Highlands industries, trimming flakes form quite a large percentage of artifacts which show signs of secondary retouch. This reinforces the idea that they are not occasional or accidental pieces but relate to particular stages in the process of creating and using an implement.

Cores

Most cores seem to have been used and retouched subsequent to their being cores and are included in the implement analyses.

Apart from these, there are only a few chunks and large flakes which have been used haphazardly as cores. The flaking seems to be entirely *ad hoc* with no attempt at preparing platforms or even consistent use of a single platform. No particular study of cores has been made. It is interesting to note that, in regard to its cores, the industry fits well within the Southeast Asian tradition (Walker and Sieveking 1962:113).

Waste Stone

Waste stone comprises all pieces of stone upon which no traces of secondary retouch or use were observed. Nearly all are flakes but a number of shattered, amorphous lumps are included. It is probable that some of these stones were used as tools, but short of examining all pieces under a microscope, this cannot be detected. However, most of this stone probably represents the unused by-product of knapping.

At all sites, samples were analysed to see whether the size of the waste material changed over time. The sizes were defined by fitting the stones into squares with sides measured in half inch units. The stones were laid with the largest dimension down, normally the bulbar surface for flakes.

Plate 1   Batari: A) environment, viewed from north.   The cave lies left of
             the foot of the foreground spur.   B) cave entrance.
             C) west face of square D3-4: horizontal scale in 20 cm.

10

III EXCAVATIONS AT BATARI, LAMARI RIVER VALLEY

THE SITE

Batari (B65) is the name given by the Tairora of Himarata village to a
small cave on the track from Himarata to Oraura, 6°36'S, 145°56'E. The site
lies about 5 miles (8 km) on a bearing of 195° from Obura Patrol Post, at an
altitude of 4200 ft (1300 m) (fig.1). Geologically the area falls within
the Lamari Conglomerate whose volcanics, tuffaceous sandstones and
calcarenites cover most of this region. Lenses of calcarenite up to 3 miles
long and 200 ft (60 m) thick are found within the Conglomerate (Dow and Plane
1965:12-14). The topography is extremely steep, with many rapidly incising
rivers. The hills are all grass-covered, mostly with *Imperata cylindrica*
and associated grasses; a few casuarina (*Casuarina papuana*) and pine
(probably *Araucaria*) trees grow close to streams and some rainforest can be
seen at the tops of the higher peaks. Gardens occur on river banks, as
irregular patches on hillsides and adjacent to the rainforest (pl.1a).
The area is sparsely populated.

Batari lies in a natural bridge of calcarenite over the Sorera River,
a fast-flowing tributary of the Lamari River. The bridge is formed at the
most easterly point of a strike belt of calcarenite which bears NW and SSW
from this spot. Where it crosses the river the calcarenite is about 60 m
wide, and on its east and west sides rises almost sheer for some 40 m above
the river. The cave is on the eastern side of the bridge, about 25 m above
the river (pl.1b). Its internal horizontal dimensions are about 15 x 7 m,
excluding a large pit falling to the river at the northern end (fig.3a-c).
The southern third of the cave is a 6 x 5 m chamber with 2-3 m of headroom
and without fallen blocks encumbering the present floor. The rest of the
cave is more irregular in both floor and roof and in the northern part there
is a steep slope towards the pit. When I visited Batari in the dry season
it was quite dry inside, with only occasional drips of water falling from the
roof in the central part of the cave. Many small stalactites can be seen on
the roof, particularly outside the southern entrance, while the eastern walls
are mostly formed of stalagmitic flowstone.

The cave has three entrances, one at the south end and two at the
northern end. The main entrance is the southern one, about 3 m wide and
3.5 m high. The northern entrances are smaller, more inaccessible and lie
just inside the dripline. All entrances are sheltered by casuarina and pine
trees, but even without these the sun would shine into the cave only for an
hour or two in the early morning.

The formation of the cave has not been studied by a geologist, but its
position and general shape suggest that the river may have run through it in
earlier times. This is reinforced by the presence in the lower part of the
deposit of many small river-rolled pebbles, unmodified by human agency.
Consolidated accumulations of similar pebbles can be seen in other crevices of
the natural bridge. From the configuration of the roof and walls and the
presence of fallen blocks just outside the present entrances, it seems likely
that there has been some opening-up of the forward part of an earlier, more
extensive cave. This collapse must have occurred many years ago as there are
no calcarenite blocks at the foot of the cliff below the cave.

There is a collection of fossilised bones incorporated in a small area of
the lower part of the stalagmitic eastern wall. The fauna represented is
similar to that found in the area at present (M.D. Plane pers. comm.) and the
deposit probably records a predator's den in the earlier cave.

Human occupation is indicated by many rock paintings outside the cave,
while inside there is a positive ochre handprint on the back wall of the
north part. Only the southern chamber, however, contains an archaeological

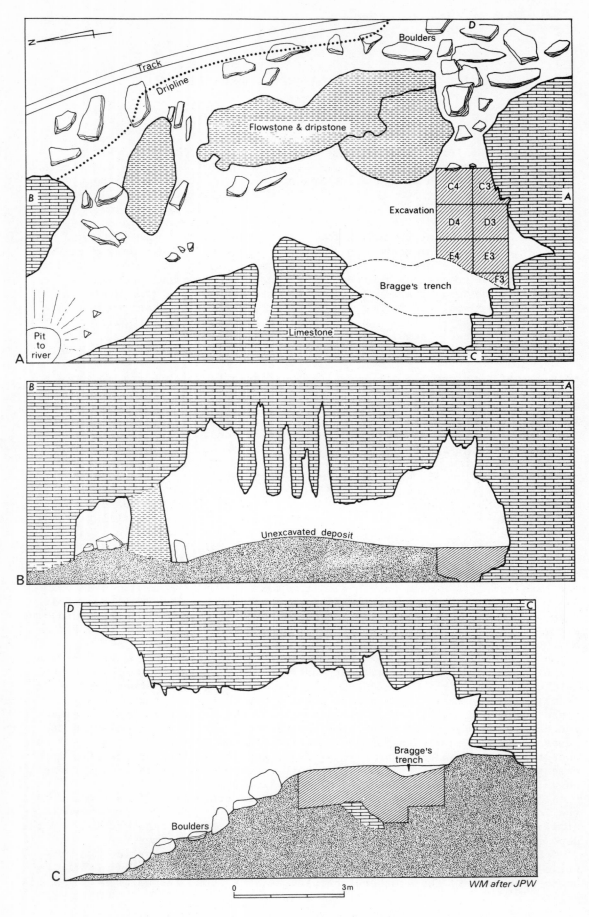

Fig.3   Batari: A) plan;   B,C) sections of cave

deposit, and its walls are heavily smoke-blackened.   Men from Himarata said
the cave was nowadays used only as an occasional shelter during gardening or
travelling.   There are certainly some legends connected with the cave and
rock-bridge but time and interpreter problems defeated my attempts to record
these.

Discovery and Excavation

Batari was located in 1962 by L. Bragge, then Cadet Patrol Officer with
the Department of District Administration, while he was on patrol.   He spent
one morning at the site and with local labourers excavated a trench approximately
4 x 1.5 x 1 m along the back wall of the southern chamber.   From this he
recovered two axes and seven flaked tools.   Mr Bragge was most helpful in
discussing his work and kindly donated the material he recovered from Batari
to the collection I excavated.

In April 1964 I made a small test excavation (White 1965b:335), the
material from which is included in the present analysis.   In June 1965 a
larger excavation was made.   The deposit was excavated as a series of levels
conforming to the general configuration of the hearth complex (see below),
which sloped down towards the front of the cave in squares C3 and C4 (fig.3c).
Excavation started just inside the southern entrance and moved into the cave.
This both increased the light for working and allowed the stratigraphy of
at least one face to be studied prior to excavation.

An area of 7 m^2 was excavated to a maximum depth of 160 cm.   Large
calcarenite boulders and encroaching walls hampered the lower part of the
excavation and, allowing for these, my excavation contained only about
5.7 m^3 of undisturbed deposit.   In addition about 2 m^3 of Bragge's infill
were removed and sieved to produce a large quantity of archaeological
material whose stratigraphic position is entirely unknown.   Only a few
important pieces such as axes and shell artifacts have been included in this
analysis, labelled 'unstratified'.   I estimate that about half the deposit
in Batari has now been removed.

The excavated soil could not be kept and used to backfill my excavation
because of the confined working space within and outside the cave.   Where
undisturbed deposit remained, a stone wall was built in front of it, but
otherwise the trench was left open.

Stratigraphy (fig.4a,b; pl.1c)

Only one major stratigraphic feature was observable in any profile at
Batari.   This was a white, black and cream complex of hearths which
stretched unbroken over the entire area of the excavation just below the
surface.   It and the material sealed beneath it were clearly undisturbed.
Above the hearth was a very fine dry grey sediment about the consistency of
flour, containing some cultural material.   It probably includes a good deal
of material thrown up from Bragge's trench, as well as *in situ* post-hearth
cultural material.   Owing to the softness of the floor, the two have been
thoroughly mixed together and the whole must therefore be considered as
unstratified.   Some heaps of bird-dung on the present surface show the cave
is now only intermittently visited.

The hearth complex, 1-13 cm thick, formed a hard, crusty layer over
most of the excavation, tailing out to a thin white ash along the south wall
of the cave.   The top of this complex lay 4-10 cm below present ground
surface.   There appear to be at least two periods of burning in this complex,
but I have no evidence as to the time between them.   One hearth could be
traced over at least 4 m^2 and must have been a very large fire.   The complex
is largely ash, with some burnt soil and carbonised wood; it contained only
two implements and a few animal bones.

Below the hearth complex, the deposit was a fine calcareous silt, with
some rounded granules of slightly cemented silt and a few angular calcarenite
fragments.   At greater depths the deposit became damper, darker and rather
more gritty, but retained the same high quantity of fine particles.   The
silt was alkaline throughout with a field pH ranging from 6.5 to 8.   Stones

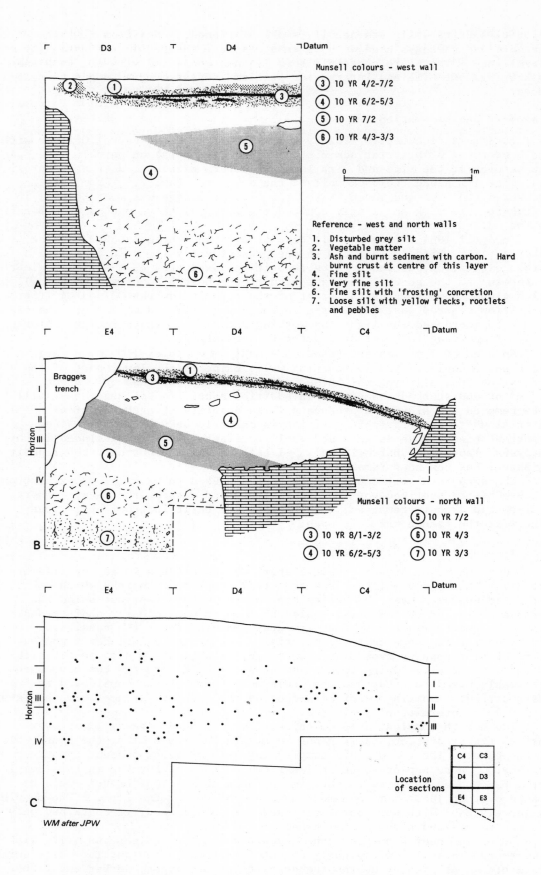

Datum

D3   D4   Datum

Munsell colours - west wall

③ 10 YR 4/2-7/2
④ 10 YR 6/2-5/3
⑤ 10 YR 7/2
⑥ 10 YR 4/3-3/3

0   1m

Reference - west and north walls

1. Disturbed grey silt
2. Vegetable matter
3. Ash and burnt sediment with carbon. Hard burnt crust at centre of this layer
4. Fine silt
5. Very fine silt
6. Fine silt with 'frosting' concretion
7. Loose silt with yellow flecks, rootlets and pebbles

E4   D4   C4   Datum

Bragge's trench

Horizon
I
II
III
IV

Munsell colours - north wall

③ 10 YR 8/1-3/2 ⑤ 10 YR 7/2
④ 10 YR 6/2-5/3 ⑥ 10 YR 4/3
       ⑦ 10 YR 3/3

E4   D4   C4   Datum

Horizon
I
II
III
IV

Location of sections

C4	C3
D4	D3
E4	E3

WM after JPW

Fig.4 Batari: A) stratigraphy of west wall; B) north wall; C) plot of implements from C4-E4 against north wall

14

were rare immediately beneath the hearth but small calcarenite cobbles and river-rolled pebbles of other materials became increasingly frequent with depth. Little carbon was seen at any level. Directly beneath the hearth the colour ranged from 10 YR 7/2 to 10 YR 5/3 on the Munsell scale. From 30 to 50 cm below this there was a consistent slight whitening of the deposit. Below this the colour darkened to 10 YR 4/4 and patches of calcium carbonate 'frosting' concreted the earth slightly. Many bones and stones in the lower part of the deposit were partly covered with calcareous concretions.

From 90 cm below the hearth several different layers of earth were banked against the south wall of the cave in squares F3 and parts of E3. In general fairly hard-packed, their colours ranged from 10 YR 7/3 to 10 YR 5/2, with one patch showing many yellow flecks. These earths were stone-free and without cultural material, although some spicules of carbon were collected from them. They were only some 40 cm thick and were not investigated in detail.

At the base of the excavation was a fine dark loose silt, without concretions but with many plant roots. Its colour was 10 YR 3/3 and it contained very slight traces of human occupation.

The deposit in this site can plausibly be derived from:

1. weathering of the parent calcarenite, which produced some of the grits (Cornwall 1958:30-1);

2. transport of fine-grained sediments by percolating ground water;

3. human and animal transport of soil and organic material;

4. perhaps some sediments remaining from the old river level.

The banked-up soils in E3 and F3 might well relate to this last cause. The very fine silt has probably accumulated in the cave through lack of wind or water removal combined with fairly intensive human occupation. The absence of features in the deposit is probably caused by occupational activity, for in a powdery soil even limited activity would rapidly remove hearths, ash lenses, pits, etc. A vertical soil column was taken but has not been analysed.

Division of the Material

In the absence of visible stratigraphy throughout most of the deposit or natural subdivision of the archaeological material (fig.4c; tables 9-11), the deposit has been divided into four arbitrary horizons (numbered from the top down) for the purposes of analysis. It is assumed that deposition below the hearth complex is likely to lie generally parallel with it and, within this framework, approximately equal and statistically significant numbers of flaked-stone tools have been placed into each horizon (table 11). The volumes of the horizons are:

Horizon I	(HI)	1.8 m^3
Horizon II	(HII)	1.1 m^3
Horizon III	(HIII)	1.0 m^3
Horizon IV	(HIV)	1.8 m^3

The top of Horizon I is the top of the hearth complex (fig.4c).

Artifact Joins

Ten pairs of stone artifacts broken in antiquity were joined together. Seven came from the same square and excavated level, and a further two came from adjacent levels. The tenth came from two levels separated by 20-30 cm, belonging to Horizons I and III. This reinforces the point that the horizons probably do no more than separate the archaeological material into groups, *most* of whose members are in the correct stratigraphic relationship.

Dating

Three radiocarbon dates are available from Batari (Polach *et al.* 1968:191-2).

ANU-39: 850 ± 53 BP

This is the age of 20 gm of wood charcoal from the hearth complex at the top of Horizon I. The sample was collected from a small area on the north wall of E4 after the excavation was complete. This date gives a *terminus ante quem* for all *in situ* material.

ANU-38a (carbonate): 3470 ± 60 BP

ANU-38b (acid-insoluble fraction): ≥ 8230 ± 190 BP

These ages refer to a sample of about 500 gm of unidentifiable food-bone remains which came from the upper part of Horizon IV, 75-100/110 cm below the surface in squares E3 and E4.

The ANU laboratory points out that the acid-insoluble fraction, normally called 'collagen', comprises the material remaining after the carbonate has been removed and the excess acid washed off the residue. The laboratory considers that the real age is most reasonably thought of as being equal to or greater than ANU-38b.

ANU-40: 16,850 ± 700 BP

This date comes from 6.3 gm of wood charcoal collected in the lower part of Horizon IV, 95-120 cm below the surface in square E3. This carbon was clearly within a matrix containing cultural material, but it was not in a hearth or other man-made feature. It was at the same level as and only 20 cm laterally from undisturbed natural sediments which also contained carbon, though in much smaller pieces. There is therefore a possibility that the dated carbon, which was the only carbon to occur in any quantity below the hearth complex, was derived from the natural sediments. ANU-40 will therefore not be accepted as being validly associated with the earliest occupation of the cave, though the possibility that this was so must be borne in mind.

The radiocarbon dates suggest that the deposit at Batari was built up quite slowly, averaging 1 cm per 50 years. This may be compared with a rate of 1 cm per 20 years at Kafiavana and is consistent with the protected nature of the cave and the absence of human features within the deposit.

FAUNA

Domestic Animals

Pig (*Sus scrofa*) was the only domestic animal noted. All remains came from the top horizon and all except two pieces from the hearth complex. A total of seventeen identifiable bones was present, comprising three teeth, ten phalanges and one each of atlas, scapula, metapodial and phalange. At least one adult animal and one piglet were present, but it is impossible to say whether the animals were domestic or feral.

Wild Animals

Table 1 sets out the minimum numbers of wild animals in each horizon, based on mandibles. If the site is considered as a whole, then at least 173 animals were present; this rises to 186 if each horizon is considered separately.

It can be seen that macropodids, cuscus (*Phalanger* spp.) and ring-tailed possums (*Pseudocheirus* spp.) make up the bulk of the fauna. There is no marked change over time in the relative proportions of animals present, though the samples are too small to be significant. This limits the environmental inferences which can be drawn. Most of the animals are forest dwellers (Appendix 1) and the grassland animals such as *Thylogale* are not concentrated in the recent horizons as might be expected, assuming that the grasslands are fairly recent. The fauna suggests that most hunting took place in a forest environment which today is several hours walk from Batari. The faunal remains may therefore suggest that during the occupation of this site the forest was rather closer to the cave, although the wide altitudinal range and long distances over which many Highlanders hunt must be remembered (R.N.H. Bulmer, B. Craig pers. comms).

In general, the picture of economic life at Batari is one of unspecialised hunting, exploiting a wide range of fauna. Most animals were brought to the cave for butchering, as is shown by the number of jaws. For square's E3 and E4 mandibles and maxillae expressed as a percentage of total number of identifiable bone per horizon are: HI, 10.8% of 306; HII, 11.0% of 137; HIII, 6.0% of 217; HIV, 12.3% of 1086.

It is noticeable that domestic animals form only 1% of the total number of animals present, and 5% of the animals in the top horizon. By comparison with present conditions, this seems to underrate the importance of domestic animals considerably. Two explanations seem possible: either domestic animals have become much more important in this area recently, or Batari does not give a true picture of the past exploitation of domestic animals, since the cave was used largely during hunting, travelling or in time of war.

Table 1   Batari: minimum numbers of animals

Animals	I	II	III	IV	Total no. of animals
Suidae					
Sus scrofa	2	–	–	–	2
Macropodidae					
Thylogale bruijni	3	4	2	4	13
Other	4	–	5	10	19
Phalangeridae					
Phalanger spp.	7	7	3	8	25
Dactylopsila or *Dactylonax*	–	–	–	1	1
Petaurus breviceps	–	–	–	3	3
Eudromicia cf. *caudata*	–	–	–	1	1
Pseudocheirus (Pseudochirops) spp.	3	1	–	5	9
P. (Pseudocheirus) spp.	2	2	10	8	22
Peramelidae					
Genus not identified	4	2	1	4	11
Dasyuridae					
Satanellus albopunctatus	1	2	–	2	5
Megachiroptera					
Pteropus or *Dobsonia*	1	–	–	2	3
cf. *Nyctimene*	–	–	–	1	1
Syconycteris sp.	1	–	–	–	1
Genus not identified	–	–	–	1	1
Muridae					
Hyomys goliath	2	–	1	–	3
Mallomys rothschildi	–	1	–	1	2
Uromys sp.	3	2	4	3	12
Genus not identified	14	5	5	28	52
Total animals per horizon	47	26	31	82	186
No. of animals per m^3 of deposit	26.1	23.6	31	45.6	32.6

[1] Only includes mandibles of animals assessed as probably eaten by humans

Rodents

Three hundred and sixty rodent mandibles were excavated. Of these, 241 were concentrated in the top half of Horizon I in three adjacent squares (D3, E3, E4) and another 17 were close by. They were associated with many other small, entirely unbroken rodent bones and all were unburnt. The other 102 dark yellow-brown or charred rodent mandibles were scattered through the site and none occurred in the upper concentration. Many of these were broken.

It seems likely that the unburnt concentration represents the remains of owl pellets and the scattered blackened mandibles the remains of human

meals.   The latter represent a minimum of 69 animals and only they have
been included in table 1.

Birds

    Twenty-seven pieces of bone were identified as bird by J.C. Yaldwyn,
who was unable to identify most of them to generic level.   Birds form only
about 2% of the total number of identifiable post-cranial bones.   One
humerus fragment from Horizon II may be fowl, *Gallus gallus*, but the
identification is not definite.   None of the fragments is large enough to
come from cassowary; most are small, down to the size of swiftlets which
inhabit part of the cave system around Batari today.
    Many small pieces of eggshell occur, most of them cassowary egg.   The
weight of cassowary eggshell fragments averages about 0.1 gm and there are no
large fragments.   The relative amount of this shell declines in H IV (table 2),
which contrasts with the picture given by other faunal remains.   Most of the
other eggshell comes from the upper two horizons.   It has not been identified.

Table 2   Batari: distribution of cassowary eggshell

Horizon	No. of pieces	Weight in gm	Weight per m^3
I	53	6.3	3.5
II	55	6.6	6.0
III	131	16.5	16.5
IV	23	2.4	1.3
Unstratified	72	7.2	–
Total	334	39.0	6.8

Reptiles

    The reptiles were identified by R.E. Barwick.   Among the 13 fragments
he distinguished ten agamid lizards (a family which includes the 'dragons')
and one snake.   At least five animals are represented.   Table 3 shows the
distribution of fragments, which are scattered through the site.   These
animals were probably eaten (cf. R. Bulmer 1967:7).

Table 3   Batari: distribution of reptiles

Horizon	Family Agamidae	Other lizards	Snake
I	3	–	1
II	7	1	–
III	–	1	–
IV	–	–	–
Total	10	2	1

Mollusca

    Mollusca from three environments – marine, freshwater and land – were
found at Batari.   Marine shells must have been brought to the site by man,
but other molluscs could have arrived through other agencies.   However,
both freshwater and land molluscs are eaten in the Highlands today
(S. and R. Bulmer 1964:51) and the number and spread of both types within the
site suggest that humans were responsible for their presence.

Marine shells   Eight genera of marine shells were identified by D.F. McMichael.
All specimens come either from Horizon I or unstratified contexts.

Horizon I: 2 *Oliva* spp. (olive shells); 1 *Polinices* sp. (sand snail);
1 cf. *Geloina* sp. (estuarine bivalve).

Unstratified: 2 *Oliva* spp.; 2 *Nassarius* sp. (dog whelk); 3 *Geloina* sp.; 1 *?Telligarca* sp. (ark shell); 1 *Trochus* sp. (trochus); 1 *Neritina zigzag* (neritina); 1 *Dentalium* cf. *elephantium* (elephant's tusk shell).

The neritina has a small round hole worked in the back of the shell, probably for threading on a string.   These shells document the existence of a trade route with the sea coast, but none of the genera is sufficiently localised to point to any particular coast.

Freshwater shells   All 59 freshwater shells (table 4) are mussels (family Hyriidae), which are common in Highlands streams.   Most specimens are very fragmented, but four have been identified as *Hyridella* (*Nesonaia*) *guppyi aipiana* McMichael.   It is equally possible that these molluscs were initially collected for the animal or its shell.

Table 4   Batari: distribution of freshwater shells

Horizon	No. of pieces
I	19
II	4
III	?1
IV	–
Unstratified	35
Total	59

Thiaridae and Neritidae. The distribution of these shells is shown in table 5. Each family has a few species which occur in fresh water in high country, although thiarids are more common in lowland streams while nerites are essentially brack-water forms (D.F. McMichael pers. comm.).   Thus where these shells are not identified to species level, they may come from any one of a range of environments.   The thiarids include *Stenomelania* and some unidentified genera, while the nerites include a large and a small species of *Neritina*.   One nerite from Horizon II and two from unstratified contexts have holes drilled in the back.

Table 5   Batari: distribution of thiarids and nerites

Horizon	Thiarids	Nerites
I	1	2
II	2	1
III	–	–
IV	–	1
Unstratified	14	5
Total	17	9

Land snails   Two genera of landsnails have been identified.   The more common is *Geotrochus* of which McMichael says (pers. comm.) 'This landsnail group occurs in New Guinea but I know of no species from the eastern Highlands'.   Five specimens occur in HI, three in HII and one in HIII.   Fourteen occur in unstratified contexts.   The only other landsnail is one specimen of *Papuina*, found in HI.   This is a typical New Guinea landsnail, probably from the local forest.

It is possible that the *Geotrochus* specimens were imported into this area, although trade in landsnail shells is not common.   In the remote area where Batari lies it is also possible that an unidentified species of *Geotrochus* occurs naturally and its presence in the site is due either to natural causes or local gathering by humans.

Human Remains

Four well-preserved human bones were found, three in unstratified contexts and one in Horizon I. They were identified by A.G. Thorne, whose comments on each follow, the reference being to square/(spit):

D3/(1) Upper left pre-molar. Only the crown remains of this tooth, which is broken off at the root junction. The tooth is worn down to the dentine, exposing a small area of this on the buccal cusp. The tooth clearly belongs to an adult person and is quite large.

F3-4/T (Bragge's trench). Thoracic vertebra. The body of this bone is eroded and the spinous process broken. There is arthritic lipping of the bone, indicating that the individual was probably adult and not young.

C3/(1) Terminal phalange of a hand. This bone comes from one of the three middle fingers.

C4/(3) Horizon I. A fragment comprising less than one quarter of a pre-molar. Quite worn.

Occasional human bones are found in many caves in the New Guinea Highlands. They often seem to be associated with the deposition of corpses in niches in the rock rather than with secondary burial in the soil.

GROUND-STONE ARTIFACTS

Axe-adzes

Two whole axe-adzes, one broken axe-adze and one ground stone chip were excavated.

The whole specimens came from unstratified contexts. The first (fig.5a) is made in gneiss and measures 18.5 cm x 4.6 cm. It is ground on the faces and hammer-dressed or pecked on both sides. The cross-section is ovoid with slightly marked corners and the cutting edge is asymmetrically bevelled. The other axe-adze (fig.5b) measures 5.3 x 4.1 cm and is made of slatey schist. The cross-section is planilateral, though both faces are slightly convex. The cutting edge is symmetrically bevelled.

The broken specimen was excavated by Bragge who reports its depth as 'about 2 ft down in the deposit' (pers. comm.). If accurate, this would place it in my Horizon III. It is made of hornfels and is of lenticular cross-section with an asymmetrical bevel. The chip is also made of hornfels and comes from the main hearth complex.

Small Ground-stone Artifacts

Horizon I

1. C4/(4) is a broken limestone bead or button which appears to have been nearly circular (fig.5k). The cross-section is plano-convex, with the convex side possibly having a slight use-gloss. A 2 mm diameter hole has been worked from both faces through the centre, the width of the hole at each face being 5 mm. Two slight scratches in the hole suggest that a drill was used.

2. F3/(2) is a smooth, solid, regular calcite cylinder, without visible surface markings.

Unstratified

3. A solid, smooth, calcite cylinder tapering to a point (fig.5i), without visible surface markings. Tairora men from Himarata claimed that this was a septum decoration and that only one end would have been pointed.

4. A solid cylinder of very dark blue hornfels, ground in eight planes around the cylinder (fig.5h). One end is slightly tapered and smoothed

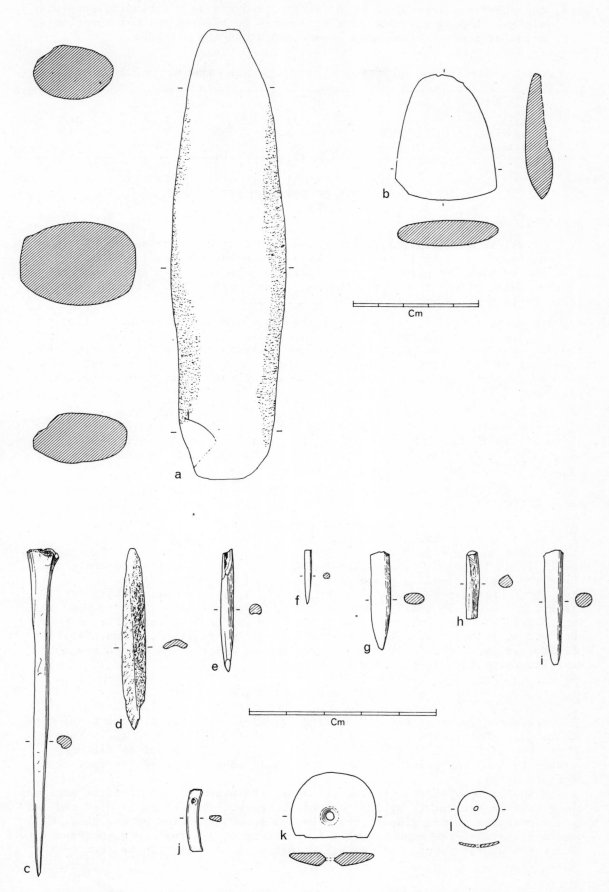

Fig.5   Batari: artifacts of ground stone (a,b,g,i,k), bone (c,d,e,f,h) and
        shell (j,l)

off, the other end is broken. The very marked traces of grinding show that the original shaping was made at right angles to the length, but superimposed fine grinding scratches run both around and along the cylinder.

Table 6 Batari: measurements of small ground-stone artifacts in mm

	1	2	3	4
Length	–	16.0	32.5	21.5
Diameter	23.0	4.5	4.5	3.6
Thickness	3.4	–	–	–

ARTIFACTS OF BONE AND SHELL

Bone Artifacts

1. A complete awl (fig.5c), made from a ?tibia with an unfused epiphysis, was found unstratified. The other end is sharpened by longitudinal grinding to a medium point. A high gloss can be seen over three-quarters of the length of the tool, with the head being unpolished. Length 91.5 mm, cross-section at 10 mm from the tip 2 x 2.5 mm.

2. A bipoint (fig.5d), found in HII, is made from a longitudinal splinter of mineralised long-bone shaft. One point is broad and slightly rounded, while at 8 mm from the other end there is a slight indentation on each side as if to hold a lashing. There is no record of bone points of this type being used recently in this area. Length 51 mm, maximum width 11.5 mm.

3. The other 13 points are 15-30 cm long. The tips range from broad, heavy examples to very fine points similar to modern needles. Three are very similar to the awl point. Their distribution is: HI, 3; HII, 1; HIII, 3; HIV, 1; unstratified, 5. Fig. 5e comes from E4/(9); 5f from E4/(2); and 5g is unstratified.

Shell Artifacts

Four shell artifacts were found, three of them in Bragge's trench. Two of these are round button-like objects with a hole drilled from one side through the centre (fig.5l). The third is a round natural tube of dentalium shell, 12 mm long and 3 mm in diameter with the ends slightly rounded. These three may well be beads of some sort.

The fourth artifact, D4/(4) from HI (fig.5j), is a thin rectangular (18 x 2 mm) piece of shell, slightly curved in one plane. Near one end a very small hole has been worked from one face to the other by drilling from both sides, probably by some form of rotating hand-drill (Williams 1940:146; cf. Semenov 1964:74). All corners are rounded and the end nearer the hole exhibits faint saw marks across one face.

OCHRE AND OCHRE KNIFE

Scattered lumps of red ochre (iron oxide) were found throughout the site (table 7). Most weigh under 7 gm, though three weigh over 10 gm. Four lumps show signs of scratching or rubbing. The ochre cannot be directly related to the rock paintings, and it may well have been used for body or artifact painting.

A short, heavy flake with ochre along both sides of one straight edge was discovered in Horizon II at the back of the cave. The ochre is dark red and is concentrated on one side of the edge. Close inspection of the ochre smears shows that the edge was used for cutting or shaving ochre, perhaps into powder for use as paint. A few slight signs of use-wear can be seen on the edge.

22

Table 7   Batari: distribution of ochre

Horizon	Weight in gm	Gm per m^3
I	32.1	17.8
II	50.2	45.6
III	6.7	6.7
IV	26.4	14.7
Unstratified	25.8	-
Total	141.2	20.2

Table 8   Batari: distribution of waste material by number

Square	Horizon I	II	III	IV	Total
C3	123	294	147	-	564
C4	214	495	248	-	957
D3	1011	954	505	21	2491
D4	385	802	990	296	2473
E3	1222	905	1251	1701	5079
E4	650	869	1216	1292	4027
F3	234	399	757	198	1588
Total	3839	4718	5114	3508	17179
Waste flakes per implement	28.0	32.3	27.2	24.4	27.9[1]
No. per m^3	2133	4289	5114	1949	3014[2]

[1] Based on total numbers of flaked implements and waste flakes
[2] Based on total number of waste flakes and total volume of deposit

Table 9   Batari: percentage distribution of waste material by size

Size In.^{2}	mm^2	Horizon I Sample 1	Sample 2	Horizon IV Sample 1	Sample 2
<0.5	<160	73.0	57.0	57.0	38.0
0.5 – 1.0	160–650	25.0	38.0	38.0	46.0
1.0 – 1.5	650–1450	1.8	5.0	4.0	11.0
1.5 – 2.0	1450–2600	0.2	-	1.0	3.0
>2.0	>2600	-	-	0.2	2.0
Total no.		385	327	563	232

Table 10   Batari: distribution of waste material by weight in gm

Square	Horizon I	II	III	IV	Total
C3	137.7	365.2	199.7	-	702.6
C4	420.3	1104.2	527.4	-	2051.9
D3	933.6	974.7	505.4	80.7	2494.4
D4	367.6	532.6	908.9	946.2	2755.3
E3	822.5	555.6	765.4	2301.5	4445.0
E4	620.5	396.4	853.3	1530.8	3401.0
F3	473.9	726.6	908.3	447.0	2555.8
Total	3776.1	4655.3	4668.4	5306.2	18406.0
Mean weight of waste material	0.98	0.99	0.91	1.51	1.07[1]
Weight of waste per m^3	2097.8	4232.0	4668.4	2947.9	3229.1[2]

[1] Total weight divided by total number of waste flakes
[2] Total number of waste flakes divided by total volume of deposit

WASTE MATERIAL

        Over 17,000 primary flakes and core-lumps showing no macroscopic traces
of secondary working or use were recovered.   Most of these are presumably
flakes produced and discarded during the manufacture of implements.   The
material is nearly all greasy chert, although there is a wide variety of
colours and textures.   Four pieces of obsidian were found towards the
front of the cave in Horizon I.   The main sources of chert are not definitely
known, but local informants said that they were several miles away up-river.
There appear to be no sources near the site.
        Waste material is in a fairly constant ratio to implements of just under
30:1, showing that knapping was regularly carried on at the site (cf. Clark
1954:96; Inskeep 1959) (table 8).   A size analysis suggests that waste
material in the basal horizon is rather larger than in the other three
horizons (tables 9-10).

FLAKED-STONE TOOLS
(fig.6)

        A total of 615 pieces of stone with secondary retouch or use-wear was
excavated from the undisturbed levels of Batari.   As already explained
(p.15), horizons were defined to include approximately equal and
statistically significant numbers within each.   The density of implements
per m^3 of deposit is therefore higher in Horizon II and Horizon III than at
the top and base of the site (table 11).   These tools have been analysed
according to both typologies.

    Table 11   Batari: distribution of flaked-stone implements

Horizon	No. of implements	No. per m^3
I	137	76
II	146	133
III	188	188
IV	144	80
Total	615	108[1]

        [1] Total number of implements divided by total volume of deposit

Standard Typology (table 12)

        According to the standard typology, the tools are mostly simple and
multi-platform scrapers made on flakes.   Most retouched edges are concave
but there is a range from straight to deeply concave.   The multi-platform
tools are often retouched cores.   They form a less important component of
the more recent industry paralleling a less concentrated use of tools, which
is also noticeable in relation to trimming flakes.   The single-platform
tools have been arbitrarily divided into classes, although the retouch ranges
from almost none to all round.   There seems to be no shift between classes
over time.
        Particular features of the tools from each horizon are:

Horizon I   Most tools are on flakes and none is large.   One is made on a
piece of obsidian and appears to be heavily used.   Two of the 'discoid'
scrapers are simply flat flakes with steep retouch round most of the dorsal
surface, while two are chunky pieces with bulbs removed.

Horizon II   The notable tools are three double-concave scrapers (fig.6c).
These have a long (1.5-2 cm), thin (<1 cm) ridged projection which juts out
from between two deeply retouched concavities.   Among the single-platform

tools there are a few deeply concave edges measuring around 20 x 3 mm.
Fig.6d is a side and end scraper, with five altered edges.

Horizon III   Of the double-concave scrapers only one is well defined and this
has retouch all round the base.   In the other two the projecting ridge is not
well marked.   The side and end scrapers tend to grade into the 'discoid' group
whose members in this horizon are small (<2.5 cm diameter) and chunky.   The
?bifacial is very lightly retouched along one side of a flake, small scalar
flakes having been detached from both faces of this edge.

Horizon IV   A few tools from this horizon are larger, including one end
scraper on a large chunky flake (7 x 5 x 4 cm) and a very large flake
(8 x 7.5 x 3 cm) in grey, non-greasy chert retouched around one end, with
pebble cortex on the dorsal surface.   This is the closest thing to a pebble
tool found at Batari, since it weighs 263 gm.   Twelve of the multi-platform
tools are very small (about 2 cm cube) and chunky.   At least eight have been
cores.   They are notable for their generally complex configuration and are
spread throughout the horizon.   Another multi-platform tool is a double-concave
scraper in one plane but is also heavily inversely retouched at the other end
(fig.6b).

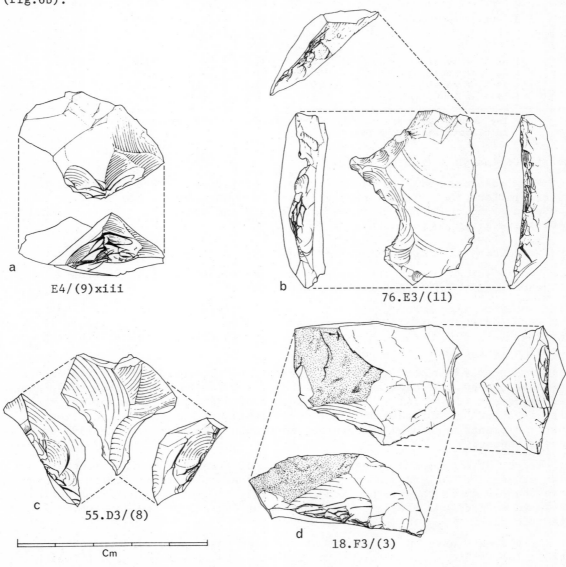

a

E4/(9)xiii

b

76.E3/(11)

c

55.D3/(8)

d

18.F3/(3)

Cm

Fig.6   Batari: flaked-stone artifacts: a) trimming flake; b) multiplane
scraper, seven altered edges; c) double concave scraper, four altered
edges; d) side and end scraper, five altered edges

Table 12   Batari: distribution of flaked-stone tool types[1]

	Horizon				Total
	I	II	III	IV	
Total tools (add 1-4)	137	146	188	144	615
1. Whole retouched tools	32	51	64	44	191
(a) Scrapers (total)	32	51	63	44	190
(i) side	7	12	12	10	41
(ii) end	3	3	8	4	18
(iii) double side	4	3	7	3	17
(iv) side and end	4	10	6	3	23
(v) side and double end	1	1	–	1	3
(vi) discoid	4	–	3	3	10
(vii) double-concave	–	3	3	–	6
(viii) multi-platform	9	19	23	20	71
(b) Bifacial retouch/use	–	–	1	–	1
2. Broken retouched tools	77	68	102	69	316
3. Utilised pieces	22	23	20	29	94
4. Cores	6	4	2	2	14
1 as % of total	23.4	34.9	34.0	30.6	31.1
2 as % of total	56.2	46.6	54.3	47.9	51.4
3 as % of total	16.1	15.8	10.6	20.1	15.3
(viii) as % of (a)	28.1	37.3	36.5	45.5	37.4

[1] The numbers vary slightly from those in White (1969) because of minor
re-classifying of the material

Attribute Analysis (tables 13-70)

An 'edge analysis' of 614 pieces was carried out.   One implement, a
multi-platform tool without pebble cortex from Horizon II, had 14 edges on
two planes and could not be incorporated into the analysis.   The numerical
tables are given on pp. 31-49.

Analyses using the implement as the basic unit

1. *Type of stone used*   The industry is made almost entirely in greasy
   chert, only 2.1-4.8% being in other material.

2. *Number of planes per implement*   In all horizons, between two-thirds and
   three-quarters of all implements are used on one plane only (table 13).
   The 20-30% used in more than one plane significantly demonstrate the lack of
   formal orientation in this industry.

3. *Number of edges per implement*   One-half to two-thirds of the implements
   have one or two edges as defined above, and few have more than three edges
   per implement (table 14).   The mean number of edges per implement for the
   site is about 2.6 and this does not vary widely between the four horizons.
   Most implements were used or reshaped more than once.   There are 1598 edges
   in the industry.

4. *Weight of implements*   There is no real difference in weight ranges
   between the horizons, except that there seem to be fewer tools weighing
   more than 10 gm in the top horizon (table 15).   Comparing the distribution
   of weights in HI and HIV, $\chi^2 = 5.30$ with four degrees of freedom, which is not
   significant.

   Implements used on two planes are heavier than those used on one plane
   (table 16).   Similarly, implements with more than two edges tend to weigh
   more than those with one or two edges (table 17).   Thus, implements with
   more planes and edges are not more 'worked out' and smaller than those with
   fewer planes and edges; rather, they have been made on larger stones giving

the opportunity for more planes and edges to be used.   This argument assumes that there are equal proportions of broken implements in each group.   This cannot be tested since numbers are too small, but its validity seems to be supported by table 18.

Analyses using the edge as the basic unit

Note that if two edges occur on an implement any measurements or observations on that implement will be duplicated.

1. *Whole implements*   Only 7-10% of the edges are made on implements which can definitely be called whole in relation to that particular edge, and only a further 11-14% of the stones are even probably whole.   With two-thirds of all edges it is unclear whether the implement is, for *that* edge, whole or not whole (table 18).

2. *Raw material*   About a third of the industry is made on stones with pebble cortex and another quarter of the edges are made on stones with some sort of cortex (table 19).   These figures are relevant to the discussion of pebble tools in chapter II.   The number of tools with pebble cortex preserved is of course only a minimum indication of the proportion of the industry actually made on river pebbles.

3. *Size and shape of implements*   Table 20 shows the weights of implements. It is noticeable that 'not whole' implements weigh much less than 'whole' implements, but 'probably whole' implements weigh significantly more: $\chi^2 = 22.09$ with 4 degrees of freedom; when $P = 0.05$, $n = 4$, then $\chi^2 = 9.49$. This suggests that 'probably whole' implements are in fact likely to be whole. Table 21 expresses the shapes of implements which are clearly whole in relation to a particular edge; table 22 of all implements not clearly broken. These tables show a marked consistency in the shape of implements throughout the deposit.   The Length/Breadth index (L/B) shows that very few have a length more than twice their breadth and about 60% are close to square.   The chunkiness of the industry is also expressed by the Breadth/Thickness index (B/Th) (table 22) which shows that breadth is less than twice the thickness in over half the industry.   The somewhat different picture given by table 21(b) may be a function of the small numbers; it may also be related to the fact that it is rather easier to assess whether a thin flake is whole than it is to assess the same for a core or lump, which is usually chunky.

4. *Flakes and cores*   About half the edges are made on definite flakes, while only a third or less are made on cores, lumps and chunks (table 23).   In this respect it could be said that the industry is primarily based on flakes. However, if the ratio of flakes to cores, lumps, etc. which result from any normal attempt to flake stone is considered (cf. Clark 1954:96), it suggests that cores and lumps are being selected for this industry.   However, it seems likely that the selection of an implement depended more on features such as suitability of edge, ease of holding the stone and so on, rather than whether it was a core or a flake.

Attributes describing the edges individually

1. *Whole/not whole*   Almost exactly two-thirds of the edges are either whole or probably whole, and this figure is highly consistent throughout the site (table 24).   There is, however, a regular decrease in the percentage of clearly whole edges and an inversely related increase in the percentage of edges from base to top of the site.   This is hardly likely to be an observer-induced change, but it is difficult to suggest any archaeological explanation for it.

2. *Base type*   Positive bulb surfaces form nearly half the bases and a further 25% are negative bulb surfaces (table 25).

3. *Preparatory flaking*   About half the edges for which this category is determinable and relevant are prepared for use by the removal of one or

more large flakes struck from the base (table 26). Almost none of the preparatory flaking is from any other point on the surface. About one quarter of the edges are not prepared.

4. *Shape of edge*   Among edges which are clearly whole, two-thirds or more are concave to some extent (table 27). This confirms the original impression of the industry as comprising mostly worked notches.

The shape of edges has been measured as the length of the chord (Lc) and the maximum distance of the edge from the chord taken at right angles from it (D). Lc is a measure of the size of the edge and Lc/D is an index of its indentation or projection. Lc/D is always zero for straight edges. The indentation index remains very stable over the whole site with nearly two-thirds of all whole concave edges being 5.9-9 (table 28). If all edges are considered (excluding those that are clearly not whole), convex edges are seen to diverge less from a straight line than concave edges (table 29).

Among the whole edges, concave edges tend to be longer than straight ones throughout the site (table 30).

5. *Retouch*   Step-flaking accounts for over 90% of all retouch in all horizons. About two-thirds of all edges are step-flaked and most other edges are not retouched at all (table 31). Most step-flaking is found on concave edges and almost none is found on convex edges (table 32(b),(c)). Light step-flaking is less restricted to concave edges than heavy step-flaking.

Nearly all step-flaked edges have acute angles with the mode at 60-79° (table 33(a),(b)). The very few edges with other unifacial flaking seem to have slightly more acute angles (table 33(c)). An early impression of the industry as consisting of right-angled to obtuse edges is not confirmed.

6. *Use-wear*   About half the edges show use-wear of the 'chattering' type and a further 10% are 'utilised' (table 34). Most of the rest show no signs of use. Thirty-eight edges scattered through the horizons show use-wear in two places. Normally both pieces of use-wear are 'chattering'.

Use-wear mostly forms a straight line along an edge: only one-third of all lengths of 'chattering' and one-quarter of all lengths of 'utilisation' are concave (table 35). Almost no 'chattering' is convex, confirming the relationship between 'chattering' and step-flaking. If only whole lengths of use-wear are considered, the relationship is even more accentuated (table 36). There is an increase in straight 'chattering' towards the top of the site.

The normal length of use-wear is under 10 mm. 'Utilisation' tends to be longer than 'chattering', with lengths up to 20 mm being common, whereas almost no 'chattering' is longer than 10 mm (table 37).

The two main types of concave use-wear are clearly distinguished by the indentation index, with 'utilisation' being much less indented than 'chattering' (tables 38-9).

Nearly all use-wear is on acute-angled edges. The mode for 'chattering' is 70-79°, while the mode for 'utilisation' is 50-59° (table 40), which probably relates to different uses of the tools. If all the angles from any one horizon are considered without reference to the type of use-wear, they are distributed in a unimodal curve. Furthermore, there is no change in the curves between the top and basal horizons, confirming the technological and functional similarity of this industry.

It is remarkable that many units of use-wear are straight when the common shape of a retouched edge is concave. This suggests that in many cases only *part* of what is usually called a functional edge is actually used at any time. Thus 'notches' in any industry may result from continual retouching of an edge rather than from any initial functional requirement. It is also probably more convenient to hold any tool in one particular way, thus tending to bring a certain point into wear more frequently.

Correlations between attributes

Some correlations may be readily inferred from the previous descriptions, but it seems useful to draw attention to three important relationships.

1. *Retouch and use-wear*   Preliminary handling of the industry suggested that
    'chattering' was concentrated on step-flaked edges.   This is not quite
    accurate as only two-thirds of all 'chattering' is found on step-flaked edges
    (table 41(a)); the reverse, however, is true - the use-wear on step-flaked
    edges is nearly all 'chattering' (table 42(a),(b)).   Two-thirds of all use-wear
    on unretouched edges is 'chattering' (table 42(c)), but nearly all 'utilisation'
    is found on unretouched edges (table 41(b)).

2. *Retouch and 'chunkiness'*   There is a definite, if slight, tendency for
    edges without retouch to occur on thinner implements than edges with
    step-flaking (table 43), though retouch type is not related to the B/Th index
    (table 44).

3. *Size of implement and angle of retouch*   There is no clear relationship
    between the weight of an implement and its angle of retouch.   For
    implements with light or heavy step-flaking there are the same ranges of
    preferred weights and angles, especially 10-19 gm and 60-79°, and these do not
    form sharply defined units (table 45).

Attempts to define 'types'

The most interesting aspect of this industry is the apparent stability of
all its features throughout the entire period of occupation.   This might be
expected in features which relate directly to activities, such as the shape and
size of use-wear, but those which are not so directly related to technical
necessities, like the shape and size of implements, might be expected to alter
to some extent.

Before the implements were described it was apparent that formal types
were not easily definable; it is not unexpected therefore that they remain
elusive.   There do, however, seem to be at least two clusters of attributes
which may begin to define 'types'.   The clearest division in the tables so
far is between the two types of use-wear, 'chattering' and 'utilisation'
(table 40).   Edges with these two types of wear have therefore been made the
basis for further study, although the number of 'utilised' edges is quite small.
It is already clear that units of 'chattering' and 'utilisation' tend to
have different angles (table 40) and that the former is often associated with
step-flaking retouch (table 41).   It can also be shown that the shape and
length of these types of use-wear are generally different (tables 46-7), while
the length and shape of the edge on which they are found is also likely to be
different (tables 48-9).   'Utilised' edges do not carry preparatory flaking
(table 50) and they are much more likely to be made on flakes than are edges
with 'chattering' (table 51).   Further, the implements themselves differ in
thickness and weight, with 'utilised' edges being on thinner, lighter implements
(tables 52-3).   These associations suggest that there is a difference, possibly
a functional one, between two groups of tools (cf. White 1968a).

A further attempt at characterising tool groups has been made by
investigating the properties of retouched and unretouched edges with
'chattering'.   The tables suggest that these two groups differ but this is
far less marked than the division based on use-wear groups.

There is a slight but consistent difference in the angle of use-wear
(table 54).   The shape of lengths of use-wear changes markedly through the
four horizons (table 55).   The reasons for this are not clear.   'Chattering'
found on unretouched edges tends to be a little longer (table 56).
Preparatory flaking is more likely to be associated with retouch than with
lack of it (table 57), but almost precisely the same numbers are made on
flakes and core/lumps (table 58).   The implements without retouch tend to
be slightly lighter and thinner than those which are step-flaked (tables 59-60).

Another method of making these types more explicit - and one which
ignores any influences of temporal change - is to combine the data from all
four horizons.   Tables 61-70 set out the results of doing this and three
features emerge clearly.   They probably relate to functional variation within
the industry (cf. White 1968a).

One is that the three groups (edges with 'chattering', with 'chattering' without step-flaking, and with 'utilisation') are distinguishable, particularly by the distribution of their weights, with the less retouched implements being lighter. The second criterion is that shapes of edges vary in a way use-wear shapes do not seem to. Three-quarters of all step-flaked and 'chattered' edges are concave, but only half the unretouched 'chattered' edges are this shape. At least one-quarter of 'utilised' edges are convex. The third feature is that half the 'chattered' edges are less than 5 mm long, whether they are associated with retouch or not. Only seven per cent of 'utilised' edges are so short.

Summary

Both the initial assumption and the methodology of this typology are open to challenge, with the assumed identification of use-wear types clearly being the first point of attack. Nevertheless both ethnographic and archaeological data strongly support a functional rather than a formal classification and the methods used here try to construct an objective basis on which work can proceed.

TRIMMING FLAKES

Trimming flakes (fig.6a) are a constant component of the industry and there is an average of one for every two flaked implements (table 71). It is interesting that the ratio of implements to trimming flakes increases from 1.85:1 to 2.63:1 from the lowest to the topmost horizon. This suggests that the implements were used less intensively in more recent times.

HAMMERS

Three river pebbles showing traces of use as hammers were recovered, one from Horizon III and two from Horizon IV (table 72). The latter two are both broken pebbles and it is not clear whether they were used as hammers before or after being broken. The porphyritic rocks used are dense and not brittle. They tend to bruise rather than fracture owing to the presence of large soft crystals in a dense ground matrix. This is probably why they were chosen for use as hammers.

The absence of hammer stones from the upper levels of the site may mean either that they were deposited in other parts of the site, or that chert pebbles, originally used as hammers, were later used as cores or implements and cannot therefore be recognised as hammers now.

CONCLUSION

The period at which Batari was first occupied is unknown. However, in terms of the dated occurrence elsewhere in the Highlands of such artifacts as ground axes, marine shell and pigs, about 8000 years ago (ANU-38b) is a reasonable estimate. Sampling error may account for the absence of some implement types in the lower levels. However, throughout the history of Batari the confined dry space of the occupied area was subject to a good deal of treadage and scuffage so that features in the deposit were obscured and some material was displaced.

The earlier occupants of the site left only limited material, in the form of flaked-stone tools and animal bones. Apparently only wild animals were eaten then, and we may assume they were hunted with weapons made by the stone tools found on the site. The middle levels of occupation show little change; very similar retouched tools, though in larger numbers, continue to be found, while the same animal species were brought back and eaten.

It is only within the upper horizon, deposited perhaps within the last 3000 years, that different artifacts are found - axe-adzes, grooved and ground stone and marine shell. Stone-knapping continued to occur and, as in earlier times, suitable chert had to be brought from some distance. Pigs began to supplement the meat part of the diet, but there is no evidence about the other types of food eaten. Some 750-1000 years ago some very large fires were lit in the cave, after which it seems to have been largely abandoned. Owl pellets show that the human occupation was sporadic, although later occupation may have been obscured in the very soft topmost level.

Generally speaking, the artifacts from Batari show a greater similarity with Aibura than with other sites. The retouched implements are similar to those found at Aibura below levels dated to 770 ± 100 BP, while the presence of small grooved and ground stone and shell artifacts also links the two sites. The absence of waisted blades, clearly quadrangular-sectioned axe-adzes, pebble tools and tools with use-polish is probably also significant and may point to an eastern regional aspect of the Highlands industries.

There is no sign at Batari of change either in the flaked implements or in the environment in which wild animals were hunted. This might also suggest that there was no sudden increase in the area of grasslands down to about 1000 years ago and that the pattern of site-use did not change. A diagrammatic summary of the material from Batari is included in fig. 27.

Table 13   Batari: percentage distribution of number of planes per implement

Horizon	Number of planes				No. of implements
	1	2	3	4	
I	67.9	28.5	3.6	-	137
II	78.8	19.2	0.7	1.3	146
III	79.8	18.1	2.1	-	188
IV	73.6	24.3	1.4	0.7	144

Table 14   Batari: percentage distribution of number of edges per implement

Horizon	Number of edges									No. of implements	No. of edges	Mean no. of edges per implement
	1	2	3	4	5	6	7	8	9			
I	29.2	21.2	22.6	11.0	7.3	4.4	1.5	1.5	1.5	137	381	2.78
II	40.4	27.4	14.4	10.3	5.5	0.7	-	0.7	0.7	146	325	2.23
III	28.7	36.2	12.8	9.0	6.9	2.7	2.1	1.6	-	188	477	2.54
IV	29.9	20.8	17.4	13.9	9.0	4.2	0.7	1.4	2.8	144	415	2.88
I-IV										615	1598	2.61

Table 15   Batari: percentage distribution of implement weights

Horizon	Weight in gm									No. of implements
	0-9	10-9	20-9	30-9	40-9	50-9	60-9	70-9	80-9	
I	51.1	32.1	9.5	3.7	2.9	0.7	-	-	-	137
II	41.1	28.8	13.0	7.5	4.1	0.7	3.4	1.4	-	146
III	40.1	39.9	6.4	6.9	3.7	1.1	0.5	-	0.5	188
IV	40.3	34.0	13.2	4.2	6.3	-	1.4	0.7	-	144

Table 16   Batari: percentage distribution of implement weights in relation to number of planes used

Horizon	0-9	10-9	20-9	30-9	40-9	50-9	60-9	70-9	80-9	No. of implements
(a) one plane										
I	60.2	25.8	7.5	3.2	2.2	1.1	–	–	–	93
II	45.4	26.1	13.0	7.0	3.5	0.9	3.5	0.9	–	115
III	42.7	38.0	6.0	7.3	3.3	1.3	0.7	–	0.7	150
IV	50.0	26.4	11.3	4.7	4.7	–	1.9	0.9	–	106
(b) two planes										
I	33.3	48.7	12.8	5.1	–	–	–	–	–	39
II	28.6	42.9	14.3	7.1	3.6	–	3.6	–	–	28
III	32.4	50.0	8.8	2.9	5.9	–	–	–	–	34
IV	14.3	54.3	17.1	2.9	11.4	–	–	–	–	35

Table 17   Batari: percentage distribution of implement weights in relation to number of edges used

Horizon	0-9	10-9	20-9	30-9	40-9	50-9	60-9	70-9	80-9	No. of implements
(a) one or two edges										
I	52.2	30.7	8.2	6.4	1.3	1.3	–	–	–	69
II	51.3	29.8	8.4	3.0	4.6	–	2.1	0.9	–	99
III	48.9	31.9	7.7	6.3	4.3	–	–	–	0.9	122
IV	58.4	23.8	8.0	5.2	2.3	–	1.2	1.2	–	73
(b) more than two edges										
I	47.1	35.3	11.8	1.5	4.4	–	–	–	–	68
II	17.1	29.8	21.3	17.1	4.3	2.1	6.4	2.1	–	47
III	27.3	54.5	3.0	7.6	3.0	3.0	1.5	–	–	66
IV	22.5	45.0	18.3	2.8	9.9	–	2.8	–	–	71

Table 18   Batari: percentage distribution of condition of implements, counting each edge as a separate implement

Horizon	Whole	Probably whole	Not whole	Indeterminate	No. of edges
I	10.8	11.0	13.4	64.8	381
II	7.7	13.5	12.3	66.5	325
III	9.4	14.3	14.1	62.3	477
IV	9.9	12.8	11.1	66.3	415

Table 19   Batari: percentage distribution of occurrence of cortex

Horizon	Pebble cortex	Other cortex	No cortex	Indeterminate	No. of edges
(a) counting each edge as a separate implement					
I	26.5	24.7	42.1	6.7	381
II	34.2	24.6	36.6	4.6	325
III	31.2	24.7	34.8	9.2	477
IV	26.1	24.8	41.0	8.2	415
(b) counting each implement as one					No. of implements
I	27.0	21.9	43.8	7.3	137
II	32.9	24.0	35.6	7.5	146
III	35.6	21.8	31.4	11.2	188
IV	29.8	20.8	34.9	14.6	144

Table 20   Batari: percentage distribution of implement weights, counting each edge as a
            separate implement

Horizon	Weight in gm									No. of edges
	0-9	10-9	20-9	30-9	40-9	50-9	60-9	70-9	80-9	
(a) whole implements										
I	56.1	14.6	19.5	9.8	–	–	–	–	–	41
II	36.0	40.0	4.0	12.0	–	–	8.0	–	–	25
III	40.0	37.8	4.4	8.9	4.4	4.4	–	–	–	45
IV	39.0	58.5	–	–	2.4	–	–	–	–	41
(b) probably whole implements										
I	31.0	33.3	23.8	4.8	7.1	–	–	–	–	42
II	29.6	29.6	18.2	6.8	–	–	15.9	–	–	44
III	23.5	45.6	10.3	10.3	7.4	1.5	–	–	1.5	68
IV	24.5	30.2	32.1	–	11.3	–	1.9	–	–	53
(c) not whole implements										
I	66.7	27.5	5.9	–	–	–	–	–	–	51
II	70.0	15.0	10.0	5.0	–	–	–	–	–	40
III	67.2	22.4	4.5	3.0	–	–	3.0	–	–	67
IV	56.5	19.6	23.9	–	–	–	–	–	–	46

Table 21   Batari: percentage distribution of whole implement shapes, counting each edge
            as a separate implement

Horizon	<0.5	0.5-0.99	1-1.49	1.5-1.99	2-2.49	2.5-2.99	>2.99	Not measured	No. of edges
(a) length/breadth index									
I	–	–	78.0	17.1	–	4.9	–	–	41
II	–	–	56.0	20.0	16.0	4.0	–	4.0	25
III	–	–	73.3	17.8	4.4	4.4	–	–	45
IV	–	–	63.4	26.8	4.9	2.4	2.4	–	41
(b) breadth/thickness index									
I	–	–	19.5	7.3	17.1	34.2	22.0	–	41
II	4.0	8.0	8.0	20.0	24.0	20.0	16.0	–	25
III	–	2.2	13.3	24.4	31.1	17.8	11.1	–	45
IV	–	4.9	4.9	7.3	24.4	29.3	29.3	–	41

Table 22   Batari: percentage distribution of the shape of all implements, except those
            clearly not whole, counting each edge as a separate implement

Horizon	<0.5	0.5-0.99	1-1.49	1.5-1.99	2-2.49	2.5-2.99	>2.99	Not measured	No. of edges
(a) length/breadth index									
I	–	–	63.6	27.2	4.6	1.5	1.8	1.2	330
II	–	–	63.1	21.8	10.2	3.2	0.7	1.1	285
III	–	–	64.4	27.3	4.9	1.2	0.5	1.7	410
IV	–	–	55.4	29.3	7.9	2.7	1.1	3.8	369
(b) breadth/thickness index									
I	1.5	11.8	29.7	18.8	18.5	11.8	7.9	–	330
II	1.1	10.9	30.2	30.5	19.0	3.9	4.6	–	285
III	–	9.3	22.2	36.6	17.8	11.0	3.2	–	410
IV	0.3	13.3	27.6	22.8	17.1	7.6	11.4	–	369

Table 23 Batari: percentage distribution of core and flake components of the total industry, counting each edge as a separate implement

Horizon	Core/lump etc.	Flake	Trimming flake	Indeterminate	No. of edges
I	33.9	55.4	4.2	6.6	381
II	36.9	51.4	7.1	4.6	325
III	24.7	61.8	4.2	9.2	477
IV	36.6	45.3	9.9	8.2	415

Table 24 Batari: percentage distribution of the condition of edges

Horizon	Whole	Probably whole	Not whole	Indeterminate	No. of edges
I	29.1	37.8	19.2	13.9	381
II	34.5	33.2	18.2	14.2	325
III	34.8	32.7	20.1	12.4	477
IV	38.6	28.4	18.6	14.5	415

Table 25 Batari: percentage distribution of base types of all implements, counting each edge as a separate implement

Horizon	Indeterminate	Pebble cortex	Other cortex	Break	Negative bulb	Positive bulb	Not applicable	No. of edges
I	8.9	2.9	6.8	6.3	27.0	41.2	6.8	381
II	9.9	2.2	10.8	8.0	18.8	48.0	2.5	325
III	5.5	1.7	2.7	7.6	25.0	51.4	6.3	477
IV	6.0	3.4	6.5	3.9	29.6	39.5	11.1	415

Table 26 Batari: percentage distribution of preparatory flaking of all implements, counting each edge as a separate implement

Horizon	Unclear	None	Base struck	Side/end struck	Not applicable	No. of edges
I	20.0	27.6	44.4	0.5	7.6	381
II	17.2	27.1	52.0	0.3	3.4	325
III	18.0	19.7	56.0	0.6	5.7	477
IV	18.8	20.5	49.2	0.5	11.1	415

Table 27 Batari: percentage distribution of the shape of whole edges

Horizon	Straight	Concave	Convex	Wavy	No. of edges
I	31.5	63.1	5.4	-	111
II	21.4	74.1	4.5	-	112
III	28.3	65.1	6.6	-	166
IV	24.4	66.2	9.4	-	160

Table 28 Batari: percentage distribution of the degree of indentation of whole concave edges, measured by index Lc/D

Horizon	Lc/D					No. of edges
	<3.3	3.4-4.9	5.0-9.9	10.0-19.9	>19.9	
I	2.8	9.9	64.8	21.1	1.4	70
II	3.6	13.3	61.5	19.3	2.4	83
III	3.7	13.0	66.7	16.7	-	108
IV	0.9	14.2	60.4	22.7	1.9	106

Table 29   Batari: percentage distribution of the degree of indentation or projection in relation to edge shape on all edges except those clearly not whole, measured by index Lc/D

Horizon	<3.3	3.4-4.9	Lc/D 5.0-9.9	10.0-19.9	>19.9	No. of edges
(a) concave						
I	1.8	7.7	63.4	26.0	1.2	169
II	2.4	10.0	66.0	20.6	1.2	170
III	3.0	11.6	64.7	20.8	-	230
IV	1.1	10.7	66.4	20.8	1.1	187
(b) convex						
I	-	-	43.7	50.0	6.3	16
II	-	-	38.4	46.2	15.4	13
III	-	-	35.3	64.7	-	17
IV	-	7.4	33.4	44.4	14.8	27

Table 30   Batari: percentage distribution of the length of whole edges in relation to edge shape

Horizon	0-5	6-10	11-15	Length in mm 16-20	21-25	26-30	31-35	>35	No. of edges
(a) straight									
I	37.2	31.4	11.4	8.6	5.7	5.7	-	-	35
II	45.8	33.3	12.5	8.3	-	-	-	-	24
III	25.5	38.3	23.4	6.4	-	2.1	4.3	-	47
IV	25.0	50.0	25.0	-	2.5	-	2.5	-	40
(b) concave									
I	19.7	50.7	23.9	4.2	1.4	-	-	-	70
II	6.0	49.4	27.7	13.3	1.2	1.2	-	1.2	83
III	16.6	49.1	29.6	3.7	-	0.9	-	-	108
IV	11.3	56.6	23.6	4.7	1.9	0.9	0.9	-	106

Table 31   Batari: percentage distribution of retouch types on all edges

Horizon	None	Step flaking light	heavy	Other unifacial flaking	Bifacial flaking	Other	No. of edges
I	37.0	37.5	21.3	3.7	0.3	0.3	381
II	22.8	52.3	19.9	4.3	0.3	1.2	325
III	25.4	54.7	16.4	2.9	0.4	0.2	477
IV	35.4	45.3	17.6	1.7	-	-	415

Table 32   Batari: percentage distribution of the relationship between retouch type and
            edge shape on whole edges

Horizon	Straight	Concave	Convex	Wavy	No. of edges
(a) no retouch					
I	39.7	52.4	7.9	-	63
II	37.9	44.8	17.2	-	29
III	48.3	37.9	13.8	-	58
IV	38.3	41.7	20.0	-	60
(b) light step-flaking					
I	23.5	73.5	2.9	-	34
II	16.7	83.3	-	-	60
III	19.5	76.8	3.7	-	82
IV	18.7	78.7	2.7	-	75
(c) heavy step-flaking					
I	10.0	90.0	-	-	10
II	-	100.0	-	-	16
III	-	100.0	-	-	21
IV	9.5	90.5	-	-	21

Table 33   Batari: percentage distribution of the relationship between edge angle and
            retouch type

Horizon	Angle in degrees								Not measured	No. of edges
	20-9	30-9	40-9	50-9	60-9	70-9	80-9	90-9		
(a) light step-flaking										
I	-	-	1.7	19.6	23.0	30.4	17.6	5.4	1.4	148
II	-	-	1.8	5.9	25.1	35.7	22.2	7.0	2.3	171
III	-	-	2.3	16.1	29.5	28.4	18.4	4.2	1.2	261
IV	-	0.3	2.1	6.4	32.4	33.5	16.5	6.4	2.1	189
(b) heavy step-flaking										
I	-	-	-	11.1	26.0	39.5	17.2	4.9	1.2	82
II	-	-	1.5	13.6	18.2	33.2	24.2	7.6	1.5	66
III	-	-	-	9.0	35.9	33.3	11.5	10.3	-	78
IV	-	-	2.7	8.2	32.9	39.7	12.4	2.7	1.4	74
(c) other unifacial flaking										
I	-	-	20.0	40.0	13.3	20.0	-	-	6.7	15
II	7.1	-	7.1	28.6	35.7	7.1	14.3	-	-	14
III	-	-	7.1	21.4	35.7	14.3	14.3	-	7.1	14
IV	-	-	28.6	42.9	14.3	14.3	-	-	-	7

Table 34   Batari: percentage distribution of the occurrence of use-wear on all edges

Horizon	None	'Chattering'	Bifacial	'Utilisation'	No. of edges
I	32.0	56.4	1.1	10.5	381
II	49.2	43.1	0.3	7.4	325
III	39.2	51.8	0.6	8.4	477
IV	33.7	54.0	0.7	11.6	415

Table 35   Batari: percentage distribution of the shape of use-wear types

Horizon	Straight	Concave	Convex	Wavy	No. of occurrences
(a) 'chattering'					
I	66.1	30.7	2.8	0.4	215
II	60.9	35.0	4.3	–	140
III	59.9	37.3	2.8	–	247
IV	59.8	36.2	4.0	–	224
(b) 'utilisation'					
I	55.0	25.0	20.0	–	40
II	41.7	25.0	33.3	–	24
III	57.5	22.5	20.0	–	40
IV	43.8	22.9	33.3	–	48

Table 36   Batari: percentage distribution of the shape of use-wear types, counting whole lengths of use-wear only

Horizon	Straight	Concave	Convex	Wavy	No. of occurrences
(a) 'chattering'					
I	58.7	40.2	1.1	–	92
II	55.9	42.7	1.5	–	68
III	47.5	49.5	3.0	–	101
IV	47.5	51.5	1.0	–	99
(b) 'utilisation'					
I	43.5	39.1	17.4	–	23
II	11.1	44.4	44.4	–	9
III	56.0	16.0	28.0	–	25
IV	32.0	24.0	44.0	–	25

Table 37   Batari: percentage distribution of the length of use-wear types, counting whole lengths of use-wear only

Horizon	Length in mm								No. of occurrences
	0-5	6-10	11-15	16-20	21-25	26-30	31-35	>35	
(a) 'chattering'									
I	60.5	36.5	2.0	1.0	–	–	–	–	92
II	57.0	36.2	4.2	2.7	–	–	–	–	68
III	53.4	30.4	13.3	1.9	1.0	–	–	–	101
IV	47.0	49.0	2.9	–	1.0	–	–	–	99
(b) 'utilisation'									
I	–	41.5	20.8	16.7	12.5	8.3	–	–	23
II	–	44.5	11.1	33.3	11.1	–	–	–	9
III	12.0	24.0	28.0	20.0	4.0	8.0	4.0	–	25
IV	4.0	12.0	36.0	20.0	12.0	8.0	8.0	–	25

Table 38 Batari: percentage distribution of the degree of indentation, measured by index Lc/D, on concave whole lengths of use-wear, in relation to use-wear type

Horizon	<3.3	3.4-4.9	Lc/D 5.0-9.9	10.0-19.9	>19.9	No. of occurrences
(a) 'chattering'						
I	5.4	16.2	70.3	8.1	–	37
II	13.8	24.1	51.7	10.3	–	29
III	8.0	16.0	62.0	14.0	–	50
IV	2.0	17.7	74.5	5.9	–	51
(b) 'utilisation'						
I	–	–	44.4	44.4	11.1	9
II	–	–	50.0	50.0	–	4
III	–	–	50.0	50.0	–	4
IV	–	–	16.7	50.0	33.3	6

Table 39 Batari: percentage distribution of the degree of indentation, measured by index Lc/D, on all concave lengths of use-wear, except those clearly not whole, in relation to use-wear type

Horizon	<3.3	3.4-4.9	Lc/D 5.0-9.9	10.0-19.9	>19.9	No. of occurrences
(a) 'chattering'						
I	4.8	17.7	66.1	11.3	–	62
II	9.5	19.0	56.2	14.3	–	42
III	8.8	15.0	62.5	13.8	–	80
IV	2.7	17.3	70.5	9.3	–	75
(b) 'utilisation'						
I	–	–	40.0	50.0	10.0	10
II	–	–	40.0	60.0	–	5
III	–	–	42.9	57.1	–	7
IV	–	9.1	27.3	45.5	18.2	11

Table 40 Batari: percentage distribution of edge angles in relation to use-wear type

Horizon	20-9	30-9	40-9	50-9	Angle in degrees 60-9	70-9	80-9	90-9	Not measured	No. of occurrences
(a) 'chattering'										
I	–	0.4	2.2	17.0	20.8	33.0	17.0	6.1	3.5	230
II	–	0.7	0.7	6.1	22.4	33.3	26.5	7.5	2.7	147
III	–	0.8	1.6	11.8	26.7	31.0	18.8	5.1	3.7	255
IV	–	1.3	5.2	10.4	24.4	28.7	15.7	10.0	4.4	230
(b) 'utilisation'										
I	7.3	17.1	17.1	26.8	12.2	9.8	4.9	4.9	–	41
II	4.2	12.5	8.3	37.5	8.3	25.0	4.2	–	–	24
III	12.5	12.5	15.0	20.0	20.0	7.5	7.5	2.5	2.5	40
IV	8.2	24.4	16.3	26.5	12.2	6.1	4.1	2.0	–	49

Table 41   Batari: percentage distribution of the relation between use-wear and retouch

| Horizon | Retouch type | | | No. of occurrences |
	None	Step-flaking light	heavy	
(a) 'chattering'				
I	46.5	34.2	19.4	228
II	44.7	44.0	11.2	150
III	37.8	47.7	14.4	243
IV	44.9	42.4	12.6	229
(b) 'utilisation'				
I	92.8	4.8	2.4	42
II	95.4	4.6	–	22
III	92.0	8.0	–	38
IV	97.9	2.1	–	49

Table 42   Batari: percentage distribution of the relation between retouch and use-wear

| Horizon | Use-wear type | | | No. of occurrences |
	'Chattering'	Bifacial	'Utilisation'	
(a) light step-flaking				
I	97.4	–	2.6	81
II	98.5	–	1.5	67
III	97.5	–	2.5	129
IV	100.0	–	–	97
(b) heavy step-flaking				
I	95.7	–	4.3	47
II	100.0	–	–	17
III	100.0	–	–	35
IV	100.0	–	–	29
(c) no retouch				
I	71.4	2.7	25.8	148
II	74.5	1.1	24.4	89
III	71.0	1.6	27.4	129
IV	66.6	2.0	31.4	155

Table 43 Batari: percentage distribution of implement thickness in relation to retouch type on all implements except those clearly not whole, counting each edge as a separate implement

Horizon	0-5	6-10	11-15	16-20	21-25	26-30	31-35	36-40	>40	Not measured	No. of edges
(a) light step-flaking											
I	5.5	41.7	26.0	14.2	8.7	3.2	0.8	-	-	-	127
II	4.5	24.2	32.0	18.3	9.2	7.2	2.0	1.3	0.6	0.6	153
III	7.1	36.6	31.7	13.0	7.1	3.1	0.9	0.4	-	-	224
IV	6.0	20.2	27.4	26.8	11.9	1.8	3.6	1.8	-	-	168
(b) heavy step-flaking											
I	4.6	41.5	20.0	21.5	4.6	7.7	-	-	-	-	65
II	1.9	17.3	30.8	28.8	15.4	5.8	-	-	-	-	52
III	5.1	23.7	50.8	13.5	5.1	1.7	-	-	-	-	59
IV	5.1	25.4	30.5	28.8	6.8	1.7	-	1.7	-	-	59
(c) no retouch											
I	19.5	30.5	22.6	14.1	7.8	2.3	0.8	0.8	-	1.6	128
II	21.4	12.9	24.3	20.0	11.4	4.3	4.3	-	1.4	-	70
III	14.4	40.5	16.2	17.1	3.6	1.8	6.3	-	-	-	111
IV	24.1	27.8	27.8	10.2	2.9	3.7	2.2	-	-	1.5	137

Table 44 Batari: percentage distribution of the breadth/thickness index in relation to retouch type on all implements except those clearly not whole, counting each edge as a separate implement

Horizon	<0.5	0.5-0.99	1.0-1.49	1.5-1.99	2.0-2.49	2.5-2.99	>2.99	No. of edges
(a) light step-flaking								
I	-	11.8	32.3	16.5	17.3	11.8	10.3	127
II	0.7	11.1	32.0	28.8	19.6	4.6	3.3	153
III	-	10.3	19.6	38.0	17.9	12.9	1.3	224
IV	0.6	16.8	33.6	23.9	16.2	1.8	7.2	167
(b) heavy step-flaking								
I	4.6	12.3	35.4	12.3	20.0	13.8	1.5	65
II	-	3.8	34.6	40.4	21.2	-	-	52
III	-	3.4	18.6	50.8	11.9	13.6	1.7	59
IV	-	5.4	40.5	28.4	6.8	10.8	8.1	74
(c) no retouch								
I	1.6	12.5	25.8	24.2	17.2	10.2	8.6	128
II	2.9	15.7	24.3	30.0	14.3	5.7	7.1	70
III	-	10.0	31.5	21.6	23.4	5.4	8.1	111
IV	-	13.1	16.8	18.3	20.4	14.6	16.8	137

Table 45 Batari: percentage distribution of the relation of retouch angle and implement weight on all implements with light step-flaking, excepting those implements clearly not whole and counting each edge as a separate implement

Angle in degrees	Weight in gm									No. of edges
	0-9	10-9	20-9	30-9	40-9	50-9	60-9	70-9	80-9	
(a) horizon I										
30-9	-	-	-	-	-	-	-	-	-	-
40-9	2.4	-	-	-	-	-	-	-	-	3
50-9	8.1	9.8	2.4	-	-	-	-	-	-	25
60-9	5.7	14.6	3.2	1.6	-	-	-	-	-	31
70-9	9.8	12.2	5.7	1.6	0.8	-	-	-	-	37
80-9	3.2	5.7	3.2	0.8	2.4	-	-	-	-	19
90-9	3.2	1.6	1.6	-	-	-	-	-	-	8
										123
(b) horizon II										
30-9	-	-	-	-	-	-	-	-	-	-
40-9	-	1.3	-	-	-	-	-	-	-	2
50-9	1.3	3.4	-	0.7	-	-	-	-	-	8
60-9	6.0	10.2	4.7	1.3	1.3	0.7	0.7	-	-	37
70-9	8.2	9.5	4.0	5.4	6.8	0.7	2.7	0.7	-	56
80-9	6.0	4.7	5.4	3.4	1.3	-	2.0	-	-	34
90-9	0.7	2.7	1.3	2.0	0.7	-	-	-	-	11
										148
(c) horizon III										
30-9	-	-	-	-	-	-	-	-	-	-
40-9	0.9	0.9	0.4	-	-	-	-	-	-	5
50-9	4.5	10.3	0.9	0.9	-	-	-	-	-	37
60-9	12.1	15.2	1.4	0.9	0.9	-	-	-	-	68
70-9	4.5	14.4	4.0	2.7	1.8	0.9	-	-	0.9	64
80-9	1.8	11.7	1.4	1.8	1.4	-	-	-	-	40
90-9	1.8	1.8	-	-	-	-	-	0.9	-	9
										223
(d) horizon IV										
30-9	-	0.6	-	-	-	-	-	-	-	1
40-9	0.6	1.2	-	-	-	-	-	-	-	3
50-9	2.4	1.2	2.4	0.6	-	-	-	-	-	11
60-9	10.4	12.8	6.7	3.7	0.6	-	-	-	-	56
70-9	3.1	19.6	5.5	1.8	3.7	-	0.6	0.6	-	57
80-9	1.8	6.1	1.2	1.2	3.7	-	0.6	-	-	24
90-9	1.2	2.4	1.2	1.2	0.6	-	-	-	-	11
										163

Table 46 Batari: percentage distribution of the shape of use-wear types, counting whole and probably whole lengths of use-wear only

Horizon	Straight	Concave	Convex	No. of occurrences
(a) 'chattering'				
I	61.6	36.5	1.9	159
II	57.8	37.6	4.9	109
III	51.7	45.9	2.4	168
IV	51.4	46.7	1.9	154
(b) 'utilisation'				
I	52.9	26.4	20.6	34
II	33.3	33.3	33.3	15
III	58.4	19.4	22.2	36
IV	41.1	23.1	35.9	39

Table 47   Batari: percentage distribution of the length of use-wear types, counting whole and probably whole lengths of use-wear only

| Horizon | Length in mm | | | | | | | No. of occurrences |
	0-5	6-10	11-15	16-20	21-25	26-30	>30	
(a) 'chattering'								
I	55.4	39.0	3.1	2.5	–	–	–	159
II	53.2	34.9	10.1	1.8	–	–	–	109
III	53.6	32.2	12.5	1.2	0.6	–	–	168
IV	44.8	50.0	3.9	0.6	0.6	–	–	154
(b) 'utilisation'								
I	–	44.2	20.6	17.7	8.8	8.8	–	34
II	20.0	40.0	6.7	26.7	6.7	–	–	15
III	11.1	33.3	22.2	19.4	5.6	5.6	2.8	36
IV	5.1	17.9	35.8	17.9	12.8	5.1	5.1	39

Table 48   Batari: percentage distribution of the length of edges in relation to use-wear type, counting whole and probably whole edges only

| Horizon | Length in mm | | | | | | | No. of edges |
	0-5	6-10	11-15	16-20	21-25	26-30	>30	
(a) 'chattering'								
I	32.0	43.6	18.4	6.1	–	–	–	147
II	22.8	45.7	22.8	6.7	1.0	1.0	–	105
III	31.2	38.8	24.8	4.5	–	0.6	–	157
IV	20.1	63.3	13.9	2.8	0.7	–	–	144
(b) 'utilisation'								
I	–	41.2	23.5	17.6	8.8	8.8	–	34
II	11.8	41.2	11.8	23.5	5.9	5.9	–	17
III	5.6	38.8	22.2	19.5	2.8	8.3	2.8	36
IV	5.0	17.5	35.0	20.0	12.5	5.0	5.0	40

Table 49   Batari: percentage distribution of the shape of edges in relation to use-wear type, counting whole and probably whole edges only

Horizon	Straight	Concave	Convex	Wavy	No. of edges
(a) 'chattering'					
I	37.2	61.2	1.4	–	147
II	32.4	61.0	4.8	1.9	105
III	33.8	63.1	3.2	–	157
IV	31.2	66.0	2.8	–	144
(b) 'utilisation'					
I	50.0	26.5	23.5	–	34
II	29.4	35.3	35.3	–	17
III	52.7	25.0	22.2	–	36
IV	45.0	20.0	35.0	–	40

Table 50   Batari: percentage distribution of the type of preparatory flaking in relation to use-wear type

Horizon	Unclear	None	Base struck	Side/end struck	Not applicable	No. of occurrences
(a) 'chattering'						
I	16.7	31.2	51.1	0.9	–	215
II	14.4	29.5	56.1	–	–	139
III	19.9	18.3	59.8	1.2	0.8	246
IV	20.1	22.3	55.4	0.9	1.3	224
(b) 'utilisation'						
I	2.5	35.0	2.5	–	60.0	40
II	12.5	33.0	12.5	–	41.7	24
III	7.5	27.5	10.0	–	55.0	40
IV	4.2	8.3	4.2	–	83.3	48

Table 51   Batari: percentage distribution of core and flake components of the industry in relation to use-wear type, counting each edge as a separate implement and excluding those clearly not whole

Horizon	Not determinable	Core/lump etc.	Flake	Trimming flake	No. of edges
(a) 'chattering'					
I	4.3	43.8	48.2	3.7	187
II	0.8	35.7	56.4	7.1	126
III	3.3	29.7	62.8	4.2	212
IV	3.0	44.3	46.3	6.5	201
(b) 'utilisation'					
I	–	17.9	76.9	5.1	39
II	–	31.8	59.1	9.1	22
III	2.6	7.7	84.5	5.1	39
IV	8.5	4.3	59.6	27.7	47

Table 52   Batari: percentage distribution of the thickness of implements in relation to use-wear type, counting each edge as a separate implement and excluding those clearly not whole

| Horizon | Thickness in mm | | | | | No. of edges |
	0-9	10-9	20-9	30-9	40-9	
(a) 'chattering'						
I	8.0	63.1	23.6	5.3	–	187
II	9.5	50.8	30.2	7.1	2.4	126
III	7.6	63.5	23.2	5.7	–	212
IV	9.5	54.7	29.8	5.0	1.0	201
(b) 'utilisation'						
I	38.5	41.0	18.0	–	2.6	39
II	45.4	36.0	9.1	9.1	–	22
III	35.9	53.8	7.7	2.6	–	39
IV	42.6	48.7	8.5	–	–	47

Table 53   Batari: percentage distribution of the weight of implements in relation to use-wear type, counting each edge as a separate implement and excluding those clearly not whole

Horizon	0-9	10-9	20-9	Weight in gm 30-9	40-9	50-9	60-9	70-9	No. of edges
(a) 'chattering'									
I	39.1	39.1	12.3	4.8	4.3	0.5	–	–	187
II	23.8	33.3	15.9	15.9	5.6	–	1.6	4.0	126
III	26.9	53.3	4.2	7.1	3.8	2.8	1.9	–	212
IV	24.6	44.7	18.4	4.0	6.9	–	1.5	–	201
(b) 'utilisation'									
I	58.9	25.6	7.7	5.1	2.6	–	–	–	39
II	68.2	9.1	9.1	9.1	4.5	–	–	–	22
III	58.9	30.8	2.6	5.1	–	2.6	–	–	39
IV	44.7	42.6	10.6	–	2.1	–	–	–	47

Table 54   Batari: percentage distribution of the angle of 'chattering' use-wear in relation to retouch type

Horizon	20-9	30-9	40-9	Angle in degrees 50-9	60-9	70-9	80-9	>89	Not measured	No. of occurrences
(a) no retouch										
I	–	1.0	3.9	16.5	25.2	25.2	12.6	14.6	1.0	103
II	–	4.3	2.9	14.5	32.2	29.0	20.3	7.2	–	69
III	–	2.2	4.5	15.7	29.2	28.1	7.9	12.4	3.4	89
IV	–	3.0	10.0	13.0	20.0	19.0	16.0	14.0	5.0	100
(b) step-flaking										
I	–	–	0.8	16.1	16.9	41.1	19.4	5.6	–	124
II	–	–	–	2.9	18.8	37.6	29.0	11.6	–	69
III	–	–	0.6	9.9	25.6	32.5	24.4	5.8	1.2	172
IV	–	–	0.8	8.6	28.1	35.2	16.4	9.4	1.6	128

Table 55   Batari: percentage distribution of the shape of use-wear in relation to retouch type, counting whole and probably whole lengths of use-wear only

Horizon	Straight	Concave	Convex	No. of occurrences
(a) no retouch				
I	53.7	43.7	2.5	80
II	58.0	32.0	10.0	50
III	52.6	43.8	3.5	57
IV	53.9	41.3	4.8	63
(b) step-flaking				
I	72.2	26.4	1.4	72
II	58.6	39.7	1.7	58
III	51.4	46.7	1.9	107
IV	48.3	51.7	–	87

Table 56   Batari: percentage distribution of the length of use-wear in relation to retouch type, counting whole and probably whole lengths of use-wear only

| Horizon | Length in mm | | | | | No. of occurrences |
	0-5	6-10	11-15	16-20	21-25	
(a) no retouch						
I	55.0	36.3	5.0	3.7	–	80
II	56.0	24.0	14.0	6.0	–	50
III	49.1	36.8	10.5	3.5	–	57
IV	38.1	50.8	7.9	1.6	1.6	63
(b) step-flaking						
I	58.3	40.3	1.4	–	–	72
II	53.4	43.1	3.5	–	–	58
III	57.0	29.9	12.2	–	0.9	107
IV	48.3	50.6	1.1	–	–	89

Table 57   Batari: percentage distribution of preparatory flaking in relation to retouch type

Horizon	Unclear	None	Base struck	Side/end struck	Not applicable	No. of occurrences
(a) no retouch						
I	14.6	46.6	37.8	1.0	–	103
II	15.9	39.1	44.9	–	–	69
III	21.3	35.9	41.6	1.1	–	89
IV	16.9	32.0	48.5	2.0	–	101
(b) step-flaking						
I	19.4	17.5	62.1	1.0	–	103
II	15.9	24.6	59.4	–	–	69
III	19.1	9.9	69.7	1.3	–	152
IV	23.3	15.8	60.8	–	–	120

Table 58   Batari: percentage distribution of core and flake components of the industry in relation to retouch type, counting each edge as a separate implement and excluding those clearly not whole

Horizon	Core/lump etc.	Flake	Trimming flake	Not measured	No. of edges
(a) no retouch					
I	43.9	48.3	4.4	3.3	91
II	39.1	53.1	6.2	1.6	64
III	31.6	58.2	5.1	5.1	79
IV	40.2	44.6	9.8	5.4	92
(b) step-flaking					
I	47.1	44.8	2.3	5.8	87
II	37.1	53.2	9.7	–	62
III	28.9	64.8	3.9	2.3	128
IV	47.2	49.1	2.8	0.9	106

Table 59   Batari: percentage distribution of the thickness of implements in relation to retouch type, counting each edge as a separate implement and excluding those clearly not whole

| Horizon | Thickness in mm | | | | | No. of edges |
	0-9	10-9	20-9	30-9	40-9	
(a) no retouch						
I	12.1	58.2	25.3	4.4	-	91
II	18.8	35.9	34.4	9.4	1.6	64
III	3.8	62.0	24.1	10.1	-	79
IV	15.2	62.0	15.2	7.6	-	92
(b) step-flaking						
I	3.5	66.6	23.0	6.9	-	87
II	4.8	58.1	27.0	6.5	3.2	62
III	10.1	64.1	22.6	3.1	-	128
IV	4.7	48.1	42.5	2.8	1.9	106

Table 60   Batari: percentage distribution of the weight of implements in relation to retouch type, counting each edge as a separate implement and excluding those clearly not whole

| Horizon | Weight in gm | | | | | | | | No. of edges |
	0-9	10-9	20-9	30-9	40-9	50-9	60-9	70-9	
(a) no retouch									
I	45.1	30.8	11.0	6.6	5.5	1.1	-	-	91
II	42.6	20.9	18.9	14.6	3.0	-	-	-	64
III	34.2	43.0	5.1	7.6	2.5	3.8	3.8	-	79
IV	33.7	41.3	12.0	3.3	8.7	-	1.1	-	92
(b) step-flaking									
I	32.2	48.3	12.6	3.5	3.5	-	-	-	87
II	12.9	43.6	19.4	12.9	8.1	1.6	1.6	-	62
III	22.6	58.6	3.9	7.0	4.7	2.3	0.8	-	128
IV	15.1	48.1	24.5	4.7	5.7	-	1.9	-	106

Table 61   Batari: percentage distribution of the angle of use-wear types

| Type of use-wear | Angle in degrees | | | | | | | | No. of occurrences |
	20-9	30-9	40-9	50-9	60-9	70-9	80-9	>89	
'Chattering' + step-flaking (C+SF)	-	-	0.5	10.0	23.0	35.2	23.2	8.2	440
'Chattering' without retouch (C-R)	-	2.5	5.6	14.4	25.0	25.8	13.3	13.3	360
'Utilisation' (U)	9.2	17.7	15.0	26.8	13.7	9.8	5.2	2.6	153

46

Table 62   Batari: percentage distribution of the shape of use-wear types, counting whole
and probably whole lengths of use-wear only

Type of use-wear	Straight	Concave	Convex	No. of occurrences
'Chattering' + step-flaking (C+SF)	56.5	42.3	1.2	326
'Chattering' without retouch (C-R)	54.4	40.8	4.8	250
'Utilisation' (U)	48.0	24.0	28.0	125

Table 63   Batari: percentage distribution of the length of use-wear types, counting whole
and probably whole lengths of use-wear only

Type of use-wear	Length in mm							No. of occurrences
	0-5	6-10	11-15	16-20	21-25	26-30	>30	
C+SF	54.3	40.2	5.2	–	0.3	–	–	326
C-R	49.6	37.6	8.8	3.6	0.4	–	–	250
U	7.2	32.0	24.8	18.4	8.8	6.4	2.4	125

Table 64   Batari: percentage distribution of preparatory flaking in relation to use-wear
type

Type of use-wear	Unclear	None	Base struck	Side/end struck	Not applicable	No. of occurrences
C+SF	19.4	16.1	63.9	0.6	–	485
C-R	19.6	36.2	43.1	1.1	–	362
U	6.5	25.3	6.5	–	61.7	154

Table 65   Batari: percentage distribution of core and flake components of the industry
in relation to use-wear type, counting each edge as a separate
implement and excluding those clearly not whole

Type of use-wear	Not determinable	Core/lump etc.	Flake	Trimming flake	No. of edges
C+SF	2.4	39.4	53.0	4.2	383
C-R	4.0	38.9	50.6	6.4	326
U	3.4	12.9	70.7	12.9	147

Table 66   Batari: percentage distribution of edge shape in relation to use-wear type, counting each edge as a separate implement and excluding those clearly not whole

Type of use-wear	Straight	Concave	Convex	No. of edges
'Chattering' + step-flaking (C+SF)	23.3	75.0	1.7	288
'Chattering' without retouch (C-R)	47.4	47.0	5.6	249
'Utilisation' (U)	46.4	25.0	28.4	127

Table 67   Batari: percentage distribution of the length of edges in relation to use-wear type, counting whole and probably whole edges only

Type of use-wear	Length in mm							No. of edges
	0-5	6-10	11-15	16-20	21-25	26-30	>30	
C+SF	17.7	51.4	25.7	4.9	-	0.3	-	288
C-R	39.8	42.6	12.0	5.2	0.4	-	-	249
U	4.7	33.1	25.2	19.7	7.9	7.1	2.4	127

Table 68   Batari: percentage distribution of base type in relation to use-wear type

Type of use-wear	Not determinable	Pebble cortex	Other cortex	Break	Negative bulb	Positive bulb	Not applicable	No. of occurrences
C+SF	7.0	2.0	6.5	7.0	28.2	49.4	-	444
C-R	9.1	4.4	9.4	5.5	35.4	36.2	-	362
U	4.4	1.3	-	3.1	12.0	17.6	61.6	159

Table 69   Batari: percentage distribution of the thickness of implements in relation to use-wear type, counting each edge as a separate implement and excluding those clearly not whole

Type of use-wear	Thickness in mm						No. of edges
	0-9	10-9	20-9	30-9	40-9	50-9	
C+SF	6.3	59.3	29.0	4.5	1.0	-	383
C-R	10.5	56.4	24.8	7.9	0.4	-	266
U	38.5	47.3	11.5	2.0	0.6	-	148

Table 70   Batari: percentage distribution of the weight of implements in relation to use-wear type, counting each edge as a separate implement and excluding those clearly not whole

Type of use-wear	Weight in gm								No. of edges
	0-9	10-9	20-9	30-9	40-9	50-9	60-9	70-9	
C+SF	21.2	50.9	14.1	6.5	5.2	1.0	1.0	-	388
C-R	37.4	35.0	10.1	8.3	5.2	1.2	1.5	1.2	266
U	54.1	31.1	8.1	4.0	2.0	0.6	-	-	148

Table 71   Batari: distribution of trimming flakes

Square	Horizon				Total
	I	II	III	IV	
C3	1	10	5	–	16
C4	3	13	12	–	28
D3	17	16	9	–	42
D4	1	3	15	4	23
E3	11	18	32	43	104
E4	15	7	18	27	67
F3	4	5	10	4	23
Total	52	72	101	78	303
Ratio of implements to trimming flakes	2.63	2.02	1.86	1.85	2.03[1]

[1] Based on total number of implements and trimming flakes

Table 72   Batari: distribution of hammers

Reference[1]	Horizon	Material	Weight in gm
39.E4/(9)	III	Hornblende-porphyry	480.6
97.E3/(11)	IV	Porphyry	125.9
116.E3/(13)	IV	Porphyry + pyrite crystals	171.1

[1] Numbers given in this form refer to 'catalogue number. Square/(spit)'.

Plate 2   Aibura: A) environment, viewed from north.   The bush-covered
          outcrop left of centre contains the cave.   B) main chamber,
          looking north.   Scale in 20 cm.   C) northern 3 m of west
          wall.   Scale in 20 cm.

IV   EXCAVATIONS AT AIBURA, LAMARI RIVER VALLEY

THE SITE

Aibura (A64) is the name given by Tairora of Barabuna village to a small free-standing block of Tertiary limestone which lies 12 miles (19 km) on a bearing of 195° from Kainantu (6°26'S, 145°57'E) at an altitude of about 5300 ft (1640 m) asl (fig.1). The block rises out of a small swampy valley draining into Kondanauta Creek, a small west-flowing tributary of the Lamari River (fig.7 upper). The valley floor, in which many old garden ditches occur, is now covered with 'pitpit' (*Miscanthus floridulus*, *Phragmites karka* and *Saccharum* spp.), while shorter grasses such as *Imperata cylindrica* grow on surrounding slopes. The topography is rolling rather than steep by New Guinea standards, with many swampy patches in the river valleys. The lower levels are all grassed, with a few trees close to water courses and stands of rainforest on all surrounding peaks (pl.2a).

The limestone block appears to be an isolated relict of Omaura Greywacke (Dow and Plane 1965). It is small (approximately 60 x 25 x 15 m), the outer surface is highly irregular and well covered with trees and creepers. It is aligned approximately NW-SE and the interior is hollow, forming a cave which stretches the length of the block (fig.7 lower).

The cave is divided into four chambers. The northwestern half is a very dark tunnel with 1-2 m headroom and a flat floor. This leads to the main chamber, approximately 15 x 10 m, which is badly lit by a few small holes in the roof and some light entering from the southern entrance. There are a few stalactites and stalagmites around the edges of this chamber, but the floor is flat and the headroom is 3-4 m (pl.2b). In the southern chamber the floor is formed by a natural talus sloping in from the two entrances. The small eastern chamber also has two entrances and an irregular floor; access to it from the main chamber is difficult because of stalagmites. There is still active deposition in the cave, with small patches of stalagmitic concretion being formed on the present floor. There are not many water drips in the dry season, but the floor is very damp and floor wash apparently occurs in the wet season.

Human use of the cave is clear from a large number of black and white paintings in the east and south chambers and on the south wall of the main chamber. The paintings are mostly abstract designs, with circles and an irregular triangle with two projections from its apex being the only recurring patterns. One very clear female figure occurs in a very small cave on the west side of the outcrop (White and White 1964).

Discovery and Excavation

Aibura was probably first visited by J.A. Rae in 1945 (Bena Patrol Report 26 of 44/45, a reference I owe to A. Radford). It was visited by A. Vincent (Summer Institute of Linguistics, New Guinea Branch) in 1961 and reported to V. Watson who was recording archaeological data as part of the University of Washington Microevolution Project (Watson 1963). At her suggestion, on 16 April 1964, I excavated a 1.2 x 1 m pit to a depth of 1.6 m in the main chamber and found sixty-one flakes and lumps, including fifteen retouched implements, in a matrix of dark, wet silty loam (White 1965b:335). Since the primary purpose of this pit was to see whether the site had stone artifacts in an undisturbed stratigraphic context, it was dug rather quickly and the soil was not carefully sieved. The material from this pit is included in the main analysis.

The western part of the main chamber was excavated in four weeks during August, 1964 (White 1965a:43-8). A total of 15 m² was removed, 12 of them as

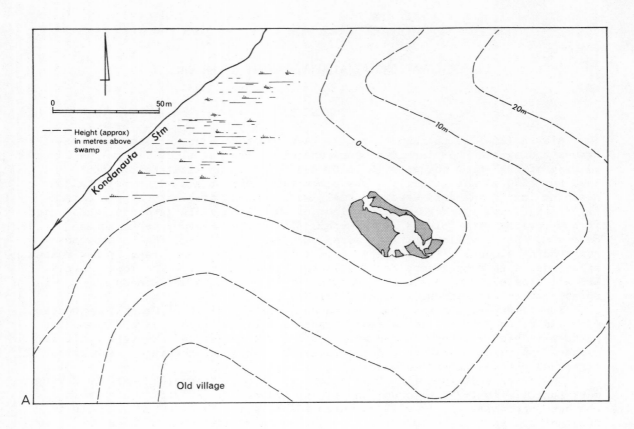

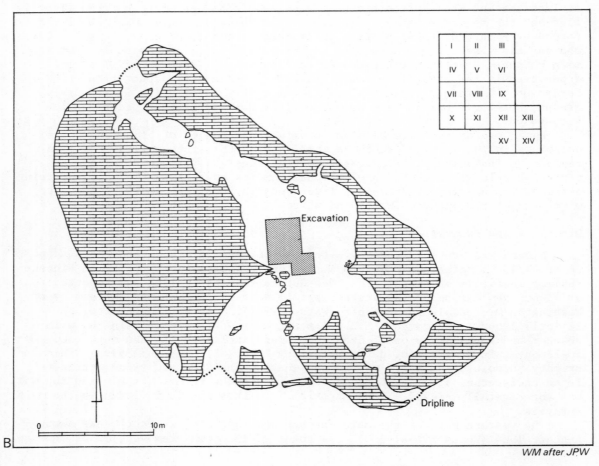

Fig.7   Aibura: locality map and plan of cave

a 4 x 3 m rectangular trench taken down to the sterile base at 140 cm (maximum).
The 3 m^2 extension trench showed no stratigraphic features: it therefore does
not appear on the drawn sections or plans of features.   The test pit was
incorporated into the main excavation.   In all, about 13.5 m^3 of deposit were
removed, perhaps one-eighth of the archaeological deposit.   Most excavation
was done by the author, although two Tairora youths dug for a few days under
close supervision.   The site was removed in metre squares and as a series of
levels (spits), conforming to the pattern of ash lenses and other visible
stratigraphic features.   These varied from 5 to 20 cm in depth and the levels
varied accordingly, but all were roughly horizontal.

Stratigraphy (fig.8a-c; pl.2c)

The surface of the excavated area sloped slightly towards the north with
a maximum fall of 30 cm and a mean fall of about 20 cm.   The soil was very
damp and dark, with a field pH of 6-8 throughout.   The main excavation showed
that ash lenses were distributed over the whole area but were thicker in the
northwestern part.   They consisted largely of well-packed white to cream ash
intermixed with some burnt soil and carbon.   Most were almost horizontal,
tending to tail out or even curve upwards slightly at the edges, as if they had
been spread and slightly redeposited by water.   They occurred for about 50 cm
below surface in the east and 60 cm below surface in the west of the trench
and were intercalated with damp blackish silt.   There was a concentration of
artifacts at about 40-5 cm below the surface, while many postholes occurred in
the top 35 cm.   Scattered through the lenses were occasional concreted patches
clearly formed by dripping water.

Below the lenses there was about 80 cm of fine dark silt with a little
grit.   It appeared to have been washed free of ash lenses, but a few
concentrations of carbon remained.   A second concentration of artifacts occurred
about 10-20 cm below the lowest ash lenses.   The sterile basal deposit was a
well-compacted, granular, yellow-brown to grey soil with a relatively high
component of grits.   This deposit was cut into by a channel running
approximately north through the excavation and also dipped parallel to this
channel along the west wall.

In the northeast corner of the trench there was only a thin deposit of
soil below the ash lenses.   Beneath this soil was a stiff, almost sterile clay,
which was sharply differentiated from the surrounding soil.   In the southwest
corner of the trench, especially square X, bedrock was found 60 cm below
surface, sloping down steeply to the north and east.

Several processes probably formed the deposits in Aibura.   The lowest
sterile material was at the same level as the swamp outside the cave, and
probably contained similar material with additions of grit due to cave
dissolution: its surface was probably shaped by water solution.   The dark, wet
silt above this was possibly deposited by both water and human action followed
by some resettling and washing due to water-table fluctuations.   The washing
was apparently very gentle since carbon and a high component of fine soil
remained.   The silt is bracketed by two radiocarbon dates (p.57) which suggest
that it accumulated over some 2,000 years.   The origin of the thick bank of
clay remains a problem but its location is likely to represent a long-term
pool.   The fact that few artifacts are incorporated in the clay reinforces
the suggestion that all washing within the cave was gentle.

The ash lenses are explicable as a series of occupations, partly spread
and compacted by gentle water action.   Most lenses have formed within the last
600-1000 years, since they lie above radiocarbon sample GaK-622.

Many postholes and a pit were found in the western half of the excavation.
The majority of the postholes lay within 15 cm of the surface and three clearly
defined alignments were noted (fig.9a).   Two of them ran almost precisely
parallel with the west wall of the cave and one ran at right angles to this,
at the southern end of the excavation.   The largest diameter among the
aligned holes was 10 cm.   All posts were set vertically or tilted slightly
towards the west.   Below 15 cm, postholes were fewer and concentrated in the
northeast corner.   Only one probable alignment was found, set approximately

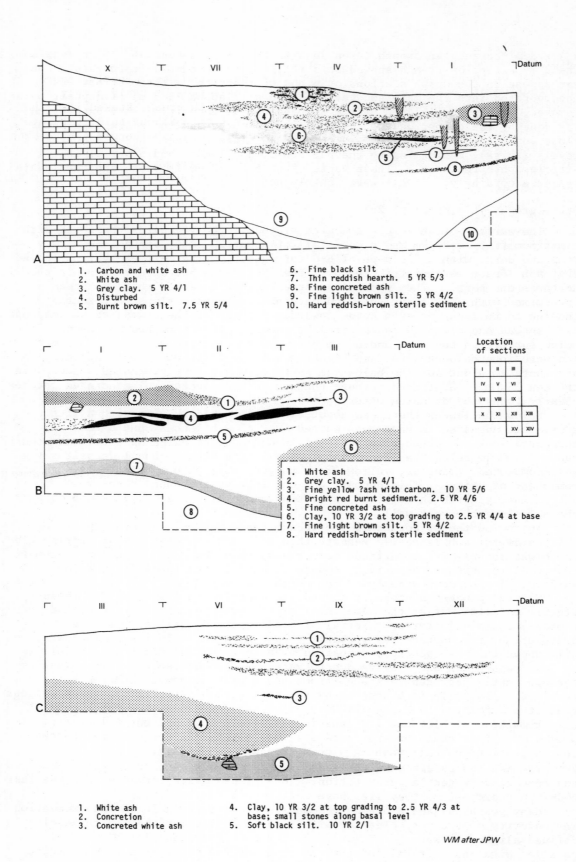

A
1. Carbon and white ash
2. White ash
3. Grey clay. 5 YR 4/1
4. Disturbed
5. Burnt brown silt. 7.5 YR 5/4
6. Fine black silt
7. Thin reddish hearth. 5 YR 5/3
8. Fine concreted ash
9. Fine light brown silt. 5 YR 4/2
10. Hard reddish-brown sterile sediment

Location of sections

I	II	III
IV	V	VI
VII	VIII	IX
X	XI	XII	XIII
	XV	XIV

B
1. White ash
2. Grey clay. 5 YR 4/1
3. Fine yellow ?ash with carbon. 10 YR 5/6
4. Bright red burnt sediment. 2.5 YR 4/6
5. Fine concreted ash
6. Clay, 10 YR 3/2 at top grading to 2.5 YR 4/4 at base
7. Fine light brown silt. 5 YR 4/2
8. Hard reddish-brown sterile sediment

C
1. White ash
2. Concretion
3. Concreted white ash
4. Clay, 10 YR 3/2 at top grading to 2.5 YR 4/3 at base; small stones along basal level
5. Soft black silt. 10 YR 2/1

WM after JPW

Fig.8   Aibura: A) stratigraphy of west wall;   B) north wall;
        C) east wall

parallel to the cave's western wall (fig.9b).

Most of these postholes, and especially the alignments, clearly record the erection of structures within the cave. These were probably simply lines of branches, which may have been interwoven with brush, staked into the ground and leaning against the wall. Villagers from Barabuna said that this cave was used as a refuge in pre-European times, and the shelters may have been used then. Temporary shelters of this kind have been seen in rockshelters used for overnight stops south of this area (P.J. Thomas pers. comm.).

A large pit was also found, starting about 10 cm below the surface (fig.9a). Irregular at the top, it became a square with rounded corners (approximately 18 x 18 cm) by 30 cm below the surface and maintained this shape until the base was rounded off at 75 cm below the surface. The pit was filled with loose grey ashy silt containing only one stone flake. At some time later a round posthole, 12 cm in diameter, was dug in the southwest corner of the original pit. Neither of these features can be associated with any complex of postholes and the purposes for which they were dug are unclear. The pit is about the right shape and size for a small cooking pit but the absence of any heating stones makes this unlikely, although heating stones are sometimes taken away for re-use. There were no signs of extra organic material in the fill, such as might suggest use as a latrine, while latrines themselves are still unusual among the Tairora.

The third feature was a congregation of small limestone boulders about 25 cm below the surface in square I. The excavation just included the 20 boulders, which looked as if they were placed in position rather than simply dumped. The size, raw material and condition of these stones preclude the suggestion that they were used for pit-cooking or stone-working. They are not obviously linked with a hearth or with a particular posthole alignment. They are also unlikely to be a roof-fall, since there is no obvious gap in the roof at this point and in this case one would expect one big, and several small rocks, all dumped in a heap (J.N. Jennings pers. comm.). I am unable at present, therefore, to suggest an explanation for this feature.

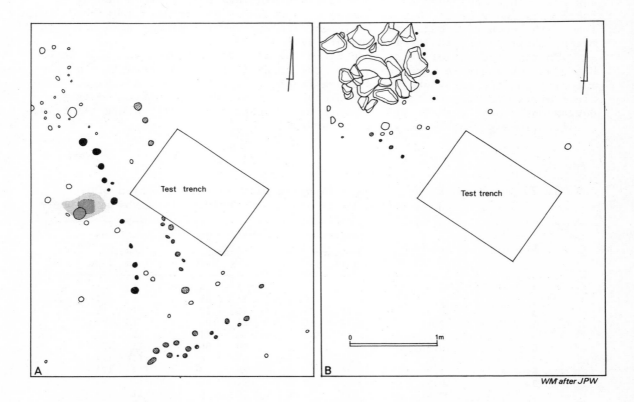

WM after JPW

Fig.9   Aibura: main excavation.   A) postholes at level 1;   B) postholes
        at level 2 with boulders at level 3

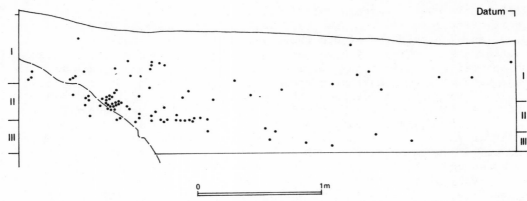

Fig.10   Aibura: implements from squares I, IV, VII and X plotted on west
wall (section A)

Division of the Material

The two divisions in the visible stratigraphy of the excavation, the ash
lenses and the lower black silt, can be seen over most of the main 4 x 3 m
excavation and can be observed in the distribution of some artifacts (fig.10).
The distribution of all flaked implements and waste stone by metre squares
and spits (table 73) indicates that there are two concentrations of material
in squares I-IX, separated by level 5.   This is confirmed by the presence of
marine shell and pottery down to level 4 only.   The faunal material, however,
is concentrated in levels 3 and 4, with the amount declining rapidly below this.

Squares X-XV, at the south end of the site, show a unimodal distribution
of all artifactual material.   To see whether a division could be made to
parallel that already seen elsewhere, five attributes of the flaked implements
were examined by excavated levels.   Use-wear type and retouch type and angle
suggested that the upper horizon should contain levels 1-3, while weight of
implements and whether they were made on a flake or a core lump suggested levels
1-4.   The number of edges per implement did not vary.   It was also noted that
marine shell occurs in level 4 in this part of the site.

To take account of these disparities as well as to divide the site into
horizons for analysis three horizons were created, based on inspection of the
material and the attribute tests above (table 73).   For other analyses, where
finer divisions are necessary, the excavated levels have been treated as
equivalent over the whole site.   This may distort the final picture slightly,
but it allows a finer separation of material.

Table 73   Aibura: volume of deposit by levels, and distribution of
implements, waste stone and horizons by level and square

Level	Volume in m³	Implements Squares		Waste stone Squares		Horizons Squares	
		I-IX	X-XV	I-IX	X-XV	I-IX	X-XV
1	1.6	1	5	5	4	I	I
2	1.6	7	16	11	24	I	I
3	1.9	28	28	40	47	I	I
4	2.1	17	61	17	104	I	I
5	1.7	9	49	14	71	II	II
6	0.8	47	43	49	36	II	III
7	1.0	51	1	49	6	II	III
8	1.0	34	1	27	3	III	III
9	0.5	15	0	22	0	III	–
10	0.8	13	0	20	0	III	–
11	1.0	2	0	7	0	III	–

56

Artifact Joins

Twenty-five artifacts which had been broken in antiquity were rejoined to make eleven whole pieces. All joining fragments except one came from the same square and spit: the odd pair came from adjacent spits and diagonally adjacent squares. Although numbers are small, they suggest that there has not been very much movement of material within the excavated deposit, which is consistent with other evidence.

Dating

Two radiocarbon determinations were obtained (Kigoshi and Kobayashi 1966:71-2).

GaK-622: base HI, square VII, level 4   770 ± 100 BP

GaK-623: lower HIII, square IX, level II 3800 ± 110 BP

GaK-622 dates wood carbon from the lower part of the ash lenses, at 50 cm below the surface. GaK-623 comes from lumps of carbon found in the lowest level of the black silt (depth 122 cm).

FAUNA AND FLORA

Domestic Animals

Pig (*Sus scrofa*) occurred only within some 30 cm of the surface. Eight definite and three probable pig bones and teeth were found, comprising at least one adult and one juvenile. The following bones were identified: one each of scapula, calcaneum, distal tibia, distal humerus, ?tibia and ?rib. The five teeth were: two pre-molars, one PM^3, one DM_3, one ?molar. Six of the bones occurred within level 1, three in level 2 and two (including one questionable bone) in level 3. It cannot be determined whether the animals were domestic or feral. All bones lie well above the level of GaK-622, 770 ± 100 BP.

Dog (*Canis familiaris*) was recorded from level 1 only, where one PM_3 was found.

Wild Animals

A wide range of animals was found. The identifiable post-cranial bones have been counted and the non-identifiable bone has been weighed, but other analyses follow the procedures previously described. Over the whole of the site the fauna was concentrated in Horizon I. If the fauna was analysed only in terms of the three horizons several important facts would be obscured through lack of a sufficient number of units. All analyses are therefore based on excavated levels treated as equivalent over the whole site.

J.A. Mahoney identified 287 rodent mandibles from this site. He divided the small murids into three or four genera and nine species, and gave data for the length of the lower three molars in each (table 74).

Table 74   Aibura: rodents

Genus	Species	Length M_{1-3} (mm)
Pogonomys	A	5.0
	B	6.1
	C	6.8
Rattus	A	6.5
	B	*c.* 5.2
	C	*c.* 4.8
Melomys or *Pogonomelomys*	A	6.0
	B	5.9
	C	8.0 (M^{1-3} only)

From the mandibles (except for *Pseudocheirus (Pseudocheirus)* whose preserved maxillae outnumbered its preserved mandibles) it is calculated that the site, treated as a whole, contains 450 animals, in the form of: 152 small rodents, 115 macropodids, 145 phalangers, and 38 other animals. The minimum number rises to 502 (including 166 small rodents) if the calculation is based on the mandibles within each excavated level (spit) over the whole site.

Of the 502 animals, 360 are identifiable to generic level and the rest may be given at least family status. Table 75 sets out the minimum number of animals in each spit, while table 76 summarises these data in terms of the percentage of animals in each level which each major animal group forms.

Table 75 Aibura: minimum numbers of animals

Animals	Adult or Juvenile	Levels							Total no. of animals by levels[1]	Total no. of animals in whole site[2]
		1	2	3	4	5	6-7	8-11		
Macropodidae										
Thylogale bruijni	A	1	5	15	10	5	–	1	37	35
	J	–	6	19	8	3	1	–	37	31
Dorcopsulus sp.	A	–	–	3	3	4	1	–	11	10
	J	–	–	–	1	2	–	–	3	2
Dendrolagus sp.	A	–	1	1	–	–	–	–	2	2
	J	–	–	–	–	–	–	–	–	–
Phalangeridae										
Phalanger spp.	A	–	1	15	17	18	8	–	59	52
	J	–	–	1	3	2	–	–	6	6
Pseudocheirus (Pseudochirops) spp.	A	–	1	–	8	4	3	–	16	11
	J	–	–	1	–	–	–	–	1	1
P. (Pseudocheirus) spp.	A	–	1	4	8	4	2	–	19	15
	J	–	–	3	2	2	–	–	7	6
Dactylopsila or *Dactylonax*		–	–	1	3	–	–	–	4	2
Petaurus breviceps		–	–	1	–	1	2	–	4	2
Eudromicia cf. *caudata*		2	–	2	2	–	–	–	6	6
Dasyuridae										
Antechinus sp.		–	–	1	1	–	–	–	2	1
Satanellus albopunctatus		–	–	1	–	–	1	–	2	2
Peramelidae										
Peroryctes or *Echymipera*		–	1	5	7	1	1	–	15	14
Megachiroptera										
Pteropus or *Dobsonia*		–	1	–	–	–	–	–	1	1
Muridae										
Hyomys goliath		–	1	–	4	2	–	–	7	5
Mallomys rothschildi		–	–	–	2	1	–	–	3	2
Anisomys imitator		–	–	–	1	1	–	–	2	2
Uromys sp.		–	1	–	2	1	–	–	4	2
Pogonomys A sp.		6	5	13	4	2	–	–	30	20
Pogonomys B sp.		–	–	2	–	1	–	–	3	2
Pogonomys C sp.		–	–	1	–	1	–	–	2	2
Rattus A sp.		5	3	8	2	4	1	–	23	21
Rattus B sp.		–	–	2	–	–	–	–	2	2
Rattus C sp.		1	–	–	–	–	–	–	1	1
Melomys or *Pogonomelomys* A sp.		12	9	14	3	3	1	–	42	41
Melomys or *Pogonomelomys* B sp.		1	–	4	–	–	–	–	5	5
Melomys or *Pogonomelomys* C sp.		–	–	3	1	–	–	–	4	4
Unidentified macropodids		–	4	22	7	2	–	–	35	35
Unidentified phalangerids (mostly cuscus?)		–	1	21	13	6	2	1	44	44
Unidentified rodents		9	12	17	10	4	2	–	54	54
Unidentified other		–	3	2	–	4	–	–	9	9
Totals										
Macropodids		1	16	60	29	16	2	1	125	115
Phalangerids		2	4	49	56	37	17	1	166	145
Small rodents		34	29	64	20	15	4	–	166	152
Other		–	7	9	17	10	2	–	45	38
Total animals		37	56	182	122	78	25	2	502	450

[1] Minimum numbers calculated by level
[2] Minimum numbers calculated on site as a whole

Table 76 Aibura: percentage distribution of animals

Level	Macropodids	Phalangerids[1]	Small rodents	Other	Total no.
1	2.7	–	91.9	5.4	37
2	28.6	3.6	51.8	16.1	56
3	33.0	20.3	35.3	11.5	182
4	23.8	27.0	16.4	32.8	122
5	20.5	33.4	19.2	26.9	78
6-7 } 8-11 }	11.1	40.7	14.8	33.3	{ 25 2

[1] Including unidentified phalangerids (mostly cuscus?)

Three features of this fauna are noticeable. One is the sheer number of animals present, which contrasts strongly with the artifactual situation. The second is the concentration of animals in and above level 5. There is almost no lower concentration of faunal material to parallel the lower horizon of artifacts, which, since the bone there is in good condition, may point to a change in site use. Third, within the upper horizon there is a steady decline and disappearance of cuscus, a rise in rodents from level 4 to level 1, a rise in macropodids to about level 2, and a corresponding decline in other animals in level 3 and above. These changes occur mostly within the last 1000 years.

Since there is no evidence that these changes represent changing hunting patterns, certain inferences may be made:

1. The decline and disappearance of cuscus (*Phalanger* spp.) which is primarily an arboreal animal (cf. S. and R. Bulmer 1964:50) may document an increase in grasslands. The increase in macropodids, especially *Thylogale*, probably supports this hypothesis (see Appendix 1).

2. The dominance of small rodents in level 1 may relate to the small numbers in the sample or to the fact that nowadays it is mostly youths that hunt around the site and large animals are rarely caught. However, the dramatic rise in the relative importance of rodents between level 4 and level 1 may well be related to an 'overkill' of larger animals in the area as increasing agricultural populations exerted more pressure on the natural environment.

3. The environmental picture given by the small rodents themselves, however, is unclear. Mahoney (pers. comm.) is inclined to regard *Pogonomys* as perhaps a tree dweller, but *Rattus* is clearly non-arboreal. The other genera are not defined sufficiently well for discussion. However, since there is no change over time in the relative proportions of the two named genera they do not document any ecological shift.

4. The balance between adult and juvenile animals is generally about normal for a hunting economy. At Aibura, with the exception of *Thylogale bruijni*, there are four or more adults to one juvenile, comparable with a ratio of 3:1 or more in other parts of the world (e.g. Clark 1954; Higgs 1962:272).

5. The steady rise in the percentage of mandibles in relation to other bone is most noticeable (table 77). By levels 4–2 it is higher than one would expect for a site to which animals were brought before butchering (cf. Batari). However, even today the villagers preserve in their huts many mandibles of larger animals caught by hunting. If this were the practice in prehistoric times, it would explain not only why mandibles are so common but also why they outnumber maxillae to such an extent.

Table 77   Aibura: distribution of mandibles and other bone[1]

Level	A. no. of mandibles	B. no. of identifiable bones	A as percentage of A + B	Weight of unidentifiable bone in gm
1	3	44	6.4	57.8
2	36	111	24.5	307.9
3	150	436	25.6	1392.6
4	145	574	20.2	1486.2
5	79	416	16.0	905.1
6	21	145	12.7	305.0
7	2	35	{9.3}	104.2
8	2	4		45.1
9	–	2	–	5.0
Total	438	1767	19.9	4608.9

[1] Small rodents are excluded since some of them may have been caught in the cave

Birds

Those bones identified as bird were submitted to J.C. Yaldwyn for identification of domestic fowl.   He reports that one tibia from level 3 is very likely to be fowl (*Gallus gallus*), while two femurs and a tibia from levels 4, 5 and 6 respectively may be fowl.   This suggests that fowl may be several hundred years old in this part of the Highlands (cf. Bulmer 1966a:26).

The other thirteen bones all came from level 3 and above.   They include long bones, pelves and metatarsals.   R.J. Scarlett inspected all bones recovered from levels 2, 4 and 6.   He reported one distal phalange of probably cassowary in Square II/Level (2) and an anterior fragment of sternum, about pigeon size, in VIII/(6).   A few other fragments of bird bone were noted. It is clear that cassowary and other birds were not commonly brought to Aibura, in contrast to the picture from sites in the Western Highlands (Bulmer 1966a:94,118).

Twenty-three fragments of cassowary eggshell were found, weighing 9.3 gm. Nine large fragments (5.2 gm) were found close together and may come from one eggshell.   The other fragments were mostly in the six southern squares and were spread through levels 3 (6 fragments), 4 (4 fragments) and 5 (5 fragments).   It is possible, but unlikely, that only one shell is represented.

Reptiles

Four reptile fragments were identified by R.E. Barwick.   They are the right maxilla of an agamid lizard from IV/(8) and three fragments of snake, subfamily Pythoninae, from adjacent squares in levels 4-5.   These animals were probably eaten (R. Bulmer 1967).

Mollusca

Mollusca from three environments, marine, freshwater and land, were found at Aibura (table 78).   All have been identified by D.F. McMichael.

Table 78   Aibura: distribution of mollusc fragments

Type of shell	1	2	3	Level 4	5	6	Total
Marine Shell:							
Trochus niloticus L. (commercial trochus)	4	2	2+1?	1+4?	–	–	9+5?
Cypraea annulus L. (ringed money cowry)	2	1	1	–	–	–	4
Ovula ovum L. (egg cowry)	1	–	–	–	–	–	1
Nassarius thersites Brugiere (plicated dog whelk)	–	–	1	1	–	–	2
Charonia tritonis L. (trumpet shell)	–	–	–	1	–	–	1
Oliva sp. (olive shell)	–	–	–	2	–	–	2
Cymatium s.l. or *Murex* s.l.	–	1	–	–	–	–	1
Freshwater mussels:							
Velsunio sentaniensis Haas	–	–	–	–	1	–	1
Hyridella (Nesonaia) guppyi aipiana McMichael	1	1	1?	–	1?	–	2+2?
Unidentified	3	4	12	13	3	1	36
Land snails:							
Helicina sp., near *coxeni* Brazier	–	–	1	–	–	–	1
Chloritis (Disteustoma) sp., near *dinodiomorpha* Tapp. Can.	–	–	1	–	–	–	1
Chloritis (Disteustoma) sp., near *lepidophora* Kobelt.	–	–	3	–	–	–	3
Kendallena broadbenti (Brazier)	–	–	1	–	–	–	1
Sulcobasis sp.	–	–	1	–	–	–	1
Family Camaenidae	1	–	2	–	–	–	3

Marine shells   Twenty-five pieces of marine shell were found in and above level 4.   Seven genera are represented, with the commercial trochus shell being most common.   No shells have been altered by human action.   McMichael (pers. comm.) points out that the presence of the ringed money cowry, presumably a trade object, is somewhat unexpected, since the more widely used form at the time of European contact was the money cowry.

Freshwater shells   Two genera of freshwater mussels were identified amongst the 41 fragments but 36 fragments remain unidentified.   Freshwater mussel shells occurred down to level 6, were concentrated in levels 3 and 4, and declined above this.   It is not known whether this decline reflects local ecological changes.   One piece of shell has a small hole drilled through it.

Land snails   Ten fragments of land snail shell were recorded, nearly all from level 3.   Of the five genera represented, four are of the camaenid family which form the typical local land snails.   It seems likely that most of these snails were naturally incorporated into the deposit.

Human Remains

Scattered and mostly broken remains of several, possibly three, individuals were found, but nothing approximating to a burial was noted.   The bones are described in detail by L. Freedman (Appendix 2) and details of the bone associations are also discussed there.   All individuals appear to have been placed in the cave before 700-1000 years ago.

Floral Remains

Pollen analysis   Eight soil samples covering the whole depth of the site were tested to see whether they contained pollen grains.   J.M. Matthews (pers. comm.) reports that all samples were treated with acridin orange 0.1% solution and then examined with a fluorescence microscope, but no pollens were observed in any sample.

Carbon   Two samples of wood carbon from the lower levels of the site were thin-sectioned and examined by the Division of Forest Products, CSIRO.   The sample from level 7 was from one of the Lauraceae, probably *Cryptocarya*, a large furry-leaved tree that grows up to 30 m in height.   This tree prefers well drained soils and is normally only found in rainforest (J. Flenley pers. comm.).   The sample from level 12 was *Bambusa* sp., a bamboo.   Bamboos grow around most village sites and are one of the essential woods in village life.
It would be too much to infer that these two carbon identifications indicate a more wooded environment during earlier occupation of the site, especially since this material has passed through a cultural filter, but it is interesting to consider this evidence in conjunction with the faunal data.

EXOTIC ARTIFACTS

Recent Objects

A yellow bead and some blue trade-store paint from the top 2-3 cm of the deposit show that the site had been used subsequent to European trade goods entering this area, about 1930 (Watson 1964:1).

Pottery

Fourteen sherds of pottery were found in level 3 and two in level 4, while two pieces of shaped clay were found in level 2.   Sherds were found over the whole excavation but were concentrated towards the southern end.   J.R. Specht distinguished the following groups:

1. Two body sherds of fine thin hand-made ware. That from Square III/Level
    (3) is red (5 YR 4/6), grit-filled, 4-5 mm thick. XIV/(3) i is 5 YR 5/3
in colour, 3.5-4 mm thick.

2. Four body sherds of fine thin (2.5-3.5 mm) blackish-grey ware found in
    quite close association: XV/(3) (two sherds), XIV/(3) ii, and 22.IX/(3);
note regarding the latter 22 is the individual catalogue number of the object.

3. The ten remaining sherds are much more heterogeneous than the other two
    groups and are simply coarse hand-made pottery. Two of the three rim
sherds come from open-mouthed bowls with incurved (VIII/(3)) and everted
(X/(4)) rims respectively. The latter is decorated with finger-nail
impressions and a parallel pair of wavy lines on the rim (fig.11a). On the
other two sherds (VIII/(3) and XII/(3)) the rim has probably been made by
pulling up a flap of clay and folding it over (fig.11b).
    239.XIII/(3) is an ornamented shoulder sherd of a large open-mouthed pot
in a sandy fabric. The body is marked on the outside with a line of angled
impressions probably made with a piece of wood. Above this is a wavy relief
band. The neck is decorated with incised cross-hatching.
    The other six sherds are mostly red-brown in colour and all are
undecorated. Thicknesses range from 4.5 to 10.5 mm. Find spots and, where
appropriate, individual catalogue numbers are: 60.III/(3) i and ii, VI/(3),
VIII/(3), 22.IX/(3) and VII/(4).

4. The two fragments of ?burned clay in IX/(2) are red (2.5 YR 6/6) and
    concavo-convex in section as though pressed against a curved object. On
the inside of one is a small deep impression which looks rather like a bamboo
node. These fragments are probably just slightly burnt clay without additives
and may be some kind of daub.

    This pottery is almost certainly foreign to the Tairora as there are no
records of pottery making in the area nor are sherds commonly found there.
The only recorded pottery making in the Highlands is among a few Agarabi
villages bordering on the Ramu Fall (Watson 1955; Coutts 1967). Watson
reports that two forms are made:

1. a high-necked jar with slightly everted rim and pointed base, decorated on
    the lower part of the neck and the flat lip;

2. a small globular form which has a short everted rim and flat lip.
    Decoration is on the exterior rim and shoulder.

Motifs include incised parallel wavy lines, parallel horizontal lines and
straight rows of punctate dots. Incising is done with sticks. The average
thickness of ten Agarabi sherds was five-eighths in. (16 mm). Pots are made
by coiling and smoothing. A local clay containing some sand and angular
particles is used and no filler is added. Colours range from tan to grey-black
and often occur on the same spot.
    From Watson's description it seems likely that some of the Aibura sherds
are of this type of pottery, for example, the rim sherds in Specht's group 3.
Agarabi people say that their pots are traded to the Tairora and some have
been seen there (Watson 1955:126; Grove 1947:9-10). Pottery said to come
from the Markham valley is also used today in Barabuna and other Tairora
villages. The mean thickness of 15 sherds collected at Barabuna is 10.2 mm,
with a range of 7-13 mm, which is as thick as most sherds of group 3 but
thicker than sherds of groups 1 and 2
    A petrological examination of six sherds was made by C.A. Key (Appendix 3).
The sherds fall into two groups of which the larger (four sherds) contains
similar raw material to Agarabi-type pottery, although the latter is much
thicker and less well fired. All four sherds are from Specht's group 3.
Another sherd, XIV/(3) i from Specht's group 1, apparently contains marine
shell fragments and was made on the coast. The sixth sherd, 239.XIII/(3)
from Specht's group 3, contains raw material unlike either the Agarabi or the
Yabob (Madang) sherd available for comparison. On the basis of its decoration,

62

however, I think that it may well have been made somewhere in the Markham valley, possibly at a site from which comparative material is not yet available.

This examination suggests that pottery came into Aibura from a variety of sources, including the coast some 80 miles (130 km) away. The extent of this prehistoric trade is unexpected, especially when such bulky and fragile objects as pots are involved.

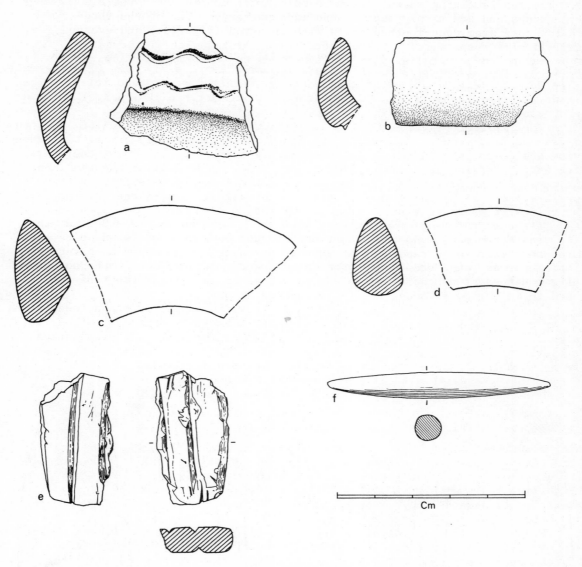

Fig.11   Aibura: potsherds (a,b) and artifacts of ground stone (c,d) ·and calcite (e,f)

GROUND-STONE ARTIFACTS

Axe-adzes

One whole axe-adze, five broken pieces and three fragments were found between levels 2 and 6, and one possible specimen was found in level 7. According to identifications provided by J.M.A. Chappell (pers. comm.), nine pieces are of low-grade metamorphic rocks such as hornfels, while one fragment (112.XI/(4)) is of slatey schist. No particular source for the axe-stone was located and these rocks are common in the area.

254.XV/(6) (fig.12b) is a wholly ground axe with a planilateral cross-section, length 6.0 cm, maximum width 3.1 cm at 2 cm from the cutting edge, thickness 0.8 cm.   One side tapers slightly towards the butt, but the other bends sharply at about the mid-point of the axe.   The butt is 1.2 cm wide and squared.   The cutting edge has been formed by alternate bevelling in such a way that when the edge is viewed end-on, it has a marked twist about the centre-point.

The eight broken axes and fragments were found in levels 2(1), 3(3) and 4(4).   Four pieces have a lenticular cross-section and one (249. XV/(3)) has definite sides (fig.12a).   Two specimens including the flat-sided one are asymmetrically bevelled, a third symmetrically so.   All pieces are partially or wholly ground.

217.IV/(7) (fig.12c) is a curious, elliptically ground blade, length 14 cm, width 4.7 cm, thickness 0.8 cm.   This implement is possibly made of a thermally altered tuff (e.g. rhyolite) which may have weathered after deposition.   There is an outcrop of rhyolite six miles (about 10 km) north of Kainantu (McMillan and Malone 1960:map 1).

The implement's cross-section is lenticular with double bevelling on both sides and flat faces.   All edges are sharp and symmetrically bevelled.   When viewed side-on, the whole artifact has a slight propellor shape.   There are traces of abrasion at the mid-point of one side.   One half of the implement is covered with small black lumps of ?mastic or gum-like material, and traces of this occur along one side (opposite the abrasion) down to the cutting edge. No traces of wear are visible under a 10x lens.

Although this implement is very similar in form to some New Guinea axes, the fine sharp edges and the occurrence of ?gum suggest that it may have been used as a knife or scraper rather than an axe-adze.   The depth at which the implement was found precludes European influence.   There seem to be no records of gum-hafted stone tools in the Highlands, although a light smear of gum is used in making some wooden artifacts such as arrows.

There are, of course, too few axes at this site to allow comparisons with other collections from either this area (e.g. Adam 1953) or the Highlands as a whole.   It is worth noting that, where this can be observed, planilateral cross-sections are found on two of the seven axes, but these implements appear to be much less square than those from the Western Highlands.

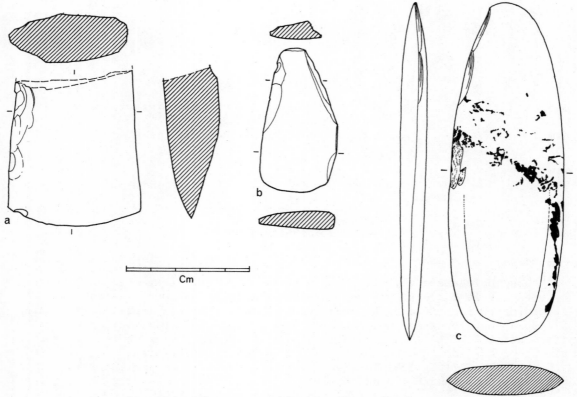

Cm

Fig.12   Aibura: ground-stone axe-adzes

Small ground-stone artifacts

1. Three fragments of stone annuli. Two of these (82.VII/(4), fig.11c; 246.XIV/(3), fig.11d) are made of marble and have external radii of 72 mm and internal radii of about 40 and about 61 mm respectively. The inner hole is pecked, or pecked and ground, from both faces (cf. Blackwood 1950), while the outer edge is semi-sharp. The thickest part of the artifact is towards the central hole (maximum thickness 14 and 13 mm respectively). The third piece is a small flat flake of ground shale with part of a ground circle (diameter 44 mm) visible on the outer edge (XII/(2)). One face of this flake is ground flat for a width of about 20 mm and the grinding then cuts away suggesting an outer circle. These pieces may be clubheads (White 1965a:45), although the size of the central hole in all cases is larger than that of any modern clubhead.

2. Two fragments (68.VIII/(4); 4.IX/(1), fig.11e) of stone, one marble and one calcite, show traces of grooving and snapping.

3. VII/(3) is an irregularly-shaped, smoothed piece of tuff, clearly a broken fragment. It is similar to modern stone-axe whetstones.

4. 28.XII/(3) is a large triangular-sectioned, long flake of hornfels, 133 x 44.5 x 19 mm. One side is ground, the other sides are flake surfaces. The edge between the ground side and the base has small chips removed, apparently through use.

5. A double-ended cylindrical point made of calcite (233.XV/(2), fig.11f), with length of 60 mm and maximum diameter of 7 mm. This artifact may be compared to the calcite cylinders found at Batari and is probably a septum decoration.

ARTIFACTS OF BONE AND SHELL

Fifteen bone, two tooth and two shell artifacts were excavated, giving an interesting picture of the technology employed at Aibura. The nineteen artifacts are concentrated in the upper levels and are scattered over the excavated area.

Bone Artifacts

1. 230.XIV/(1) (fig.13m); 129.XII/(5) (fig.13k) are two bone points, made of straight lengths of long-bone shaft. Both are ground asymmetrically at the point.

2. XII/(2) (fig.13j) is an unground, slightly curved fragment of bat long bone with a small (1 mm diameter) hole cut into the medullary cavity. The technique used to make the hole was to cut across the bone with a sharp blade and then cut down from either side. The same technique is seen on similar bones used as needles in the Highlands recently. The diameter of this specimen is 1.8 mm and its length 42 mm.
    X/(3) (fig.13l) is a highly polished fragment of long bone about the same diameter as the needle. Both ends are snapped off.

3. XI/(2) (fig.13h) is a metapodial worked to a very fine sharp point at one end but with the unfused proximal end unworked. Length 42 mm.

4. 42.VI/(3) (fig.13e). A bone bipoint made from a sliver of long-bone shaft. Length 92 mm. The black remains of what seems to be a band of gum covers about 17 mm around the centre of the tool. The gum band suggests that this point may not be a septum decoration.

5. XIV/(3) is a small shaft of polished long bone tapering towards one end, possibly part of a bone point.

6. 5.X/(2) is a broken spatula in ?cassowary long bone, 118 x 18 x 5 mm. Both faces are ground at one end to form the spatulate tip. Both ends are broken and chewed, not by rodents. Spatulae now found in the Highlands are used for scraping taro and cleaning pandanus, but this specimen is too fragile for these purposes.

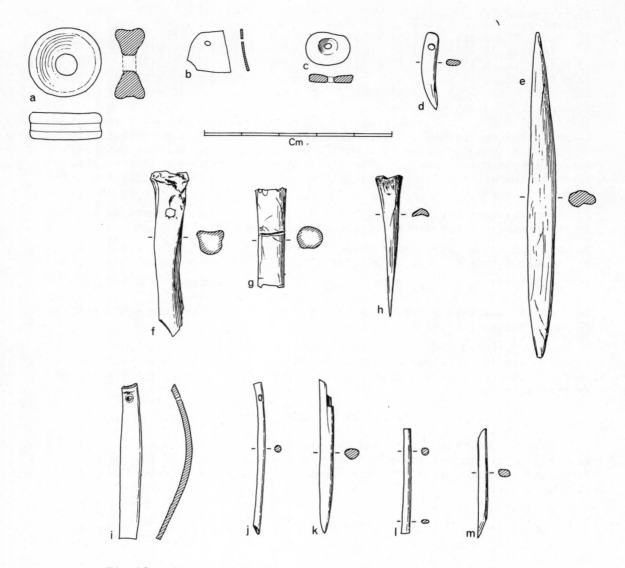

Fig.13   Aibura: artifacts of bone (a,d-m) and shell (b,c)

7.   40.IV/(3) is a shaft of bird bone ground at the tip until it is nearly
     flat.   The other end has been cut laterally and intentionally broken just
before the epiphysis.   The tip has been ground diagonally rather than around
or along the bone.   Length 83 mm.

8.   II/(3) is a small sliver of long-bone shaft with one corner ground and
     polished.

9.   XII/(3) (fig.13f).   Proximal end and part of a shaft of a ?macropodid
     metapodial, with a small (2.5 mm) hole just below the epiphysis.   The
hole is nearly square, but the technique of manufacture cannot be determined.

10.   XIV/(3) (fig.13g) is a tubular fragment of bird long bone (6.5 mm
      diameter) with a deep V-sectioned groove around it about half-way along
its 28.5 mm length.

11.   V/(7) (fig.13i) is a rib of lenticular cross-section with a small hole
      bored with a rotary motion from both faces.   The bone was scratched
across one face before being broken.   Its dimensions are 43 x 5.5 x 1.5 mm.
This object was probably a pendant.

12.   XV/(3) is a cuscus mandible with a round hole pierced in the ascending
      ramus.   Similar holes are pierced in cuscus mandibles today to hang them

up in the houses.   This specimen probably documents the same practice in prehistoric times, already inferred from the faunal remains.

13.   87.XII/(4) (fig.13a) is a biconcave annular bead made possibly from a shark vertebra, diameter 19.5 mm, thickness 7.2 mm, diameter of the central hole 6.8 mm.   The corners are highly polished and the whole bead gives the appearance of having seen much use.

Tooth Artifacts

1.   XV/(1) (fig.13d) is a cuscus incisor with a hole (2.2 mm diameter) drilled through from mesial to distal surface.   Drilling probably occurred from both faces but this is not clear.   This is almost certainly a neck ornament.

2.   235.XV/(2) is a boar's tusk, broken laterally as well as at both ends.   Although unworked, it is included because of the widespread use of unworked tusks as nose ornaments in this area today.

Shell Artifacts

1.   19.XII/(3) (fig.13c) is a flat-sectioned, oval shell bead 12 x 9 mm with a 1.5 mm central hole drilled from both sides.

2.   76.IV/(4) (fig.13b) is an irregularly-shaped nacreous piece of freshwater mussel shell, approximately 14 x 11 mm with a 1 mm diameter hole drilled from both sides through it near one edge.   It is clearly decorative.

These artifacts suggest that Aibura was more than a simple stop-over camp.   The presence of needles, awls, spatulae and ornaments all point to the fact that the cave was probably used for some length of time, or fairly regularly, as a place where extractive or craft activities could occur.   Craft activities of various kinds are an everyday occupation for men in most Highlands societies (e.g. Gardner and Heider 1968:26).

Table 79   Aibura: distribution of bone and shell artifacts

Level	Bone	Shell	Tooth	Total
1	1	-	1	2
2	3	-	1	4
3	8	1	-	9
4	1	1	-	2
5	1	-	-	1
6	-	-	-	-
7	1	-	-	1

COLOURING MATERIALS

At least seven different colouring materials were found.   Most seem to be orange, pink, red, red-brown and yellow-brown iron oxides, but there is also a creamy white which is possibly a clay or shale.   Four pieces, one each of pink, white, orange and red-brown, show signs of rubbing.   The white piece has a deep tapering groove for 15 mm along one side.   Table 80 sets out the distribution of colouring material in general.

In the context of the cave, only the white colouring material was recognised as paint by local people.   It was found in levels 3 and 7, mostly in level 3.   Other colours were probably used as body paint or on *art mobilier*.   The sources of this material are not known.

WASTE MATERIAL

Only 587 flakes and lumps of stone without traces of secondary retouch or use were recovered, including test pit material.   The waste material is spread through the site in a very similar way to the flaked implements, with perhaps a slightly greater concentration in the southwest corner.

An analysis of the waste material (table 81) shows that there is a virtual absence of very small flakes, suggesting that normal kinds of stone knapping only rarely occurred at the site. This is confirmed by an implement/waste ratio of 1 : 1.4.

Table 80   Aibura: distribution of colouring material

Level	Number	Weight in gm
1	1	0.2
2	3	5.6
3	15	186.1
4	4	9.9
5	3	21.9
6	1	2.9
7	7	58.2
8	–	–
9	1	13.1
10	2	35.5
Total	37	333.4

Table 81   Aibura: distribution of waste material by size[1]

Level	<0.5 in.	0.5-1.0 in.	1.0-1.5 in.	1.5-2.0 in.	>2.0 in.	Total
(a) squares I-IX						
1	1	3	1	–	–	5
2	1	8	1	1	–	11
3	4	26	10	–	–	40
4	2	9	5	–	1	17
5	2	5	5	1	1	14
6	1	20	20	4	4	49
7	–	13	19	14	3	49
8	1	11	11	4	–	27
9	1	10	4	5	2	22
10	1	2	8	7	2	20
11	–	–	3	3	1	7
Total	14	107	87	39	14	261
(b) squares X-XV						
1	1	2	–	–	1	4
2	1	13	6	3	1	24
3	4	27	14	1	–	46
4	5	70	22	5	2	104
5	3	41	22	3	2	71
6	2	14	15	4	1	36
7	–	4	1	1	–	6
8	–	1	2	–	–	3
Total	16	172	82	17	7	294

[1] Excluding test pit material

FLAKED-STONE TOOLS
(fig.14)

A total of 456 implements with secondary retouch or use-wear and cores was excavated at Aibura. They seem to be naturally disposed in two horizons over some of the site, but, as has been outlined earlier, have been grouped into three horizons for analysis. The tools have been analysed by both methods described in chapter II, but the test pit material has been excluded from the attribute analysis.

Standard Typology (table 82)

Most of the tools are scrapers and their morphology does not alter visibly

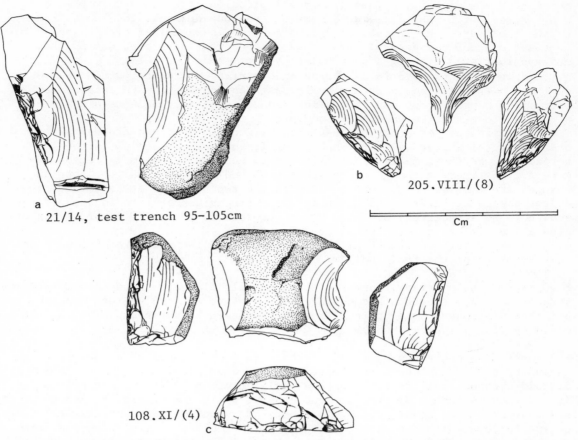

21/14, test trench 95-105cm

b

205.VIII/(8)

Cm

108.XI/(4)

c

Fig.14   Aibura: flaked-stone artifacts: a) side scraper, three altered edges;
b) double-concave scraper, five altered edges; c) double-side and
end scraper, four altered edges

Table 82   Aibura: distribution of flaked-stone tool types

		Horizon		Total
	I	II	III	
Total tools (add 1-4)	105	232	119	456
1. Whole retouched tools	15	85	51	151
(a) Scrapers (total)	15	84	51	150
(i) side	3	15	19	37
(ii) end	-.	10	4	14
(iii) double side	1	5	1	7
(iv) side and end	1	7	3	11
(v) side and double end	–	3	1	4
(vi) discoid	–	9	4	13
(vii) double-concave	1	3	4	8
(viii) core	–	1	–	1
(ix) multi-platform	9	31	15	55
(b) 'Bifacial' retouch/use	–	1	–	1
2. Broken retouched tools	31	113	52	196
3. Utilised pieces	59	31	7	97
4. Cores	–	3	9	12
1 as % of total	14.3	36.6	42.9	33.1
2 as % of total	29.5	48.7	43.7	43.0
3 as % of total	56.2	13.4	5.9	21.3
(ix) as % of (a)	60.0	36.9	29.4	36.4

throughout the deposit. They give the impression of being cruder than at other sites, with many implements made on odd-shaped chunks and lumps. Many of the tools are made on pebbles and as such could be called pebble tools, but none are outside the general size range of the other scrapers, nor is there any apparent selection of a particular type of stone for them.

Implements are made in a heterogenous variety of cherts, often of poor quality. The flaking is irregular in position and scrappy in appearance. There is a range of retouch from almost none, especially on some side scrapers, to extensive on discoid scrapers.

Two main changes occur between the horizons. Utilised flakes make up half the total number of tools in Horizon I, but only about 10% in the lower horizons. Further, multi-platform scrapers seem to become more common in more recent times, although the numbers involved are very small. Both these changes are similar to those occurring in the top horizons at Kafiavana; they do not appear at Batari, which, on this and the evidence of radiocarbon dates, ceased to be effectively occupied at or before 1000 BP. The lower levels of Aibura are similar to all levels at Batari.

Table 82 sets out the tool types according to the standard typology and some comments on the tools follow:

Horizon I   The multi-platform tools are heavily flaked, and the double-concave scraper is also retouched around the side opposite the projection. Most utilised pieces are small thin flakes, but two are heavy chunks of stone and could be planes (White 1968a).

Horizon II   Among the side scrapers there is a wide range of shapes and sizes, including some heavy chunks. There are also four deepish notches. The discoid scrapers include three with a small unretouched projection at one end. Six of these scrapers are rounded and chunky, while the others are irregular and flatter. The double-concave scrapers are unretouched apart from this, except for one which has some retouch on another plane. The multi-platform scrapers are very variable in size and shape; a few of the smaller ones seem to have been used as cores. The unretouched cores have only two or three flake scars each.

Fig.14c illustrates a double-side and end scraper, with four altered edges, (108.XI/(4)), from this horizon.

Horizon III   The side scrapers are mostly lightly retouched and only three have deep notches. The double-concave scrapers all have the typical double concavity separated by an unretouched projection (e.g. fig.14b, 205.VIII/(8)). All nine unretouched cores are pebbles with very few flakes removed: the material is poor quality.

Attribute Analysis (tables 83-113)

A study of the attributes of all stone artifacts·showing retouch or use-wear was made according to the method described in chapter II. Particular comparisons with Batari and Kafiavana sites will be made throughout. Numerical tables are given on pp. 74-82.

Analyses using the implement as the basic unit

1. *Type of stone*   Various poor quality cherts provide nearly all of the stone used, especially in Horizon I (table 83).

2. *Number of planes per implement*   In all horizons about three-quarters of all implements were used on one plane only (table 84). There are about the same proportion of multi-plane implements as at Batari. The slightly higher numbers at both these sites when compared to Kafiavana may reflect similar problems in obtaining raw material.

3. *Number of edges per implement*   A total of 1205 altered edges was observed (table 85). The number of edges per implement shows a steady if slight decrease from HIII to HI: the change is similar to that seen in

Kafiavana.   In HII and HIII about 20% of implements have more than four edges which is slightly higher than at Kafiavana and may reflect more re-use of implements.

4. *Weight of implements*   In HI, two-thirds of the tools weigh less than 10 gm which is a much higher number than elsewhere.   In the lower horizons the tools normally weigh 10-30 gm and the number weighing less than 10 gm declines markedly (table 86).   This changing picture is similar to that found in the upper four horizons of Kafiavana.   In this attribute, the whole of Batari compares fairly closely with HII at Aibura.

Implements used on two planes seem to weigh rather more than those used on one (table 87) and the same is approximately true in relation to edges (table 88).   There is no absolute difference, but a suggestion that larger implements were chosen for re-use.

Analyses using the edge as the basic unit

1. *Whole implements*   The number of implements which can be called 'whole' in relation to a particular edge is low (table 89), although very few are definitely 'not whole'.   The percentage of whole implements is about the same as at Batari and the rise in this percentage in Horizon I is paralleled at Kafiavana, HI-II.

2. *Raw material*   A third or less of the implements retain some pebble cortex, and other cortex is also quite common.   The lower two horizons are similar to Batari in this respect.   HI is unlike any other site in that two-thirds of its implements are without cortex (table 90).

3. *Size and shape of implements*   The weights of 'whole' and 'probably whole' implements are similar so that the latter are likely to be whole (table 91). HI is unique in that most implements weigh less than 10 gm.   Otherwise, implements mostly weigh less than 30 gm, which is similar to the other sites.
    The Length/Breadth (L/B) indices of HII-III are similar to other sites; in HI, however, the index is rather higher and the implements become more 'blade'-like.   Upper horizon implements are also slightly less chunky (tables 92-3).

4. *Flakes and cores*   While the use of flakes is common in HI, there is a very high percentage of cores and lumps used in HIII (table 94).   This suggests that, in the lower levels, stone was used without much flaking on site.

Attributes describing the edges individually

1. *Whole/not whole*   Except for Horizon I about half the edges are 'whole' or 'probably whole' (table 95).   The balance between these two groups is very different from Kafiavana and more similar to Batari.   HI at Aibura is aberrant in having a high number of whole edges.

2. *Base type*   Table 96 shows that flake surfaces were commonly used for bases.   The increased percentage of 'not applicable' in HI relates to the rise in used but unretouched pieces.

3. *Preparatory flaking*   About half the edges of HII and HIII are prepared by the removal of one or two large flakes struck from the base (table 97). HI, however, shows the expected high number of 'not applicable' as a result of the used but unretouched category.

4. *Shape of edge*   Two-thirds of the 'whole' and 'probably whole' edges in HII and HIII are concave, while in HI nearly two-thirds are straight or convex (table 98).   This difference is much more marked than at Kafiavana. Table 99 shows that different shapes of edges tend to be about the same length (6-15 mm).   The picture is similar to that found in Batari, whereas at Kafiavana all edges tend to be longer, with very few being less than 5 mm.
    The indentation index does not vary through the site (tables 100-1). There are more concave edges than at Kafiavana suggesting that, as at Batari,

the material is more heavily retouched and/or used.

5. *Retouch*   Nearly all retouch is step-flaking.   Nearly three-quarters of
   all edges in HI are not retouched, whereas three-quarters of all edges
below this are step-flaked (table 102).   The absence of retouch in HI is more
marked than in other sites.

   Most step-flaked edges are concave, but about 20% are straight (table 103(b);
see also (c)).   Edges without retouch, on the other hand, are frequently
straight (table 103(a)).

   Nearly all edges are acutely angled, with the degree of retouch apparently
not increasing the angle of the edge (table 104).

6. *Use-wear*   Just over half the edges in the lower two horizons show use-wear,
   but over 80% show this in HI.   As at Kafiavana, the percentage of edges
with 'chattering' does not decrease in HI, which suggests that the activity
producing this effect continued unabated in more recent times.   This also
points out that there is no *necessary* correlation between 'chattering' and
step-flaking and that the two must be, in general, the product of different
actions performed on the altered edge (table 105).

   About half of all 'chattering' is concave and the other half straight
(table 106(a)).   This is similar to the picture found at Kafiavana but differs
from Batari, which suggests that differences are not related to present
cultural boundaries.   The shape of 'utilisation' is split approximately in
the proportion 2:1:1 between straight, concave and convex (table 106(b)).
This is similar to both Batari and Kafiavana.

   The normal length of 'chattering' is under 10 mm and for 'utilisation'
it is 6-20 mm (table 107).   About half the 'chattering' at Aibura is 6-10 mm
long and this is similar to the situation at Kafiavana.   The high percentage
of 'utilisation' whose length is 6-10 mm is more similar to Batari than
Kafiavana.

   Where use-wear is concave, 'chattering' is more indented than 'utilisation'
(table 108).   There are general similarities within the horizons of Aibura
and with the other sites.

   Use-wear is nearly all on acute-angled edges (table 109).   The mode for
'chattering' is 70-89° in HII and HIII but 60-79° in HI.   The mode for
'utilisation' is 40-59°.   The picture is similar to that found in other sites.

Correlations between attributes

1. *Retouch and use-wear*   Tables 110 and 111 show that there is a high
   correlation between 'chattering' and step-flaking.   The tables however,
suggest that this correlation is largely one-way, for while 'chattering' is
often found on unretouched edges, use-wear on step-flaking is always
'chattering'.

2. *Retouch and 'chunkiness'*   Edges without retouch may be on slightly thinner
   implements than those with step-flaking, but there is very little
difference (table 112) except in edges less than 6 mm long.   This may relate
to the mechanics of step-flaking.

   Implements with unretouched edges are slightly less chunky than those
with step-flaking (table 113).   The unretouched implements are much chunkier
than at Kafiavana and this is true, to a lesser extent, of the step-flaked
tools.

Summary

   The most important differences are between Horizon I and the lower
horizons in respect of weight and shape of implements, the number with
secondary retouch and the shape of edges.   The standard typology brought out
some of these differences but they have been made more precise by the attribute
analysis.   This is especially noticeable in relation to the features of used
but unretouched flakes, which differ grossly from the other tools.   This
major change is similar to that seen in the upper horizon of Kafiavana and is
expressed in similar ways.   Apart from this change there is no other obvious

way in which the industry changes through time.

The similarities of Aibura are generally with Batari, the other site in the Lamari valley. This refers to features like bases, preparatory flaking and weight, which do not relate to used but unretouched flakes. Some of the similarities may relate to difficulties in obtaining adequate supplies of good raw material. Some features clearly do not relate to this, such as number of 'whole' implements, the length of edges, the indentation indices of edges and the chunkiness of unretouched implements. These may express some regional similarity, but whether this is cultural, mechanical or imposed by the raw material is not clear.

TRIMMING FLAKES

There is an average of one trimming flake for every 5.2 flaked implements. The number of trimming flakes is low but may be explained by the fact that stone working was apparently very rarely carried out at Aibura.

Table 114 suggests that implements were rarely re-used in the upper horizon. This is consistent with the fact that step-flaked tools, which produce trimming flakes, are less common in Horizon I.

HAMMER

One small fragment of river pebble apparently used as a hammerstone was found in IV/(7).

CONCLUSION

The use of Aibura began about 4000 years ago and continued until modern times. The character of the occupation appears to have been basically similar throughout and was probably always sporadic in this dark, wet cave, although the artifactual evidence suggests that it was more than casual when it did occur.

The early occupation is marked only by a few stone implements and wild animal remains. The implements are crudely made and rather larger than those that occur later; they were not manufactured at the site. There is some suggestion that the site may have remained unoccupied for a period after this, and possibly the human remains were deposited during this phase.

The second phase of occupation (Horizon I) began 1000 years ago or less. In this level the occupation takes on a more definite structure: ash lenses are preserved while postholes show that structures, perhaps lean-to shelters, were made. Faunal remains suggest that grasslands were increasing around the site. A wide variety of artifacts was used, including trade items from scores of miles away. Manufacturing techniques included smoothing, grooving and snapping of stone and drilling and polishing of bone and shell, but the flaking of stone implements did not occur. Retouched stone tools declined in importance and became much smaller, while unretouched flakes were more commonly used. Wild animals, including birds and reptiles, continued to provide most of the meat eaten; domestic pig and hen were scarce, while dog remained absent until the most recent levels. This faunal picture may not truly represent the resources since pigs were probably available for food during the entire period of occupation (see chapter V).

The cultural remains at Aibura seem to be more similar to those from Batari than from sites further west. This is seen especially in the flaked stone implements, such as the rare double-concave scrapers, and in certain attributes of the retouched tools. It is also expressed in the absence of pebble tools and waisted blades; one unground waisted blade made of weathered tuff was found on the road near Barabuna village, but this is the only artifact of this kind reported east of the Chimbu-Asaro divide. Parallels between Aibura and Batari also occur in the small grooved and ground stone and bone artifacts. However, there is also a striking similarity in the recent material from Aibura and Kafiavana, both of which show a marked rise in the use of unretouched stone implements and a decline in retouching. This change appears to be complete by the ethnographic present when retouched tools do not seem to be made throughout the Highlands (White 1967, 1968a, 1968b; Strathern 1969). No intelligible explanation for this change can be given yet, but it does seem to be a marker which runs across other areal divisions.

A diagrammatic summary of the material from Aibura is given in fig. 27.

Table 83   Aibura: percentage distribution of types of stone used

Horizon	Chert	Non-chert	No. of implements
I	96.2	3.8	105
II	85.2	14.9	229
III	81.8	18.2	110

Table 84   Aibura: percentage distribution of number of planes per implement

Horizon	Number of planes					No. of implements
	1	2	3	4	5	
I	78.1	16.9	5.7	–	–	105
II	72.9	20.1	6.1	0.4	0.4	229
III	71.8	23.6	3.6	0.9	–	110

Table 85   Aibura: percentage distribution of number of edges per implement

Horizon	Number of edges									No. of implements	No. of edges	Mean no. of edges per implement
	1	2	3	4	5	6	7	8	9			
I	41.9	26.7	17.1	8.6	4.6	–	1.0	–	–	105	222	2.1
II	26.2	24.5	17.5	13.1	5.7	8.3	3.9	–	0.9	229	672	2.9
III	34.5	20.9	15.5	8.2	7.3	9.1	1.8	0.9	1.8	110	311	2.8
I-III										444	1205	2.72

Table 86 Aibura: percentage distribution of implement weights

Horizon	Weight in gm													No. of implements
	0-9	10-9	20-9	30-9	40-9	50-9	60-9	70-9	80-9	90-9	100-9	110-9	>119	
I	68.6	17.1	4.8	1.9	1.9	1.0	-	3.8	1.0	-	-	-	-	105
II	32.6	28.4	13.5	11.4	4.8	1.8	2.6	1.8	1.3	0.4	1.3	-	-	229
III	14.6	22.7	16.4	12.7	9.1	9.1	5.5	1.8	2.7	1.8	-	0.9	2.7	110

Table 87 Aibura: percentage distribution of implement weights in relation to number of planes used

Horizon	Weight in gm													No. of implements
	0-9	10-9	20-9	30-9	40-9	50-9	60-9	70-9	80-9	90-9	100-9	110-9	>119	
(a) one plane														
I	72.0	14.6	4.9	2.4	1.2	1.2	3.7	-	-	-	-	-	-	82
II	38.3	24.6	10.8	13.2	4.8	1.8	2.4	1.8	1.2	-	1.2	-	-	167
III	13.9	26.6	13.9	13.9	5.1	11.4	7.6	1.3	2.5	2.5	-	1.3	-	79
(b) two planes														
I	58.8	23.5	5.9	-	5.9	-	-	5.9	-	-	-	-	-	17
II	17.4	37.0	21.7	6.5	4.4	2.2	4.4	2.2	-	2.2	2.2	-	-	46
III	15.4	15.4	26.9	3.9	23.1	3.9	-	3.9	3.9	-	-	-	3.9	26

Table 88 Aibura: percentage distribution of implement weights in relation to number of edges used

Horizon	Weight in gm													No. of implements
	0-9	10-9	20-9	30-9	40-9	50-9	60-9	70-9	80-9	90-9	100-9	110-9	>119	
(a) one or two edges														
I	72.3	13.9	2.8	2.8	1.4	1.4	-	5.6	-	-	-	-	-	72
II	42.2	26.7	9.5	10.3	2.6	1.7	3.4	0.9	0.9	0.9	0.9	-	-	116
III	16.4	19.7	16.4	13.1	6.6	11.5	8.2	1.6	3.3	1.6	1.6	-	-	61
(b) more than two edges														
I	60.8	24.2	9.1	-	3.2	1.7	-	-	3.2	-	-	-	-	33
II	23.0	30.1	17.7	12.4	7.1	1.7	1.7	2.7	1.7	-	1.7	-	-	113
III	12.3	26.5	16.4	12.2	12.2	6.1	2.0	2.0	2.0	2.0	-	-	6.1	49

Table 89   Aibura: percentage distribution of condition of implements, counting each edge as a separate implement

Horizon	Whole	Probably whole	Not whole	Indeterminate	No. of edges
I	16.7	18.5	2.7	62.2	222
II	8.8	6.9	6.6	77.8	672
III	5.5	15.1	4.8	74.6	311

Table 90   Aibura: percentage distribution of occurrence of cortex

Horizon	Pebble cortex	Other cortex	No cortex	Indeterminate	No. of edges
(a) counting each edge as a separate implement					
I	14.9	13.1	66.2	5.9	222
II	31.7	30.8	31.2	6.2	672
III	34.7	24.1	37.9	3.2	311
(b) counting each implement as one					No. of implements
I	14.3	13.3	62.8	9.5	105
II	31.9	30.6	30.1	7.4	229
III	40.0	24.5	30.0	5.5	110

Table 91   Aibura: percentage distribution of implement weights, counting each edge as a separate implement

Horizon	Weight in gm 0-9	10-9	20-9	30-9	40-9	50-9	60-9	70-9	80-9	90-9	100-9	110-9	>119	No. of edges
(a) whole implements														
I	86.5	10.8	-	-	-	-	-	2.7	-	-	-	-	-	37
II	39.0	37.3	8.5	8.5	5.1	-	1.7	-	-	-	-	-	-	59
III	35.3	5.9	11.8	35.3	5.9	-	-	-	-	5.9	-	-	-	17
(b) probably whole implements														
I	85.4	9.8	-	-	-	-	-	2.4	2.4	-	-	-	-	41
II	34.8	30.4	8.7	-	8.7	4.4	2.2	6.5	-	-	4.4	-	-	46
III	12.8	19.2	14.9	8.5	6.4	17.0	-	4.3	4.3	8.5	-	4.3	-	47

Table 92   Aibura: percentage distribution of whole implement shapes, counting each edge as a separate implement

Horizon	<0.5	0.5-0.99	1-1.49	1.5-1.99	2-2.49	2.5-2.99	>2.99	No. of edges
(a) length/breadth index								
I	–	–	32.4	51.4	16.2	–	–	37
II	–	–	72.9	20.3	3.4	3.4	–	59
III	–	–	76.5	17.7	–	5.9	–	17
(b) breadth/thickness index								
I	–	5.4	13.5	37.8	16.2	10.8	16.2	37
II	–	6.8	5.1	30.5	27.1	3.4	27.1	59
III	–	11.8	11.8	11.8	29.4	–	35.3	17

Table 93   Aibura: percentage distribution of the shape of probably whole implements, counting each edge as a separate implement

Horizon	<0.5	0.5-0.99	1-1.49	1.5-1.99	2-2.49	2.5-2.99	>2.99	Not measured	No. of edges
(a) length/breadth index									
I	–	–	70.7	14.6	9.8	–	2.4	2.4	41
II	–	–	73.9	26.1	–	–	–	–	46
III	–	–	89.4	8.5	2.1	–	–	–	47
(b) breadth/thickness index									
I	–	2.4	14.6	22.0	22.0	17.1	22.0	–	41
II	–	2.2	4.4	26.1	23.9	34.8	8.7	–	46
III	2.2	2.2	14.9	31.9	17.0	14.9	17.0	–	47

Table 94   Aibura: percentage distribution of core and flake components of the total industry, counting each edge as a separate implement

Horizon	Core or lump	Flake	Trimming flake	Indeterminate	No. of edges
I	25.2	65.4	3.6	5.9	222
II	47.7	43.4	2.7	6.3	672
III	53.4	41.2	2.2	3.2	311

Table 95   Aibura: percentage distribution of the condition of edges

Horizon	Whole	Probably whole	Not whole	Indeterminate	No. of edges
I	42.3	27.5	3.6	26.6	222
II	22.5	30.5	15.2	31.8	672
III	27.7	30.2	6.8	35.4	311

Table 96   Aibura: percentage distribution of base types of all implements, counting each edge as a separate implement

Horizon	Indeterminate	Pebble cortex	Other cortex	Break	Negative bulb	Positive bulb	Not applicable	No. of edges
I	5.9	0.9	1.4	5.9	34.7	27.0	24.3	222
II	9.2	7.1	8.6	7.6	26.0	35.6	5.8	672
III	4.5	9.7	8.0	7.7	36.3	31.2	2.6	311

Table 97   Aibura: percentage distribution of preparatory flaking of all implements,
counting each edge as a separate implement

Horizon	Unclear	None	Base struck	Side/end struck	Not applicable	No. of edges
I	12.6	40.5	22.1	0.5	24.3	222
II	17.3	22.5	54.0	0.5	5.8	672
III	19.3	24.4	53.4	0.3	2.6	311

Table 98   Aibura: percentage distribution of edge shapes

Horizon	Straight	Concave	Convex	Wavy	No. of edges
(a) whole edges					
I	41.5	39.4	19.2	–	94
II	28.5	66.9	4.6	–	151
III	23.3	73.3	3.5	–	86
(b) probably whole edges					
I	47.5	47.5	4.9	–	61
II	30.2	66.8	2.9	–	205
III	29.8	66.0	4.3	–	94

Table 99   Aibura: percentage distribution of the length of whole and probably whole edges
in relation to edge shape

Horizon	Length in mm								No. of edges
	0-5	6-10	11-15	16-20	21-25	26-30	31-35	>35	
(a) straight									
I	19.1	51.5	19.1	7.4	1.5	1.5	–	–	68
II	25.7	44.7	19.1	7.6	2.9	–	–	–	105
III	33.3	50.0	10.4	4.2	2.1	–	–	–	48
(b) concave									
I	13.6	53.0	28.8	4.5	–	–	–	–	66
II	10.9	54.2	24.6	9.2	0.4	0.4	–	–	238
III	5.6	50.4	32.8	8.0	3.2	–	–	–	125
(c) convex									
I	4.8	38.1	38.1	19.1	–	–	–	–	21
II	–	46.2	30.8	7.7	–	7.7	7.7	–	13
III	–	57.1	28.6	–	14.3	–	–	–	7

Table 100   Aibura: percentage distribution of the degree of indentation of whole and
probably whole concave edges, measured by index Lc/D

Horizon	Lc/D					No. of edges
	<3.3	3.3-4.9	5.0-9.9	10.0-19.9	>19.9	
I	1.5	10.6	69.6	18.2	–	66
II	0.4	12.6	63.9	23.1	–	238
III	0.8	16.0	65.6	17.6	–	125

Table 101 Aibura: percentage distribution of the degree of projection of whole and probably whole convex edges, measured by index Lc/D

Horizon	<3.3	3.3-4.9	Lc/D 5.0-9.9	10.0-19.9	>19.9	No. of edges
I	–	14.3	38.1	42.9	4.8	21
II	–	–	46.2	46.2	7.7	13
III	–	14.3	57.2	28.6	–	7

Table 102 Aibura: percentage distribution of retouch types on all edges

Horizon	None	Step-flaking light	Step-flaking heavy	Other unifacial flaking	Bifacial flaking	Other	No. of edges
I	71.2	24.8	1.4	1.8	–	0.9	222
II	25.7	62.5	9.7	1.9	0.2	–	672
III	20.3	64.6	12.5	2.3	0.3	–	311

Table 103 Aibura: percentage distribution of the relationship between retouch type and edge shape on whole and probably whole edges

Horizon	Straight	Concave	Convex	Wavy	No. of edges
(a) no retouch					
I	50.8	32.5	16.7	–	120
II	49.0	42.0	9.0	–	100
III	53.8	35.9	10.3	–	39
(b) light step-flaking					
I	21.8	75.0	3.1	–	32
II	22.6	76.1	1.4	–	213
III	21.7	76.6	1.7	–	115
(c) heavy step-flaking					
I	–	100.0	–	–	1
II	15.2	81.8	3.0	–	33
III	4.8	95.2	–	–	21

Table 104 Aibura: percentage distribution of the relationship between edge angle and retouch type

Horizon	20-9	30-9	40-9	50-9	60-9	70-9	80-9	90-9	100-9	>109	Not measured	No. of edges
(a) light step-flaking												
I	–	–	3.6	5.5	29.1	27.3	18.2	10.9	3.6	1.8	–	55
II	–	–	2.1	8.6	29.5	28.1	21.4	8.8	1.2	–	0.2	420
III	–	–	0.5	2.5	22.4	31.3	26.9	12.4	3.0	–	1.0	201
(b) heavy step-flaking												
I	–	–	–	33.3	–	66.6	–	–	–	–	–	3
II	–	–	–	4.6	18.5	36.9	29.2	6.2	1.5	–	3.1	65
III	–	–	–	5.1	18.0	43.6	23.1	5.1	–	–	5.1	39

Table 105   Aibura: percentage distribution of the occurrence of use-wear on all edges

Horizon	None	'Chattering'	Bifacial	'Utilisation'	No. of edges
I	16.2	52.7	0.5	30.6	222
II	45.8	47.5	-	6.7	672
III	44.7	51.8	-	3.5	311

Table 106   Aibura: percentage distribution of the shape of use-wear types, counting whole and probably whole lengths of use-wear only

Horizon	Straight	Concave	Convex	Wavy	No. of occurrences
(a) 'chattering'					
I	51.9	46.8	1.3	-	79
II	42.7	55.5	1.7	-	173
III	47.9	50.0	2.1	-	96
(b) 'utilisation'					
I	43.1	27.6	29.3	-	58
II	45.4	33.4	21.2	-	33
III	50.0	12.5	37.5	-	8

Table 107   Aibura: percentage distribution of the length of use-wear types, counting whole and probably whole lengths of use-wear only

Horizon	1-5	6-10	11-15	16-20	21-25	26-30	31-35	>35	No. of occurrences
(a) 'chattering'									
I	24.0	53.1	20.2	1.3	-	-	-	1.3	79
II	36.4	47.2	12.5	2.8	1.1	-	-	-	176
III	31.4	50.0	14.7	3.9	-	-	-	-	102
(b) 'utilisation'									
I	6.9	43.1	31.0	15.5	1.7	1.7	-	-	58
II	3.0	33.3	24.2	24.2	6.1	6.1	3.0	-	33
III	-	62.5	-	12.5	24.0	-	-	-	8

(Length in mm)

Table 108   Aibura: percentage distribution of the degree of indentation, measured by index Lc/D, on whole and probably whole concave lengths of use-wear, in relation to use-wear type

Horizon	0-3.3	3.4-4.9	5.0-9.9	10.0-19.9	>19.9	No. of occurrences
(a) 'chattering'						
I	-	8.1	81.1	8.1	2.7	37
II	3.1	13.6	66.7	15.6	1.0	96
III	-	14.6	68.8	16.7	-	48
(b) 'utilisation'						
I	6.3	-	56.2	37.5	-	16
II	-	-	45.5	54.5	-	11
III	-	-	-	100.0	-	1

(Lc/D)

Table 109   Aibura: percentage distribution of edge angles in relation to use-wear type

Horizon	20-9	30-9	40-9	50-9	60-9	70-9	80-9	90-9	Not measured	No. of occurrences
(a) 'chattering'										
I	0.9	2.6	7.7	15.4	24.8	24.8	14.5	7.7	1.7	117
II	0.6	1.3	1.3	9.1	20.7	25.1	24.5	16.0	1.6	319
III	–	–	0.6	5.0	14.9	29.2	30.4	16.2	3.7	161
(b) 'utilisation'										
I	17.6	13.2	20.6	26.5	11.8	5.9	4.4	–	–	68
II	6.7	11.1	28.9	24.4	15.6	4.4	2.2	4.4	2.2	45
III	9.1	–	36.4	–	27.3	–	9.1	18.2	–	11

Table 110   Aibura: percentage distribution of the relation between use-wear and retouch

| Horizon | Retouch type | | | No. of occurrences |
	None	Step-flaking light	heavy	
(a) 'chattering'				
I	76.9	23.1	–	117
II	43.2	47.8	9.0	324
III	35.0	54.4	10.6	160
(b) 'utilisation'				
I	100.0	–	–	67
II	100.0	–	–	43
III	100.0	–	–	10

Table 111   Aibura: percentage distribution of the relation between retouch and use-wear

Horizon	'Chattering'	Use-wear type Bifacial	'Utilisation'	No. of occurrences
(a) light step-flaking				
I	100.0	–	–	27
II	100.0	–	–	155
III	100.0	–	–	87
(b) heavy step-flaking				
I	–	–	–	–
II	100.0	–	–	29
III	100.0	–	–	17

Table 112   Aibura: percentage distribution of implement thickness in relation to retouch
type on all implements except those clearly not whole, counting each
edge as a separate implement

Horizon	Thickness in mm								Not measured	No. of edges
	0-5	6-10	11-15	16-20	21-25	26-30	31-35	>35		
(a) light step-flaking										
I	13.0	33.3	1.9	27.8	9.3	7.4	5.6	1.9	-	54
II	1.5	19.9	22.7	27.8	15.4	7.8	3.0	1.1	0.3	396
III	-	11.9	19.2	21.8	20.7	10.4	8.3	7.9	-	193
(b) heavy step-flaking										
I	-	-	-	33.3	66.6	-	-	-	-	3
II	1.7	13.6	25.4	28.8	23.7	6.8	-	-	-	59
1II	-	8.6	40.0	8.6	34.3	8.6	-	-	-	35
(c) no retouch										
I	38.3	33.0	9.1	2.6	6.5	1.9	0.6	1.3	6.5	154
II	6.8	27.0	20.2	19.6	12.3	5.5	1.8	2.4	4.3	163
III	11.7	11.7	23.4	20.0	23.4	-	1.7	8.4	-	60

Table 113   Aibura: percentage distribution of the breadth/thickness index in relation to
retouch type on all implements except those clearly not whole, counting
each edge as a separate implement

Horizon	B/Th index							No. of edges
	<0.5	0.5-0.99	1.0-1.49	1.5-1.99	2.0-2.49	2.5-2.99	>2.99	
(a) light step-flaking								
I	-	9.3	37.0	24.1	16.7	11.1	1.9	54
II	0.5	9.8	41.9	29.5	8.8	6.6	2.8	396
III	-	14.5	40.4	23.8	13.5	5.2	2.6	193
(b) no retouch								
I	0.6	8.4	16.2	31.8	16.9	13.6	12.3	154
II	-	15.9	23.9	24.6	11.0	11.0	13.5	163
III	1.7	8.3	33.3	31.7	6.7	5.0	13.3	60

Table 114   Aibura: distribution of trimming flakes

Horizon	Number	Implements per trimming flake
I	10	10.5
II	56	4.1
III	19	6.3

82

V   EXCAVATIONS AT KAFIAVANA, ASARO VALLEY

THE SITE

Kafiavana (K65) is the name given by the Yagaria people of Legaiyu village to a small, high shelter on the east bank of the Fayantina River (6°15'S, 145°27'E), about 1 mile (1.6 km) south of the Fayantina - Dunantina junction and 12 miles (20 km) S 15° E of Goroka, close to Kami estate (fig.1).

The site is within an area of Tertiary limestones, shales, greywacke and conglomerate, at the southern end of the Asaro valley about 4400 ft (1350 m) (McMillan and Malone 1960:map 1). The surrounding country lies within the Abiera land system of the CSIRO Division of Land Research report (Haantjens 1970:43). It is a region of benched and rounded ridges on unconsolidated sediments and of aggraded valley floors, very poorly drained. *Phragmites* swamp is common in the valley bottoms and the ridges carry induced grassland with local patches of garden and garden regrowth.

Kafiavana lies about half-way up the south side of Koyagu hill, an 80 m high outcrop of highly-sheared calcareous siltstone (J.G. Best, Senior Geologist, Department of Mines, Port Moresby, pers. com.), approximately 1 km in circumference (pl.3a). From outside the shelter there is a good view over the Fayantina valley to the south and southwest, while from the hilltop the country may be clearly seen for several miles in every direction except southeast.

The shelter is formed by a slightly overhanging cliff whose brow is some 10-11 m above the present floor. The area sheltered is about 43 m^2 and the maximum dimensions are 15 x 4 m (fig.15a,b). There is little protection from the rain from the south or east. The shelter faces south so that the sun does not reach over the sill in the dry season (April-October) but comes about 1 m inside the dripline during the wet.

Human occupation of the shelter was indicated by many coloured paintings on the back wall (pl.3b) and a litter of stone flakes and chips on the floor. Legaiyu men said that the shelter was occupied intermittently as a refuge during pre-European conflicts.

Discovery and Excavation

Kafiavana came to my attention in 1964 when J.D. Cole, then living at Goroka, visited it as a result of hearing reports of paintings. The floor of the shelter was then covered with chert chips. In November-December 1964, Cole dug a 3 x 1 yd (2.77 x 0.92 m) trench on the east side of the site to a maximum depth of 85 in. (218 cm), finding implements throughout. (This material is now in the University of Washington Museum, Seattle.)

This test excavation showed that Kafiavana contained a deep deposit with a sequence of concentrated human occupation. It was the only major site reported from the Asaro valley, which lies between the Chuave-Wahgi cultural area (Read 1954:12) and the Lamari valley sites discussed in previous chapters. Thus it was strategically located to provide one link in an east-west transect through the Highlands.

During March-May 1965 the author and Carmel White excavated 12 m^2 of Kafiavana (fig.15a). Ten m^2, including the inner two of Cole's squares, were removed down to basal sterile clay at 370-410 cm. The other 2 m^2 (squares F6, F7), which lay outside the drip-line, were partly removed to provide access to the trench. A total of just over 30 m^3 of deposit was removed, which is probably less than 10% of the total volume of occupation material present. The rate of excavation was about 0.5 m^3 per day. The only spits of a depth greater than 10 cm were removed in order to take account of the sloping stratigraphy of the lower part of the site.

A

B

Plate 3   Kafiavana: A) aerial view of Koyagu hill from southeast.   The site
                is at a foot of the major cliff on left.   B) shelter
                floor, looking east.   Scale in 20 cm.

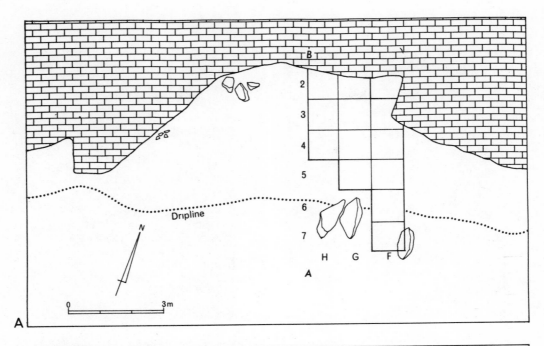

Fig.15   Kafiavana: A) plan;   B) section

Stratigraphy (fig.16a-c; pl.4a,b)

     The visible stratigraphy of the site was not a series of small, distinct layers, but some major divisions were seen.   The units of excavation were therefore generally smaller than the observable strata.   There were also marked horizontal variations.   In general, the deposit may be divided into six main stratigraphic units.

1.   0-40 cm below surface.   Recent occupation, marked by posts and postholes, hearths and pits in the inner part of the site and an increasing humus content with many roots towards and outside the dripline.

2.   40-160 cm below surface.   An undifferentiated grey-grown (10 YR 3/4 - 7.5 YR 4/2) sandy silt (Appendix 4 for mechanical analyses), containing very little macroscopic carbon but many implements and waste flakes.   Below and

Plate 4   Kafiavana: A) excavation.   Ranging pole stands in square H3.
           B) west wall of squares H2-4.

outside the dripline the deposit was variably concreted with calcium carbonate.
The soil was mostly damp with a marked division from the dry, soft soil at the
back of the shelter.

3. 160-230 cm below surface.   Heavily burnt layers of fine, hard, white,
    cream and red ash bands, containing little carbon and cultural material but
some faunal remains.   These ash bands were concentrated in squares G3-5 and
H3-4 and faded out rapidly in surrounding squares.   They were therefore only
visible in the G/H section wall (fig.16b).   Towards the front of the site,
notably in F6 and to a certain extent in G5, cultural material was common and
bone rarer.   It seems likely that the ashy areas represent the hearth and
cooking areas at this time, with tools being made and used elsewhere.   In
contrast, during the accumulation of units (2) and (4), it may be assumed that
the hearth and cooking activities were located elsewhere and the excavated
area was used for flint knapping and other craft activities.

4. The hearth levels overlay a series of different coloured (10 YR 4/1 - 10
    YR 3/4) silty sands which were most clearly seen in G2-5.   This material
was banked up against the back wall of the shelter, so that its top was at
about 200 cm below surface in G2 but at about 240 cm in G5.   These sloping
strata were not visible in the west part of H2-4 (fig.16c) where the material
was so undifferentiated as to obscure any slope; they were seen in F3-5
(fig.16a), but sloped much less steeply on the eastern side.   In the outer
part of the site the soil was heavily concreted and any incline was obscured.
These strata ended at about 310-30 cm.   They contained a large amount of
cultural material, much of it covered with concretions.
     The relative positions of these sloping strata seemed to be original, but
it is difficult to account for them in occupational terms since the slope is
quite steep.   It might be suggested that initially the slope was less marked,
but continued use of the shelter, combined with slight disturbance by run-off
water and subsidence, caused the front part of the deposit to sink.
J.N. Jennings (pers. comm.) states that he would expect more disturbance if
this were the case but admits it as a possible explanation.   Alternative
explanations are difficult to find.

5. Large numbers of finger-sized fragments of the parent rock, lying
    approximately horizontally and in some places tightly packed, were found
below 320 cm.   Patches of very fine black humus, culturally sterile and

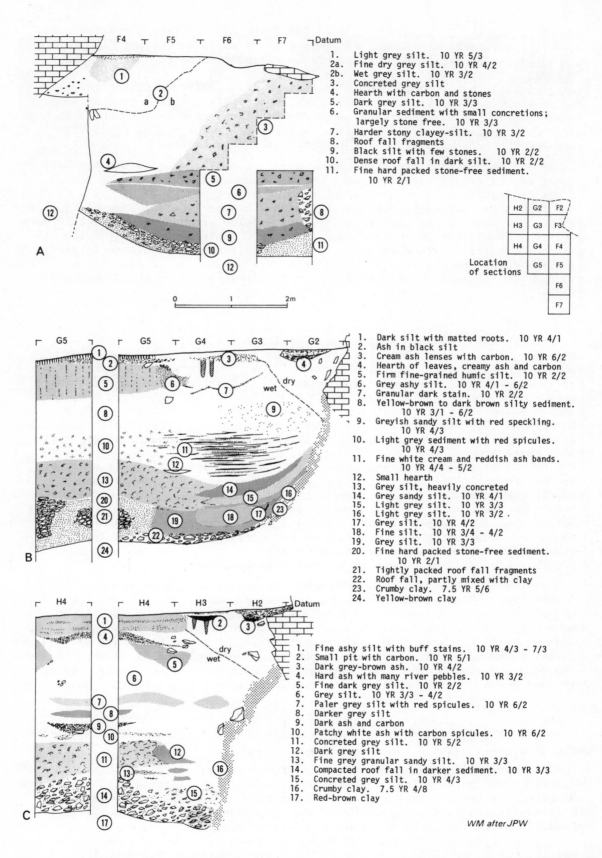

1. Light grey silt. 10 YR 5/3
2a. Fine dry grey silt. 10 YR 4/2
2b. Wet grey silt. 10 YR 3/2
3. Concreted grey silt
4. Hearth with carbon and stones
5. Dark grey silt. 10 YR 3/3
6. Granular sediment with small concretions; largely stone free. 10 YR 3/3
7. Harder stony clayey-silt. 10 YR 3/2
8. Roof fall fragments
9. Black silt with few stones. 10 YR 2/2
10. Dense roof fall in dark silt. 10 YR 2/2
11. Fine hard packed stone-free sediment. 10 YR 2/1

Location of sections

1. Dark silt with matted roots. 10 YR 4/1
2. Ash in black silt
3. Cream ash lenses with carbon. 10 YR 6/2
4. Hearth of leaves, creamy ash and carbon
5. Firm fine-grained humic silt. 10 YR 2/2
6. Grey ashy silt. 10 YR 4/1 - 6/2
7. Granular dark stain. 10 YR 2/2
8. Yellow-brown to dark brown silty sediment. 10 YR 3/1 - 6/2
9. Greyish sandy silt with red speckling. 10 YR 4/3
10. Light grey sediment with red spicules. 10 YR 4/3
11. Fine white cream and reddish ash bands. 10 YR 4/4 - 5/2
12. Small hearth
13. Grey silt, heavily concreted
14. Grey sandy silt. 10 YR 4/1
15. Light grey silt. 10 YR 3/3
16. Light grey silt. 10 YR 3/2 .
17. Grey silt. 10 YR 4/2
18. Fine silt. 10 YR 3/4 - 4/2
19. Grey silt. 10 YR 3/3
20. Fine hard packed stone-free sediment. 10 YR 2/1
21. Tightly packed roof fall fragments
22. Roof fall, partly mixed with clay
23. Crumby clay. 7.5 YR 5/6
24. Yellow-brown clay

1. Fine ashy silt with buff stains. 10 YR 4/3 - 7/3
2. Small pit with carbon. 10 YR 5/1
3. Dark grey-brown ash. 10 YR 4/2
4. Hard ash with many river pebbles. 10 YR 3/2
5. Fine dark grey silt. 10 YR 2/2
6. Grey silt. 10 YR 3/3 - 4/2
7. Paler grey silt with red spicules. 10 YR 6/2
8. Darker grey silt
9. Dark ash and carbon
10. Patchy white ash with carbon spicules. 10 YR 6/2
11. Concreted grey silt. 10 YR 5/2
12. Dark grey silt
13. Fine grey granular sandy silt. 10 YR 3/3
14. Compacted roof fall in darker sediment. 10 YR 3/3
15. Concreted grey silt. 10 YR 4/3
16. Crumby clay. 7.5 YR 4/8
17. Red-brown clay

WM after JPW

Fig.16 Kafiavana: stratigraphy, A) east wall; B) west wall G2-5 and south wall G5; C) west wall H2-4 and south wall H4

sometimes completely stone-free, were found within this level, mostly in F5 and G5. Artifacts were found within the stony areas but became less common as the number of parent rock fragments increased towards the base. The soil became increasingly clayey from 360 cm.

Jennings (pers. comm.) comments that the fine, black, stone-free soil was possibly derived from the upper part of the hill, where a similar soil is found today. It was clearly associated with large pieces of parent rock which fell as lumps and shattered on impact. Some merging of falls with parts of the surrounding deposit is apparent but incomplete.

6. By 380 cm, in most areas, a stiff, damp, yellow-brown clay was reached.
It was culturally sterile but contained many small fragments of bone.
It was at least 1 m deep and was not removed to bedrock.

The basal clay sloped upward at the back of the site and some of it clung to the back wall of the shelter up to 100 cm below ground surface. This back wall of clay was 20-120 cm thick and was very sharply differentiated from the cultural deposit. It contained only some highly mineralised bone (Appendix 5). Jennings (pers. comm.) suggests that this clay may be an old landslip surface and that the basal clay slipped some 3 m downwards prior to human occupation of the site.

Sediment Analysis

Twenty-one sediment samples were submitted to E. Schmid for analysis (Appendix 4). The samples consisted of one basal clay sample and twenty samples from a column taken at alternate 10 cm from the west wall at the south end of square H3. The analyses consisted of mechanical sorting and chemical tests. The mechanical analysis shows that the soil throughout is a silty sand. Below about 250 cm it contains a proportion of small gravel, and a few elements of this kind are also found near the surface. The samples above the basal clay all have a nearly constant amount of phosphate but a widely varying humus content.

On the basis of these analyses, Schmid and Grüninger divide the deposit into six zones. The basal clay was formed in water and laid down under pluvial conditions. The other sediments exhibit evidence of five different climatic phases, with the three humid periods being interspersed with two dry ones. The 'dry' samples occur at 295-155 cm and 95-35 cm and Schmid and Grüninger argue that the lower of these two samples must record a dry period during deglaciation subsequent to 10,000 BP.

They also draw attention to two interesting items:

1. Samples 3-20 (above 325 cm) all contain very small flakes (down to 0.1 mm
    diameter) of siliceous materials. Their presence indicates that flaking was carried out at and above the specified level. It will be seen later that the artifacts from the lowest horizon, into which samples 1 and 2 fall, exhibit a number of differences from the artifacts above. These facts may be related. It also seems to me that by studying the relative number of these micro-flakes, some determination of the local intensity of flint working could be made and workshop areas within the site delineated. This has not been done here.

2. The high humus content of samples 14-16 at the top of Horizon III may
    indicate that the site was abandoned for some time. This seems to correlate well with certain archaeological evidence for some lessening in the rate of deposition at about this level.

Whether Schmid's climatic interpretations are valid is something for soil scientists and palaeoclimatologists to discuss. J.N. Jennings and R.M. Frank consider that it is premature to make climatic inferences and that even the local conditions during deposition cannot be clearly derived from the analyses given. Their comments are included in Appendix 4.

The analyses by Schmid and Grüninger are the first to be made of the sediments in a New Guinea shelter. They give a valuable and detailed description, which confirms and supplements the field observations. In particular respects their data are helpful in considering certain problems.

Even if certain aspects of the interpretation are disputed, the report should provide a stimulus to further research.

Division of the Material

For the purposes of analysis the artifactual material has been divided into nine arbitrary horizons numbered from the surface down. These divisions attempt to take particular account of the concentrations of artifactual material, and then the need to have approximately equal numbers of implements and equal volumes in each horizon.

It will be seen from the scatter-plots (fig.17a,b), recording the position of implements which were recognised in the field (55% of the total), that three main concentrations occurred within the site. These were obscured towards the back wall (squares F3, G2, H2) and seem to be different in F6, probably for reasons already explained. These three concentrations, which were clearest in F5, G3-4 and H3-4, show variations in the quantity of stone-tool working which can also be seen in the distribution of waste stone.

The nine horizons are linked to these concentrations of material. The small uppermost implement concentration is placed within Horizons I-II, while Horizons III-V include the main upper concentration. Horizon VI contains the more sterile intermediate zone around 160-210 cm but also includes the large number of implements from square F6. The lower concentration of implements lies in Horizons VII-VIII, while all basal material is found in Horizon IX. The density of implements per m^3 is set out in table 115.

It must be pointed out that these horizons are fairly broad units which contain from 1.5 to 4.5 m^3 of deposit. This is a deliberate attempt to avoid drawing fine divisions, which neither the visible stratigraphy nor the theory of disturbance due to human treadage and scuffage within heavily occupied sites (Matthews 1964:167-71) will support.

For certain parts of the analysis only some of the squares are included. Thus, in the standard typology, the three back squares (F3, G2, H2) are omitted because of possible greater admixture in the loose soft soil and the banking up of material against the back wall. Also, some questions in the attribute analysis were asked of squares F5, G3-4 and H3-4 only, as it seemed worthwhile trying to discover if the implements which were clearly in different concentrations showed different characteristics. In all cases, however, the division into nine horizons was retained.

Table 115   Kafiavana: concentration index[1] of implements per m^3

Square	Horizon									Total
	I	II	III	IV	V	VI	VII	VIII	IX	
F3	116	165	242	56	70	107	60	80	10	-
F4	-	-	-	-	-	-	35	51	37	-
F5	-	-	-	-	25	12	17	33	13	-
F6	-	-	-	37	164	167	-	-	-	-
F7	-	-	9	5	-	-	-	-	-	-
G2	140	168	38	75	4	15	31	-	-	-
G3	129	91	157	64	29	52	105	35	-	-
G4	63	48	132	150	100	30	36	85	15	-
G5	25	14	93	68	64	70	16	90	8	-
H2	88	360	260	150	110	40	33	-	-	-
H3	100	120	147	100	48	44	117	66	2	-
H4	55	15	63	166	89	15	34	63	2	-
Index per horizon	95	118	100	100	71	49	47	52	11	-
No. of implements per horizon	164	226	351	284	325	192	165	202	45	1954
Volume of horizon in m^3	1.73	1.92	3.51	2.83	4.60	3.95	3.51	3.85	4.27	30.17

[1] Calculated by dividing number of implements per square per horizon by volume in m^3 of deposit in that unit

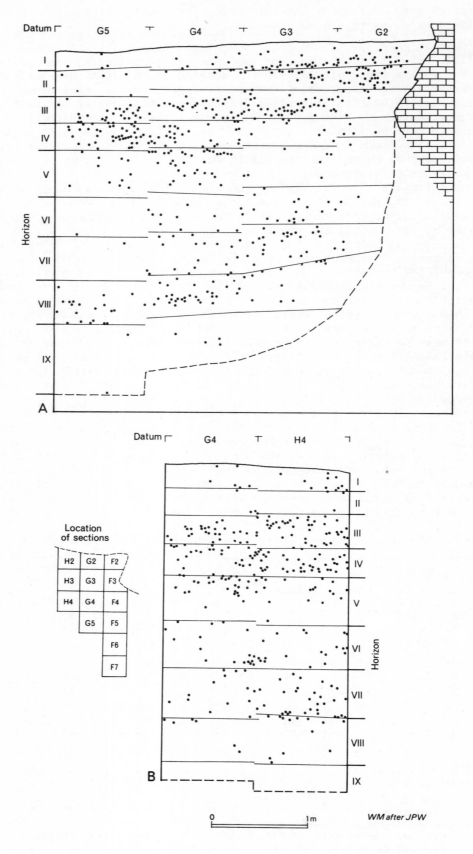

Fig.17   Kafiavana: plot of implements, A) from G2-5 or west wall; B) from G4
and H4 on south wall

90

Artifact Joins

Only nine pairs of flakes or implements which had broken in antiquity were joined together despite, or probably because of, the large amount of stone material.   Seven pairs came from the same square and spit, one pair from the same square but four spits (24-30 cm) apart and one, from adjacent squares, was vertically separated by 55 cm.   This last pair came from towards the rear of the shelter (G2, G3) where the earth was softer and this may have assisted their movement.

The number of joins is, of course, too small to use as a basis for generalisation, but it does suggest that some migration has occurred within the deposit and that it would be incorrect to analyse material in micro-stratigraphic units.

Dating

1. Four samples were submitted for radiocarbon dating, three to the ANU laboratory (Polach *et al.* 1967:22-3; 1968:192-3), one to the Institute of Nuclear Sciences, New Zealand; no official number has yet been allocated to the latter, for which the intra-laboratory reference prefixed by R is therefore used.

ANU-42: 4690 ± 170 years
This comes from wood carbon collected in square G5/spit (5) at the base of Horizon II in the upper part of the grey-brown sandy silt, at a depth 50-5 cm below the surface.   The carbon comes from the upper part of the humus horizon referred to by Schmid (Appendix 4).

R1894A (carbonate): 6180 ± 125 years
R1894B (collagen) : 9290 ± 140 years
These two dates refer to 277 gm of food bone remains collected over 8 m^2 of the site.   The sample lies between 200 and 270 cm below the surface in the lower ash bands and the material below them, but was collected over only 50 cm depth in any one square.   It spans the lower part of Horizon VI and most of Horizon VII.   The collagen date is to be preferred as closer to the true age.

ANU-20: >9500 years
This comes from three small samples of wood carbon from three adjacent metre squares of the excavation.   Each sample had close internal association and all are from the banked silty sands, at 250-70 cm below the surface in the lower half of Horizon VII.   The ANU laboratory advises that the sample was very small and 'only the younger age limit is relevant' (Polach *et al.* 1967:23).

ANU-41a (carbonate): ≥6750 ± 100 years
ANU-41b (acid-insoluble fraction): ≥10,730 ± 370 years
These dates refer to 500 gm of unidentifiable food bone remains collected from the banked silty sands 260-310 cm below the surface over 6 m^2 of the site. The dates span the lower part of Horizon VII and the upper part of Horizon VIII.   The ANU laboratory comments (H.A. Polach pers. comm.):

> After the carbonate had been evolved, the residue was allowed to settle and the excess acid washed off.   The residue was then oven-dried and combusted to give sample 41b.   This is referred to as 'collagen', but is more accurately called the 'acid insoluble fraction'.   It is generally agreed that this substance gives a valid date, but we agree with Tamers in considering it is more reasonable to think of this date as equal to or greater than the age given.

2. The basal clay has been tentatively dated by the associated fauna to Pleistocene times (Appendix 5).

Domestic Animals

Pig (*Sus scrofa*) was the only domesticated animal found. On a within-horizon basis, at least six animals, including one piglet, are represented (table 116). Most of the bones are very fragmented and are insufficient for metrical study. About half the pieces are teeth, mostly molars, and phalanges are also common. It is assumed that the animals are domestic, but they may have been feral.

Table 116   Kafiavana: distribution of pig bone

Horizon	Bone	Minimum no. of animals
I	58 fragments	>4
III	Lower incisor	1
IV	M^2 (very worn)	
	M^3? (unworn)	1 + 1?
	Prox. humerus (broken)	
V	?Astragalus (broken)	1?
Total	63	>6 + 2?

Wild Animals

The total number of animals is 95. This is calculated from the mandibles and maxillae on a within-horizon basis. A distinction has been made between adult and juvenile dentition where possible. Table 117 demonstrates that the bulk of the identifiable fauna is made up of macropodids and cuscus (*Phalanger* sp.), with a few bats and small mammals comprising the remainder. About 27 (28%) of the animals have not been identified.

Table 117   Kafiavana: minimum numbers of wild animals

Animals	I	II	III	IV	V	VI	VII	VIII	IX	Total
Macropodidae	2	–	2	2	5	3	–	2	2	18
Phalangeridae										
Phalanger sp.	1	2	2	–	4	2	–	3	1	15
Pseudocheirus (Pseudochirops) spp.	–	–	1	–	2	–	–	–	1	4
P. (Pseudocheirus) spp.	–	1	–	–	1	–	–	1	–	3
Peramelidae	–	–	2	1	–	1	–	–	–	4
Dasyuridae	–	–	–	–	1	1	–	–	1	3
Megachiroptera	–	1	1	1	1	–	–	2	2	8
Muridae										
Hyomys goliath	1	–	2	–	–	–	–	–	–	3
Uromys sp.	–	–	–	–	1	–	–	–	1	2
Small genera unidentified	1	–	2	1	–	–	–	2	1	7
Tachyglossidae										
Zaglossus sp.	–	–	–	–	–	–	–	–	1	1
Unidentified (estimated)	4	1	2	3	8	6	1	1	1	27
Total animals per horizon	9	5	14	8	23	13	1	11	11	95
No. of animals per m³ of deposit	5.2	2.6	4.0	2.8	5.0	3.3	0.3	2.9	2.6	3.1

The number of animals at different levels tends to be positively correlated with the number of implements. This is not true of Horizon VII which has few animals but contains the upper part of the lowest implement concentration.

The small number of animals found throughout the deposit is surprising and unlike other sites reported here. The most likely explanation seems to be that much bone was either destroyed or thrown out of the shelter by its occupants. Most bones in the excavation are very broken and splintered, while nearly all of them are burnt to some extent. It should also be noted

that even where many hearths occurred in combination with a slight decline in
stone-working, there is little alteration in the amount of bone present.
This suggests that the low quantities of bone are not restricted to the
excavated part of the site and the present sample is representative.

It is evident that domestic animals only become important in Horizon I,
where they form about one-third of all animals. It might be assumed that
this is a reasonable representation of their importance, particularly at a
site which is likely to have been occupied sporadically by husbandmen.
Whether the sudden increase in the number of pigs in Horizon I goes with other
economic changes remains to be demonstrated.

Fish

One fish vertebra was found in Horizon IV and three broken shark's teeth
in HII. They were probably used for decoration but show no traces of working.
Some very small fragments of fishbone were found by Professor Schmid, so that
more fish may actually have been taken to the site than were found.

Birds

Only a few fragments of bird bone were noted, none of which was cassowary.
Eggshell occurred throughout the site. Cassowary shell was concentrated
in Horizon III and particularly in square H2, but even there there was only
sufficient for one-eighth of an egg. Other unidentified eggshell was found
in limited quantities throughout the site. None of the shell had been
worked in any way.

Reptiles

All 11 reptile fragments identified by R.E. Barwick are from lizards.
Seven (minimum of four animals) are from agamid lizards, one is from a
sharp-snouted lizard, and the other three cannot be further identified.
The fragments were scattered through the site, viz. HI,2; HIII,2;
HIV,2; HV,3; HIX,2.

Mollusca

Mollusca from three environments, marine, freshwater and terrestrial,
were found throughout Kafiavana. The only naturally occurring types are
probably some land snails, which were common in the basal clay and probably
crawled into the site from time to time. All mollusca have been identified
by D.F. McMichael.

Marine shells Four genera of marine molluscs have been identified (table 118).
One other genus, *Stenomelania*, may be marine but some species live in freshwater
in higher country. The gastropod is only tentatively identified. The
presence of four *Cypraea moneta* shells in Horizon VII documents trade with the
coast some 9000 years ago, which is much earlier than had been suspected
previously.

Table 118   Kafiavana: distribution of marine shells

	Horizon								
	I	II	III	IV	V	VI	VII	VIII	IX
Geloina spp. (estuarine bivalve)	3	2	2	1	-	-	-	-	-
Oliva sp. (olive shell)	1	-	-	-	-	-	-	-	-
Nassarius sp. (dog whelk)	-	-	1	-	-	-	-	-	-
Cypraea moneta L. (money cowry)	-	1	-	-	-	-	4	-	-
Stenomelania sp.	1	-	-	-	-	-	-	-	-
Class Gastropoda	-	-	-	-	-	-	-	-	1

Freshwater shells   All these shells belong to freshwater mussels (family Hyriidae), which are common in Highland streams.   All specimens are very fragmentary and none was identified to species level.   None shows signs of working or use.

Land snails   All land mollusca are snails of the camaenid family which McMichael says occur locally.   The presence of some snails is probably fortuitous and none of the shells shows any signs of human attention.

Human Remains

Eleven pieces of human bone and teeth were discovered scattered through the site.   Four of them were close together in square G5, Horizon V, but no signs of a pit were seen.   The other bones were not in association.   The bones have been identified by A.G. Thorne.   The reference is to catalogue number (where applicable), square/(spit).

H2/(2)   Horizon I.   Two-thirds of the crown of a lower PM.   The tooth is heavily worn with substantial exposure of the dentine.

H2/(12)   Horizon III.   Five fragments of human bone, not further identifiable.

G5/(10)   Horizon IV.   A terminal carpal phalange; from one of the three middle fingers.

76.G5/(15) Horizon V.   A lumbar vertebra, highly encrusted with calcium carbonate.

77.G5/(16) Horizon V.   Clavicle, right, adult.   It is fairly robust.

G5/(17)   Horizon V.   One middle carpal phalange and one tarsal bone (not further identified).

Flora

Pollen Analysis

Four samples from 0-210 cm below surface were analysed by J.M. Wheeler and W.H. Litchfield.   They report that low concentrations were present near the surface but that few grains could be identified (Appendix 6).

Macroscopic Vegetable Matter

Three kinds of material were found in the upper part of the top horizon:

1. The lower parts of 14 wooden stakes were recovered.   These were usually sharpened at one end and had the other end cut off square and/or carbonised.   The lengths range from 3.7 to 18.5 cm and diameters range from 1.3 to 2.5 cm.   All appear to be made of straight branches, with twigs broken off but the bark left on.
    Eleven stakes were found in squares G2 and H2, and the other three were in H3 and H4.   No pattern could be seen in their distribution.   The top of one stake was 10-15 cm below ground surface but all others were at or just below the surface.   The wood of these stakes has been identified by R.W.R. Muncey.   Three are certainly *Casuarina* and 'could well be' the common species *Casuarina oligodon*.   Two others are possibly *Casuarina*.   One is a *Pittosporum*, possibly *P. ferrigineum*, a common small tree.   Two are monocotyledons and could be bamboo, while the remaining six are from three different genera of dicotyledonous trees.   All these trees grow in the area today.   The uses of these stakes are unknown.

2. Three small pieces of bark cloth similar to modern material were found on and just below the surface.

3. One flattened sleeve of fibre binding similar in every respect to the binding made over the junction of a bamboo arrowhead and its shaft was found on the surface.

POTTERY

One piece of hand-made pottery was found on the surface of the site prior to excavation. This rim sherd is reddish in colour and made of fine clay with occasional lumps of coarse filler. The rim is horizontally everted with finger indentations around the edge. On the body of the sherd there are continuous chevrons interspersed with jabbed depressions. This sherd is very similar petrographically to Aibura sherd 239.XIII/(3). Several Legaiyu men said that pottery came to them from the upper Bena Bena River area.

AXE-ADZES

Fifty-four whole and fragmentary axe-adzes were found, some in every horizon excepting VI (table 119). Thirty-seven of these specimens show signs of grinding. All whole axes and most large fragments were found in the upper part of the front of the shelter in squares F6 and F7 (fig.18i,k). Both flaked and ground axe fragments were found right to the base of the site (fig.18h,j).

Nearly all axes whose shape is determinable are lenticular in cross-section (angle of sides 60-75°), and taper towards the butt. One axe from Horizon III has narrow ground sides and might be called planilateral. Three have pointed butts, all other butts being squared-off in plan. The cutting edges are normally slightly curved in plan, with a fairly sharp corner at each end of the blade. Few axes are ground all over and many, particularly those from the upper part of the site, are coarsely flaked from river pebbles and have considerable cortex remaining on them (fig.18k).

The stone used has been identified by J.M.A. Chappell and includes several varieties of hornfels, greywackes and meta-greywackes, as well as micaeeous nephrite, andesite and slate. Most pieces do not come from identifiable quarries and were probably collected from the Fayantina River gravels. Two pieces, one each from Horizons II and III, come from the Kafetu hornfels quarry about 30 miles (50 km) northwest of Kafiavana, near Daulo Pass (Salisbury 1962:85; Chappell 1966:104).

Table 119   Kafiavana: distribution of axe-adzes

Horizon	Total	No. with grinding	Whole	Butt	Body	Cutting edge	Chips	Roughout	No. per m^3
Surface	4	–	–	1	1	–	–	2	–
I	5	4	–	1	1	1	2	–	2.9
II	14	12	1	1	2	–	10	–	7.3
III	10	6	1	3	1	–	5	–	2.8
IV	6	2	–	2	1	–	3	–	2.1
V	1	1	1	–	–	–	–	–	0.2
VI	–	–	–	–	–	–	–	–	–
VII	9	8	–	2	2	–	5	–	2.6
VIII	3	3	–	–	1?	–	2	–	0.8
IX	2	1	–	1	–	1?	–	–	0.5
Total	54	37	3	11	8+1?	1+1?	27	2	1.8

ARTIFACTS OF BONE AND SHELL

Bone Artifacts

Twenty-two bone tools and 15 pieces of worked bone were found (table 120). With one exception, all these artifacts were found towards the back of the site, near the shelter wall.

Three main classes of points have been defined, while four tools are described separately. There is no apparent change in the proportion in each class over time.

1. Six tools are made from slivers of long bone or from ribs (fig.18b). They are very asymmetrical in cross-section and have one rounded end. The other end is broken in each case. The figured specimen is from H2/(23).

2. The characteristic feature of nine points (fig.18d-f) is that the tip is formed by cutting across the medullary cavity of a shaft in the same way as in the present-day manufacture of needles in Legaiyu. However the archaeological specimens are much thicker and heavier. Of the figured specimens d is from H2/(17), the others from G2/(10).

3. Three fine points (fig.18g) are very similar to present-day needles. The figured specimen is from H2/(15).

Four bone tools are worth recording separately:

1. G3/(18), Horizon V. A very large, flat, highly polished spatulate point made from a splinter of long bone. Length 60 mm, maximum thickness 10 x 3 mm (fig.18a).

2. H3/(29), H3/(30), Horizon VI. Two flat points made from long-bone splinters cut sharply from each side to form an angular tip. One is 32.5 mm long with a thickness of 3 x 1.5 mm.

3. H3/(33), Horizon VII. A broken ?metapodial with a 3 mm diameter hole pierced through the shaft just below the proximal end (fig.18c). There are no signs of drilling around the hole but both bone surfaces show a number of lateral scratches leading into it.

Shell Artifacts

Three shells of the marine species *Cypraea moneta* (money cowry), each with a large round hole in the back, were found in Horizon VII. These holes were probably humanly made, which means that the shells may have been sewn onto fabric or strung together.

Table 120   Kafiavana: distribution of bone tools

| | | Horizon | | | | | | | | | |
		I	II	III	IV	V	VI	VII	VIII	IX	Total
Class	1	-	-	2	1	2	-	1	-	-	6
	2	1	-	2	2	2	2	-	-	-	9
	3	-	-	1	-	-	2	-	-	-	3
Other tools		-	-	-	-	1	3	-	-	-	4
Broken worked pieces		-	1	5	3	3	1	2	-	-	15
Total		1	1	10	6	8	8	3	-	-	37

OCHRE AND OCHRE STONES

Ochre, mostly red iron-oxide, was found concentrated in Horizons I-VI, with much less being found below this (table 121). The decline is sharp enough to suggest that painting was much less common in the earlier period. Nineteen pieces, mostly weighing more than 10 gm, show surface traces of rubbing or cutting, probably caused by preparing powder for making paint.

Thirty-four stones have some red ochre adhering to them. These stones were found throughout the deposit but were commoner in the upper horizons (table 122). One stone is painted with a design, but all others seem to be by-products of ochre working.

The stone with a design on it is from Horizon II. It is an oval, flattish river pebble of volcanic rock (6.6 x 3.9 x 2.4 cm) on which a double pattern has been painted (fig.19c). The lower design comprises four dark-red stripes, each 0.6-1.0 cm wide, which run from pole to pole. Two stripes are on one face, one is down one side and the other is asymmetrically placed on the other face. Superimposed on this are two pinkish-red crosses, one on each face. The uprights are set in the centre of each face and meet at the ends, while the cross-bars meet to form a circle around the middle of the stone. All the lines are about 1.1 cm wide.

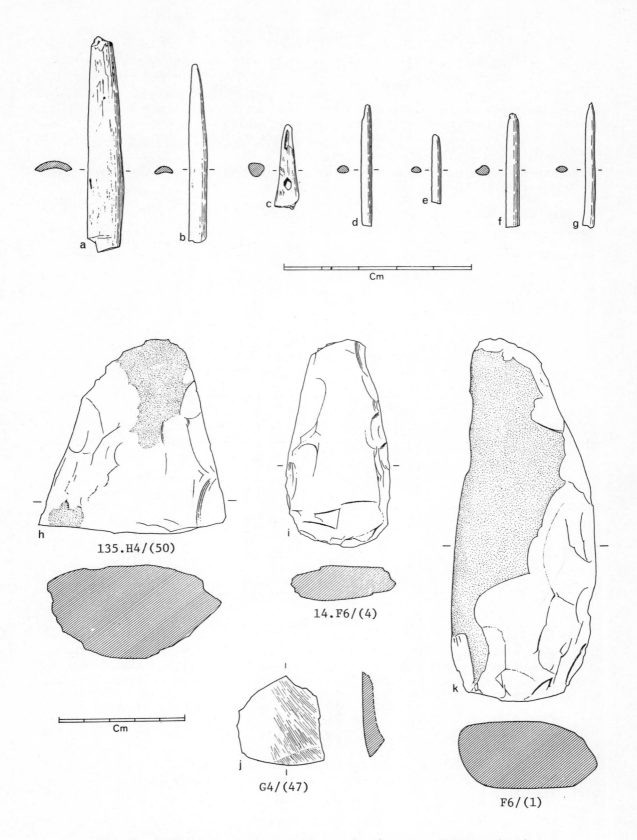

Fig.18   Kafiavana: bone artifacts (a–g) and axe-adzes (h–k)

135.H4/(50)

14.F6/(4)

G4/(47)

F6/(1)

The rest of the stones may be divided into three groups:

1. Five flakes have smears along one or both edges and seem to have been used
    for cutting or shaving ochre (fig.19b). On one the smears clearly run
    parallel to the edge.

2. Twelve stones have single dots, small patches or thin lines of ochre on
    them. The material appears to have been applied when dry. Some
    specimens may have been used to crush dry ochre to powder, but two are thickly
    covered with ochre over most of their surface.

3. Sixteen stones have large smooth smears which appear to have been applied
    wet either to corners or flat surfaces.

Table 121   Kafiavana: distribution of ochre

Horizon	Weight in gm	Gm per m^3
I	93.6	54.1
II	115.1	60.0
III	444.7	126.7
IV	314.1	111.0
V	324.8	70.6
VI	355.8	90.1
VII	35.4	10.1
VIII	88.6	23.0
IX	40.6	9.5
Total	1812.7	60.1

Table 122   Kafiavana: distribution of ochre stones

Horizon	design	Class 1	2	3	Total	No. per m^3
I	-	-	-	1	1	0.6
II	1	2	1	1	5	2.6
III	-	1	1	3	5	1.4
IV	-	1	2	3	6	2.1
V	-	-	6	2	8	1.7
VI	-	1	2	2	5	1.3
VII	-	-	-	1	1	0.3
VIII	-	-	-	1	1	0.3
IX	-	-	-	2	2	0.5

OBSIDIAN

Four pieces of obsidian were found, which, since it is not available
locally, demonstrates trade within the Highlands. Two pieces come from each
of Horizons I and II. Too little is known about Highlands obsidian to trace
these pieces to a source. Two show signs of use.

WAX

In Horizon I, 4.5 gm of a hard black waxy substance was found. It is
possibly old and dried-out plant wax, such as is used today in various craft
activities.

USE-POLISHED TOOLS

Twenty-seven pieces of stone with gloss along one margin were found,
scattered throughout the site (table 123). Study of these tools does not
suggest that their overall shape or size are particularly significant. All
whole tools can be held comfortably and none shows shaping retouch. Generally

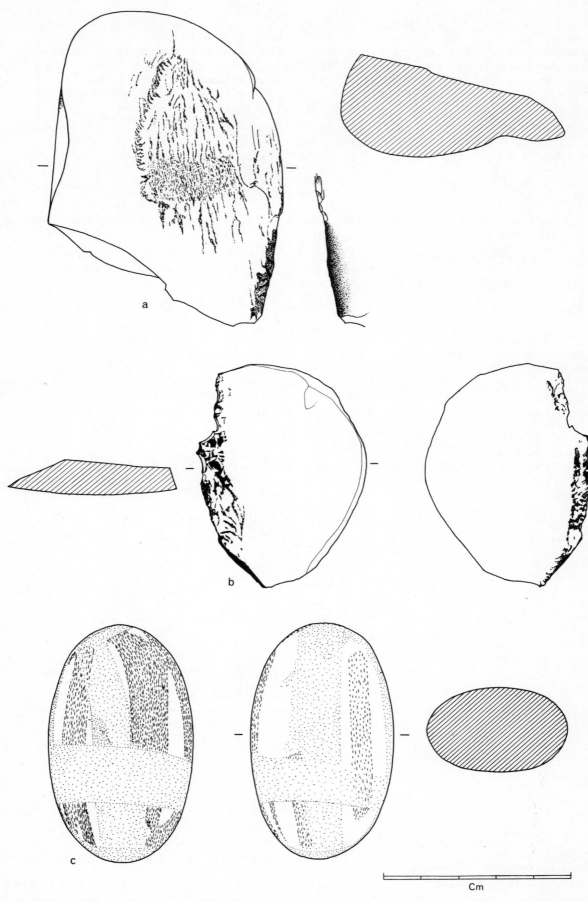

Fig.19   Kafiavana: a) use-polishing flake (19.G5/(7)), b) ochre cutter
(60.H4/(17)); c) painted pebble (29.H2/(6))

they seem to be larger than most retouched tools, but the sample is small. The majority of these tools is made in dark, fine-grained volcanic rocks without inclusions; only four are made on the red and brown chert which is the common material for retouched implements.

The use-polish has been studied with a hand-lens (10x) and binocular microscope and four different types of polish have been distinguished, based on the position, direction and intensity of gloss and wear striations. These variations may relate entirely to the way the tool was used, but they may also imply that different materials were being treated. The types are:

1. Equal wear on both sides of the edge with all striations running at right angles to the edge. Most striations are short and thick. The polish extends 4.6 mm back from both sides of the edge and then fades out rapidly (fig.19a).

2. Similar to (1) but shows a few long deep striations parallel to the edge. The wear on both sides does not seem to be equal.

3. The most marked striations occur parallel with the edge and are long and deep. Some short scratches occur at various angles to the edge. The wear is approximately equal on both sides.

4. Very similar to (1) but with nearly all wear on one side of the edge, showing that the tool was moved quite differently.

At least 16 examples of type (1) occur, while the other types are represented by only one each. In addition, eight implements have too little wear for them to be classified. Most of the edges are chipped as well as polished and two show step-flaking retouch. All edges are straight or slightly concave (indentation index <20) and the angles of these edges are acute, except for the example of class (4) wear. On two tools small areas away from the edge show light polishing on slightly projecting parts of the stone (fig.19a). It seems almost certain that this is due to movements of the hand while the tool was in use.

Some idea of the function of these tools may be deduced by comparison with data from other parts of the world (Semenov 1964). The very high gloss combined with many shallow striations is good evidence that the material being worked was plastic and not hard (Semenov 1964:115). The equal wear and right-angled striations on each side of the edge of class (1) suggest that the tool was held edge-on and pushed through soft material. In other parts of the world hide or skin-working would be a logical suggestion, but Bulmer's reminder (1966a:148) that bark cloth and other vegetable fibres needed to be prepared is probably more appropriate for the Highlands.

The wear on class (2) tools suggests that some sawing went with this type of use, while class (3) wear was primarily produced by a sawing motion. Class (4) tools were used entirely with a one-way motion so that only one side of the tool came into contact with the material.

Table 123   Kafiavana: distribution of tools with use-polish

Square	I	II	III	IV	V	VI	VII	VIII	IX	Total
F3	2	1	-	-	-	-	-	-	-	3
G2	1	1	-	-	-	-	-	-	-	2
G3	1	-	1	1	1	2	-	1	-	7
G4	-	-	-	-	-	-	-	-	2	2
G5	-	-	1	-	1	-	-	-	-	2
H2	-	2	1	2	-	-	-	-	-	5
H3	1	-	-	1	-	1	-	-	-	3
H4	-	-	-	-	1	-	-	1	1	3
Total	5	4	3	4	3	3	-	2	3	27
No. as % of total retouched implements	3.0	1.8	0.9	1.4	0.9	1.6	-	1.0	6.7	1.4
No. per m^3	2.9	2.1	0.9	1.4	0.7	0.8	-	0.5	0.7	0.9

WASTE MATERIAL

    If we make an estimate based on 25 randomly chosen spits with a mean of
530 pieces, the 480 excavated spits produced a total of about 250,000 flakes
and lumps which showed no traces of secondary working or use.   This is more
than 99%·of the stone at the site and clearly shows that it was a workshop
throughout the period of occupation (cf. Mulvaney and Joyce 1965:table 1;
Bulmer 1966a:108b).   Most of the material is chert, frequently the dark
red-brown type used to make implements.

    A size analysis was carried out on six samples, totalling 12,686 waste
pieces, selected from top, middle and basal levels (table 124).   From the
results of χ^2 tests made by W.J. Ewens, to whom I am grateful for assisting
with the interpretation of results, many highly significant differences occur
both within and between samples but these differences do not form any
consistent pattern, so that there is no consistent change in the size of
waste material throughout the site.   It may therefore be argued that there
was no significant change in flaking technique and size of raw material
throughout the occupation and also that·the presence of more large or small
flakes is due to chance factors like an extra-large core, the condition of
the pieces of stone used, personal preference over time and so on.

Table 124   Kafiavana: distribution of a sample of waste material by size

Horizon	<0.5 in.	0.5-1.0 in.	1.0-1.5 in.	1.5-2.0 in.	>2.0 in.	Total
I	1062	678	86	17	3	1846
I-II	1518	827	111	21	4	2481
III-IV	1892	930	141	19	1	2983
IV	1154	781	132	23	5	2095
VIII	1210	684	155	27	8	2084
VIII-IX	655	436	81	19	6	1197
Total	7491	4336	706	126	27	12686

FLAKED STONE TOOLS
(figs.20,21)

    A total of 1954 stones with secondary retouch or use-wear was excavated
(table 125).   These tools have been analysed by both methods outlined in
chapter II.   For the standard typology 1329 pieces were included, the tools
from the three back squares (F3, G2, H2) being excluded because of the
considerable slope and possible mixing due to increased treadage on the
softer soil.

Table 125   Kafiavana: distribution of flaked-stone implements

Horizon	F3	F4	F5	F6	F7	G2	G3	G4	G5	H2	H3	H4	Total
I	21	-	-	-	-	42	31	12	4	23	20	11	164
II	28	-	-	-	-	37	21	11	4	90	31	4	226
III	73	-	-	-	4	12	47	45	28	79	44	19	351
IV	15	-	-	8	1	15	20	45	52	45	30	53	284
V	28	-	19	82	-	1	13	49	32	37	23	41	325
VI	32	-	6	75	-	3	25	13	3	10	18	7	192
VII	12	11	9	-	-	5	38	16	8	3	47	16	165
VIII	12	22	15	-	-	-	18	41	36	-	33	25	202
IX	2	15	11	-	-	-	-	9	6	-	1	1	45
Total	223	48	60	165	5	115	213	241	173	287	247	177	1954

Standard Typology (table 126)

    Most of the tools are scrapers and their morphology does not alter
visibly throughout the deposit.   Although there are some with deeply concave

edges, none of the double-concave scrapers of the type seen at Aibura and Batari was found.   Occasional large flakes with retouch or use-wear occur but these do not seem to form a special type; Bulmer notes this at Kiowa also (1966a:88).

The major change which occurs is that retouched tools are consistently larger towards the base of the deposit (table 127).   This change is a gradual one rather than a sudden shift.   It is not restricted to a particular type but occurs within all tool classes and is irrespective of raw material, size and amount of retouch.   A similar but less definite change occurs among the unretouched but used pieces.

Three significant changes in the proportion of various tools occur:

1. In Horizons I-II flakes with use-wear are more common and the number of retouched tools declines.   This replacement of retouched by unretouched tools is similar to that found at Aibura Horizon I (<1000 years BP).

2. In the upper two horizons there is a rise in multi-plane scrapers (figs.20a, 21b,c).   Although the numbers are small, this suggests that some retouched tools were more heavily used in recent times.

3. There is the large number of pebble tools (fig.20b) in Horizons VIII-IX. Although tools made on pebbles and weighing more than 100 gm occurred occasionally throughout the site, there were many more in the lowest horizons. All are made on grey non-greasy chert and volcanic rocks rather than the normal red-brown chert.   Some of these tools appear to be cores but others are step-flaked.

Table 126   Kafiavana: distribution of flaked-stone tool types

	I	II	III	IV	Horizon V	VI	VII	VIII-IX	Total
Total tools (add 1-4)	78	71	187	209	259	147	145	233	1329
1. Whole retouched tools	27	15	67	80	116	67	53	74	499
(a) Scrapers (total)	24	13	66	79	113	67	52	61	475
(i) side	5	5	23	22	34	26	13	20	148
(ii) end	1	1	10	12	15	6	7	12	64
(iii) double side	2	1	2	6	12	4	7	2	36
(iv) side and end	3	–	10	7	13	7	7	7	54
(v) double side and end	1	–	2	3	1	5	2	5	19
(vi) discoid	–	1	3	2	1	3	3	1	14
(vii) inverse retouch	–	–	–	2	–	–	–	–	2
(viii) double end	–	–	–	–	–	–	–	1	1
(ix) core scrapers	–	–	–	–	1	–	–	–	1
(x) multi-platform	12	5	16	24	31	16	13	13	130
(b) Bifacial retouch/use	3	–	–	–	1	–	1	1	6
(c) Pebble tools	–	2	1?	1	2	–	–	12	17+1?
2. Broken retouched tools	15	22	84	94	96	51	66	109	537
3. Utilised pieces	36	33	35	33	40	26	22	42	267
4. Cores	–	1	1	2	7	3	4	8	26
1 as % of total	34.6	21.1	35.8	38.3	44.8	45.6	36.5	31.8	37.5
2 as % of total	19.2	31.0	44.9	45.0	37.1	34.7	45.5	46.8	40.4
3 as % of total	46.2	46.5	18.7	15.8	15.4	17.7	15.2	18.0	20.1
(x) as % of (a)	50.0	38.5	24.2	30.4	27.4	23.9	25.0	21.3	27.4

Attribute Analysis (tables 128-59)

An analysis of 1954 pieces of stone showing retouch or use-wear was carried out.   Details are given in the tables on pp. 110-124

Analyses using the implement as the basic unit

1. *Type of stone*   In Horizons I-VII just over half the 1954 tools are made

Table 127   Kafiavana: percentage distribution of whole retouched tools by weight

| Horizon | Weight in gm | | | | | | Number |
	0-9	10-9	20-9	30-9	40-9	>50	
I	19.0	38.0	26.6	3.8	3.8	7.6	27
II	13.3	33.3	6.7	26.6	-	20.0	15
III	13.6	24.2	33.3	12.1	6.5	9.1	67
IV	6.2	40.7	23.5	12.3	3.7	13.6	80
V	8.5	21.4	24.0	13.7	13.7	17.1	116
VI	10.5	21.0	27.0	18.7	7.5	16.5	67
VII	3.8	18.9	24.5	9.4	15.1	28.3	53
VIII-IX	2.7	13.7	13.7	16.4	8.2	45.2	74

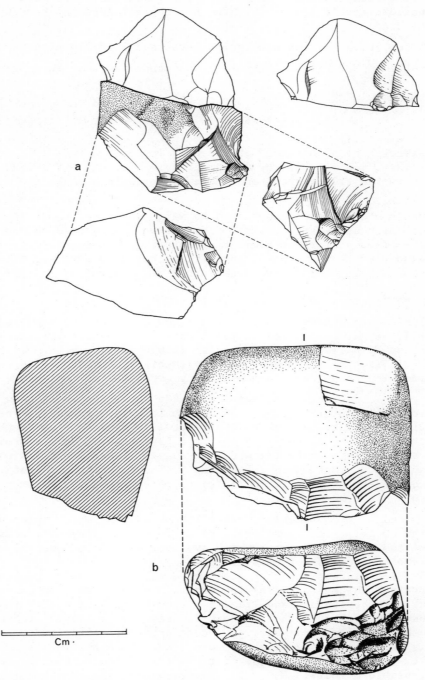

Cm·

Fig.20   Kafiavana: flaked-stone artifacts: a) multiplane scraper, two altered edges, subsequently broken and one part re-used, as top right (44, 45.F5/(26)); b) pebble tool (G5/(34))

103

on a red-brown chert, with other chert being used for about two-thirds of the rest. In the two lowest horizons, however, other sorts of stone become much more common (table 128). This probably relates to the use of pebble tools.

2. *Number of planes per implement* In all horizons about four-fifths of all implements were used in one plane only (table 129).

3. *Edges* A total of 4181 edges was observed on the 1954 stone implements (table 130). In the top six horizons about 70% of implements have one or two edges. Below this, rather more implements have more than two edges. Horizon IX is aberrant. In no horizon do more than 10% of implements have more than four edges.

4. *Weight of implements* The weight of implements increases from the top horizons down (table 131). Within this overall pattern three groups may be differentiated:

Horizon I The number of tools weighing less than 10 gm is high.

Horizons II-VII There is a slight but consistent increase in weight with depth.

Horizons VIII-IX Many more tools weigh over 130 gm and there are also slightly more tools weighing less than 10 gm than in the levels immediately above.

These differences are significant at the 0.1% level. Between HI and HIV most of the variation lies in the 0-9 gm group. Between HIV and HVIII most variation is in the >50 gm group and there is no difference in the 0-9 gm group.

Implements used on two planes tend to weigh more than implements used on one plane, although most heavier implements were only used on one plane (table 132). This picture is similar to Batari. Implements with more than two edges also tend to weigh more, suggesting that they were not selected for re-use unless they were above a certain size (table 133).

Analyses using the edge as the basic unit

1. *Whole implements* Less than 10% of all edges are on implements which can definitely be called 'whole' in relation to that particular edge, although rather more can be called 'probably whole' (table 134). With over two-thirds of all edges it is unclear whether the implement is, for *that* edge, whole or not. Horizon IX is aberrant in having many more 'whole' implements.

2. *Raw material* Over half the edges are made on stones which have some pebble cortex remaining (table 135(a)). This is, of course, only a minimum indication of the number of tools actually made on river pebbles, but even so is very high. It confirms that the Fayantina River was probably always the source of raw material and also suggests that chert was used lavishly and without continuous re-working. The contrast with Batari in this respect is quite striking. Table 135(b) relates cortex to implements using the implement as the basic unit.

3. *Size and shape of implements* Table 136 shows that most implements weigh less than 30 gm. It seems 'probably whole' tools generally weigh more than 'whole' tools. There are fewer heavy 'not whole' implements, which tends to confirm the correctness of this division.
Tables 137-8 express the shapes of implements in terms of Length/Breadth (L/B) and Breadth/Thickness (B/Th) indices. The Kafiavana implements are clearly square rather than blade-like, but tend to be flat rather than chunky, with B/Th usually greater than 2. Both indices remain fairly stable throughout the history of the site. The industry at Kafiavana is consistently less chunky and slightly more square than that at Batari, which may relate to less concentrated use of the material and to such factors as fewer multi-platform tools.

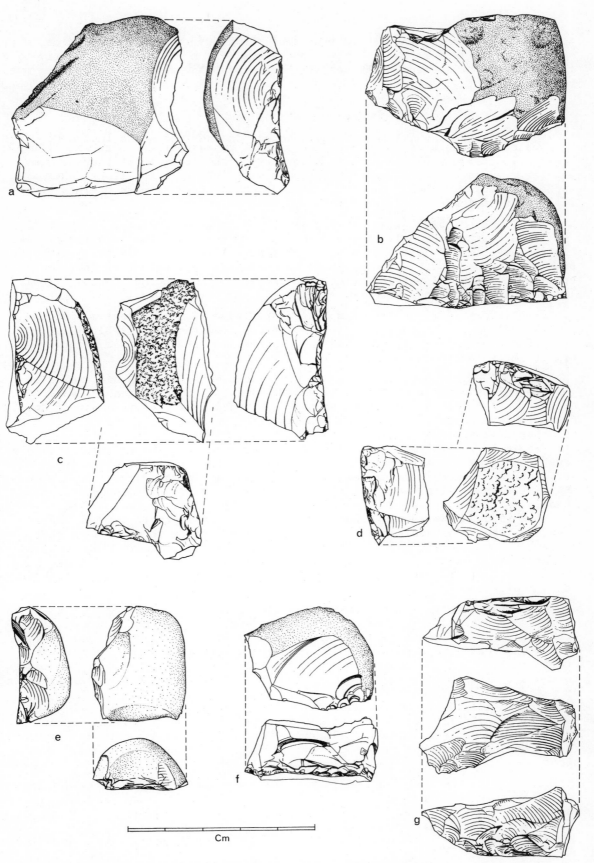

Cm

Fig.21 Kafiavana: flaked stone artifacts: a) side-scraper, four altered
edges, (151.G3/(37)); b,c) multiplane scrapers, six and five altered
edges respectively, (155.G3/(38), 150.G3/(37)); d) discoid scraper,
five altered edges (156.H3/(33)); e) side and end scraper, two
altered edges, (118.G3/(27)); f) discoid scraper, five altered edges,
(156.H3/(33)); g) double side scraper, three altered edges (110.H4/(37))

4. *Flakes and cores*   About two-thirds of the industry is made on flakes, while
     a third or less is made on cores and lumps (table 139).   The industry is
therefore primarily made on flakes, although the same proviso as at Batari must
be applied (p.27).

Attributes describing the edges individually

1. *Whole/not whole*   Between 40% and 50% of all edges are 'whole' or 'probably
     whole', and this figure is very consistent throughout the site except for
Horizon IX (table 140).   There is a contrast with Batari in that there some
20% fewer edges can be classified in these ways, while rather fewer edges are
broken at Kafiavana and more have been classed as indeterminate.   This may
imply that implements were used less fully at Kafiavana.

2. *Base type*   Table 141(a) shows that a wide range of surfaces was used as
     bases, with about half the bases being formed of positive bulbar surfaces.
The increase in pebble cortex bases in Horizons VIII-IX clearly relates to the
presence of large pebble tools, while the increased percentage of 'not
applicable' in HI-II refers to the greater use of unretouched flakes.   Table
141(b) relates base types to implements.

3. *Preparatory flaking*   About half the preparatory flaking consists of the
     removal of one or more large flakes struck from the base (table 142).
More than one-quarter of the edges are not prepared and this is a slightly
higher percentage than at Batari.

4. *Shape of edge*   Between 40% and 65% of whole edges are concave, while
     two-thirds or more of 'probably whole' edges are concave (table 143).
An inverse relationship between 'whole' and 'probably whole' is apparent among
convex edges and to a slight extent among straight edges.   These
relationships are dissimilar to those at Batari.
     Table 144 shows that straight and concave edges tend to be about the same
length (6-15 mm), while convex edges are rather longer (11-20 mm).   It is
very noticeable that straight edges at Kafiavana are a good deal longer than
those at Batari, with under 10% being less than 5 mm long, a decrease of more
than 20%.   The increase in length of concave edges is much less marked.
     The indentation index varies slightly but inconsistently through the
site (tables 145-6) and convex edges diverge less from a straight line than do
concave.   Concave edges at Kafiavana are slightly less concave than those at
Batari, which clearly suggests less retouching at Kafiavana due to greater
availability of raw material.   Convex edges appear to be much the same shape
at both sites.

5. *Retouch*   Nearly all retouch is step-flaking.   Just under two-thirds of
     all edges are step-flaked and most other edges are not retouched at all
(table 147).   Horizons I and IX have fewer step-flaked edges than the others.
Most step-flaking is found on concave edges and very little on convex edges
(table 148).   Edges without retouch are frequently straight.   Fourteen edges
in the site incorporate two types of retouch.   There is less heavy step-flaking
at Kafiavana than at Batari.
     Nearly all step-flaked edges are acutely-angled with the mode being at
60-79° (table 149).   As at Batari, other sorts of unifacial flaking occur on
rather more acute edges (table 149(c)).   Very few angles are obtuse.   There
is a clear trend towards more acute-angled step-flaked edges at the top of the
site.

6. *Use-wear*   Less than half the edges show use-wear of the 'chattering' type
     while only 10% are 'utilised' (table 150).   The rest shows no traces of
use-wear.   The number of 'utilised' edges increases in Horizons I, II and IX.
There is generally more 'utilisation' at Kafiavana than at Batari.
     Over half the 'chattering' at Kafiavana is concave, though well under half
of 'utilisation' is this shape.   One-third to one-half of both types of
use-wear is straight (table 151).   There is more straight use-wear in the
middle levels of the site than at the top and base.   In general, the percentage
of each shape of 'utilised' edge is about the same at Batari and Kafiavana but

there is about 20% more concave 'chattering' at Kafiavana than at Batari.

The normal length of use-wear is under 10 mm for 'chattering' but 6-20 mm for 'utilisation'. There is little variation in the length of either throughout the site (table 152). Where use-wear is concave, the two main types are distinct in terms of the indentation index, with 'utilisation' being less indented than 'chattering' (table 153). Use-wear is nearly all on acute-angled edges. The mode for 'chattering' is within the range 60-89° while the mode for 'utilisation' is 40-49°. There is a tendency for 'chattering' to become steeper in the lower horizons, but the same tendency is not apparent with 'utilisation' (table 154). There is a definite suggestion that 'chattered' edges at Kafiavana are steeper and 'utilised' edges are rather more acute than comparable edges at Batari.

Correlations between attributes

1. *Retouch and use-wear*   There is a clear correlation between 'chattering' and step-flaking retouch. Only about half of all 'chattering' is found on step-flaked edges (table 155(a)), but all step-flaked edges with use-wear are 'chattered' (table 156(a),(b)). While two-thirds of all use-wear on unretouched edges is 'chattering' (table 156(c)), there is a very high correlation between 'utilisation' and unretouched edges (table 155(b)). This picture is similar to that found in Batari.

2. *Retouch and 'chunkiness'*   Unretouched edges tend to occur on thinner implements than those which are step-flaked (table 157). It is especially noticeable that very few step-flaked edges are on implements less than 5 mm thick, which may relate to the mechanics of step-flaking. It also seems that implements with unretouched edges are less chunky and flatter (i.e. greater B/Th index) than those with step-flaking (table 158).

3. *Size of implement and angle of retouch*   There is no clear relation between the weight of implements and angle of their retouch, though this may be due to the small sample sizes (table 159).

Summary

It is clear that although there are changes in the industry over time, nearly all of them are only slight and might easily be overlooked. The data given in this analysis reflect the underlying stability of the industry, while allowing the changes already seen in the standard typology to be expressed more fully.

The marked divergence of Horizon IX from the norm, however, only really emerges from the attribute analysis. In the standard typology (table 126) this shows up in relation to pebble tools, but the differences in attributes which distinguish this horizon, cannot all be related to these tools. The importance of pebble tools and their by-products in Horizon IX is shown by stone type, weight and the use of pebble cortex as a base (tables 128, 131, 141). But, where sufficient numbers allow comparisons to be made, the following further differences emerge:

1. Higher percentages of whole implements and core-lumps (tables 134, 139).

2. More whole edges with less preparatory flaking on them and perhaps more convex edges (tables 140, 142, 143(a)).

3. Less step-flaking, and the angle of the step-flaked edges is less than in other horizons (tables 147, 149(a)).

4. More 'utilisation' in this horizon (table 150). There is more concave 'chattering' and it tends to be longer (tables 151(a), 152(a)); 'chattering' occurs more frequently on unretouched edges (table 155(a)).

Two sorts of variation seem to be involved. One suggests that utilised flake types play a bigger part than is shown in the standard typology (table 126): lack of retouch (table 147), more whole convex edges (table 143(a)), 'utilisation' (table 150).

The other differences are clearly not related to this: the slightly
higher percentage of core-lumps (table 139), the more acute angles associated
with step-flaking (table 149(a)) and 'chattering' (table 154(a)), more concave
and longer 'chattering' (tables 151(a), 152(a)) and the rather higher
proportion of 'chattering' on unretouched edges (table 155(a)).   It is
difficult to relate these to any one cause.   They suggest that tools may have
been used rather differently, but whether this is a consequence of the presence
of pebble tools or to other differences in the industry is not clear.   This
will only be tested by making a comparative study of flaked tools from sites
where pebble tools were also regularly produced.

TRIMMING FLAKES

Trimming flakes occur throughout the deposit and there is an average of
one for every four flaked implements (table 160).   The ratio of implements to
trimming flakes varies consistently through the site, being high in the lower
horizons, dropping sharply in Horizon VI, and then rising again in the upper
horizons.   The generally low numbers of trimming flakes reflect the ready
availability of raw material, already indicated by aspects of the attribute
analysis (e.g. table 135).   There is a strong contrast with the situation at
Batari.

HAMMERS AND ANVILS

Twenty-six hammers and four anvils were found.   The hammers are
characterised by battering on the ends or sides of river pebbles, the anvils
by battering on a flat surface.   All are made on volcanic rocks, either tuff,
basalt, diorite or a variety of porphyry.   Half the tools may be broken.
The majority of tools weigh less than 500 gm, with whole hammers weighing
83-1270 gm.   One hammer shows some powdered ochre around the area of battering.
Hammers were found throughout the site, but anvils occurred only in the lower
horizons (table 161): both tended to be found in all areas of the excavation.

CONCLUSION

Humans first occupied Kafiavana more than 11,000 years ago.   They possessed
ground stone axes and hunted wild animals.   They flaked large stone scrapers
and pebble tools and prepared ochre for painting.   The subsequent history of
the occupation can be subdivided as follows:

Phase I (about 11,000-4500 BP)

The site was intensively used.   Fires were lit and much chert was
carried up from the Fayantina River for knapping into scrapers, pebble tools
and a few axes.   In the period 9500-8000 BP fires were often made near the
eastern end of the shelter, though this area was used for stone working both
before and after this.   A range of wild animals, mammals from forests and
grasslands, birds, reptiles and fish, were brought to the site and eaten.
Pigs were present from about 6500 years ago, but whether they were kept as
domestic animals in this area or not is unknown.

The stone and bone tool-kit changed to some extent after the earliest
occupation.   Pebble tools were largely discarded, while many smaller flaked
tools were made.   The flaked tools changed in some ways, but the techniques
of making them remained much the same.   Bone tools were made and may have
been stored or discarded at the back of the shelter.   Human bones were
occasionally left at the site.   People continued to grind axes from local
stones and ochre was used for painting.   From time to time shells came along
trade routes from the coast: they were probably always valuable objects.

According to Schmid (Appendix 4), the climate was drier than at present
in the early-middle part of this phase.

Phase II (about 4500-2000 BP)

The site was probably used much less; fewer tools were deposited and the humus content of the soil increased.

Phase III (from about 2000 BP)

The flaked tools are similar to those made only within the last 1000 years at Aibura, with very common use of unretouched flakes and a marked decline in the size of tools. Along with the variations in flaked tools, axes in this upper level tended to be less well ground and were discarded at the front of the site. Bone tools were less frequently made but more marine shell came along the trade routes. Someone painted a design on a river pebble. The diet also appears to have changed, with pig being more often eaten, especially in the most recent period.

This form of use continued until very recent times, as is shown by the presence of wooden stakes and fibre arrow-bindings. The recent variations in the surviving stone tool-kit may indicate that rather different activities were being carried on compared to the earlier period or it may signify a purely formal change in the artifacts.

The long sequence at Kafiavana has a basic similarity with that at Kiowa, 20 miles (32 km) to the northwest (Bulmer 1966a). In both sites the main occupation occurs from about 10,000-4000 BP. Wild fauna predominates, but pigs are found in the later period, dogs do not occur and trade routes with the coast are open.

But there are some striking differences. For example, at Kafiavana, ground stone axes were present at least 9500 years ago and were made throughout the occupation; they show no major formal change through time and most are lenticular in cross-section. These tools are recorded only from about 6000 years BP at Kiowa. Pebble tools were found only at the earliest levels in Kafiavana and their manufacture then virtually ceased, but they were made throughout the occupation of Kiowa. Waisted blades do not occur at all at Kafiavana, although they are present from about 6000 BP at Kiowa.

It is not yet certain whether these differences are real ones, indicating the presence of the Chimbu/Asaro cultural divide in prehistoric times, or whether they are the unreal product of small-scale sampling of only two sites. I am inclined to suspect that while sampling errors may be largely responsible for the absence of ground axes before 6000 BP at Kiowa, a valid cultural division may be indicated by the relative absence of pebble tools and possibly waisted blades east of Chuave.

A diagrammatic summary of the material from Kafiavana is given in fig. 28.

Table 128   Kafiavana: percentage distribution of types of stone used

Horizon	Red-brown greasy chert	Other greasy chert	Non-greasy chert and other materials	No. of implements
I	51.2	37.2	11.6	164
II	54.9	28.8	16.4	226
III	50.1	34.2	15.7	351
IV	52.8	34.9	12.3	284
V	49.9	36.6	13.5	325
VI	54.7	29.2	16.2	192
VII	50.9	37.6	11.5	165
VIII	44.6	26.2	29.2	202
IX	35.6	17.8	46.7	45

Table 129   Kafiavana: percentage distribution of number of planes per implement

Horizon	Number of planes				No. of implements
	1	2	3	4	
I	76.8	20.1	3.1	–	164
II	77.9	17.7	4.4	–	226
III	83.2	13.7	2.3	0.9	351
IV	80.3	18.0	1.4	0.4	284
V	80.3	17.9	1.9	–	325
VI	86.5	13.0	0.5	–	192
VII	84.2	14.6	1.2	–	165
VIII	81.2	16.4	2.5	–	202
IX	82.2	17.8	–	–	45

Table 130   Kafiavana: percentage distribution of number of edges per implement

Horizon	Number of edges									No. of implements	No. of edges	No. of edges per implement
	1	2	3	4	5	6	7	8	9			
I	33.5	38.4	15.2	6.1	6.1	–	0.6	–	–	164	353	2.15
II	41.2	29.7	15.9	6.6	3.5	2.7	0.4	–	–	226	478	2.11
III	43.3	30.8	13.7	6.8	2.6	1.4	1.4	–	–	351	717	2.04
IV	43.7	29.9	14.8	6.7	2.5	1.1	0.7	0.7	–	284	580	2.04
V	36.9	34.2	15.1	6.8	3.1	1.2	1.9	0.6	0.3	325	719	2.21
VI	45.8	26.6	17.2	5.2	2.6	2.1	0.5	–	–	192	386	2.01
VII	38.2	26.1	13.9	11.5	4.9	3.6	1.2	0.6	–	165	391	2.37
VIII	37.1	22.8	21.8	7.4	6.9	2.5	0.5	–	1.0	202	482	2.38
IX	53.3	35.6	4.4	4.4	2.2	–	–	–	–	45	75	1.67
I-IX										1954	4181	2.14

Table 131   Kafiavana: percentage distribution of implement weights

Horizon	0-9	10-9	20-9	30-9	40-9	50-9	60-9	70-9	80-9	90-9	100-9	110-9	120-9	>129	No. of implements
I	45.7	23.8	16.5	6.1	4.3	1.8	-	0.6	0.6	-	-	-	-	0.6	164
II	27.8	28.3	16.4	10.6	4.9	2.2	3.1	1.3	0.9	0.9	0.4	-	-	3.1	226
III	27.6	28.2	21.1	7.7	5.1	2.6	1.1	1.4	1.1	0.6	0.3	0.6	-	2.0	351
IV	23.5	31.9	18.6	10.2	5.3	3.2	2.1	1.4	0.7	0.4	1.1	-	0.4	1.4	285
V	22.5	28.1	18.5	11.1	7.1	3.1	1.2	1.5	0.3	2.2	0.6	0.9	0.6	2.2	324
VI	21.9	30.2	17.2	13.5	8.3	3.1	2.1	1.0	-	-	1.0	0.5	-	1.0	192
VII	17.0	27.2	18.2	12.1	8.5	5.5	3.0	2.4	3.0	1.8	-	-	-	1.2	165
VIII	25.2	17.3	12.9	12.4	4.0	3.0	4.5	2.5	1.5	1.5	1.5	2.5	2.0	9.4	202
IX	20.0	13.3	11.1	17.8	4.4	8.9	-	6.7	-	-	2.2	2.2	2.2	11.1	45

Table 132   Kafiavana: percentage distribution of implement weights in relation to number of planes used

Horizon	0-9	10-9	20-9	30-9	40-9	50-9	60-9	70-9	80-9	90-9	100-9	110-9	120-9	>129	No. of implements
(a) one plane															
I	49.6	22.4	15.2	5.6	3.2	2.4	-	0.8	0.8	-	-	.	-	-	126
II	33.0	26.7	15.3	10.2	4.5	2.8	3.4	1.1	-	0.6	0.6	-	-	1.7	176
III	30.5	28.4	18.9	7.5	5.1	3.1	1.4	1.0	1.0	0.7	0.3	0.7	-	1.4	292
IV	26.2	30.6	17.5	8.7	6.1	2.6	2.2	1.8	0.9	0.4	1.3	-	-	1.8	229
V	24.6	29.6	18.1	9.6	5.4	3.1	0.8	1.9	-	2.7	0.8	0.8	0.8	1.9	260
VI	25.3	31.3	17.5	11.4	6.6	1.8	1.8	1.2	-	-	1.2	0.6	-	1.2	166
VII	18.0	26.6	17.3	13.0	8.6	5.8	3.6	2.2	1.4	2.2	-	-	-	1.4	139
VIII	29.9	16.5	13.4	13.4	3.7	3.7	2.4	1.8	1.2	-	1.2	3.1	1.8	7.9	164
IX	15.2	16.2	13.5	16.2	2.7	5.4	-	8.1	-	-	-	-	13.5	8.1	37
(b) two planes															
I	33.3	30.3	21.2	6.1	9.1	-	-	-	-	-	-	-	-	-	33
II	10.0	37.5	20.0	15.0	7.5	-	-	2.5	2.5	-	-	-	-	5.0	40
III	14.6	29.2	33.3	8.3	8.3	-	-	4.2	-	-	-	-	-	2.1	48
IV	13.7	37.2	23.5	13.7	2.0	5.9	2.0	-	-	-	-	-	2.0	-	51
V	13.8	22.4	20.6	15.5	13.8	3.4	3.4	1.7	1.7	-	-	1.7	-	3.4	58
VI	-	24.0	16.0	24.0	20.0	12.0	4.0	-	-	-	-	-	-	-	25
VII	8.3	29.2	25.0	8.3	8.3	4.2	-	4.2	12.5	-	-	-	-	-	24
VIII	3.0	24.2	9.1	9.1	3.0	-	15.1	6.1	3.0	9.1	-	-	3.0	15.1	33
IX	-	-	-	25.0	12.5	25.0	-	-	-	-	12.5	25.0	-	-	8

Table 133   Kafiavana: percentage distribution of implement weights in relation to number of edges used

Horizon	\multicolumn{14}{c	}{Weight in gm}	No. of implements
	0-9	10-9	20-9	30-9	40-9	50-9	60-9	70-9	80-9	90-9	100-9	110-9	120-9	>129	
(a) one or two edges															
I	51.7	20.3	14.4	4.1	5.1	1.7	-	0.8	0.8	-	-	-	-	0.8	118
II	35.0	26.9	15.0	10.0	3.7	2.5	1.9	1.9	0.6	0.6	0.6	-	-	1.3	160
III	33.5	28.1	16.2	7.3	5.4	3.1	1.5	0.8	1.2	0.8	0.4	0.4	-	1.5	260
IV	28.6	30.5	17.6	7.1	6.7	2.4	1.9	1.0	1.0	0.5	1.4	-	0.4	1.4	210
V	29.1	26.5	17.0	8.7	7.4	2.6	0.4	1.7	0.4	2.2	0.4	0.9	0.4	2.2	230
VI	25.9	36.0	15.1	7.9	8.6	1.4	2.2	1.4	-	-	0.7	-	-	0.7	139
VII	20.8	30.2	17.0	11.3	7.6	6.6	2.8	0.9	0.9	0.9	-	-	-	0.9	106
VIII	34.7	15.7	10.7	10.7	4.1	3.3	3.3	3.3	1.7	-	1.7	2.5	0.8	7.4	121
IX	22.5	15.0	12.5	15.0	5.0	7.5	-	5.0	-	-	2.5	2.5	-	12.5	40
(b) more than two edges															
I	30.4	32.6	21.8	10.9	2.2	2.2	-	-	-	-	-	-	-	-	46
II	10.6	31.8	19.7	12.1	7.6	1.5	6.1	-	1.5	1.5	-	-	-	7.6	66
III	11.0	28.6	35.2	8.8	4.4	1.1	-	3.3	1.1	-	-	1.1	-	3.3	91
IV	9.3	36.0	21.3	18.7	1.3	5.3	2.7	2.7	-	-	-	-	1.3	1.3	75
V	6.4	31.9	22.4	17.0	6.4	4.3	3.2	1.1	-	2.1	1.1	1.1	1.1	2.1	94
VI	11.3	15.1	22.6	28.3	7.5	7.5	1.9	-	-	-	1.9	1.9	-	1.9	53
VII	10.2	22.0	20.4	13.6	10.2	3.4	3.4	5.1	6.8	3.4	-	-	-	1.7	59
VIII	11.1	19.8	16.1	14.8	3.7	2.5	6.2	1.2	1.2	3.7	1.2	2.5	3.7	12.3	81
IX	-	-	-	40.0	-	20.0	-	20.0	-	-	-	20.0	-	-	5

Table 134   Kafiavana: percentage distribution of condition of implements, counting each edge as a separate implement

Horizon	Whole	Probably whole	Not whole	Indeterminate	No. of edges
I	5.1	23.5	9.4	62.0	353
II	4.8	19.5	7.5	68.2	478
III	5.2	17.9	8.8	68.2	717
IV	1.2	21.7	8.3	68.8	580
V	2.0	17.9	8.1	72.0	719
VI	6.0	17.6	9.1	67.4	386
VII	2.1	14.6	12.3	71.1	391
VIII	1.9	18.1	7.3	72.8	482
IX	17.3	8.0	2.7	72.0	75

Table 135   Kafiavana: percentage distribution of occurrence of cortex

Horizon	Pebble cortex	Other cortex	No cortex	Indeterminate	No. of edges
(a) counting each edge as a separate implement					
I	49.0	12.5	34.0	4.5	353
II	55.2	18.8	21.4	4.6	478
III	52.4	15.9	27.8	3.9	717
IV	57.4	14.8	25.2	2.6	580
V	48.1	20.6	26.7	4.6	719
VI	59.6	12.7	24.1	3.6	386
VII	52.9	11.3	31.0	4.9	391
VIII	60.6	6.8	26.5	6.0	482
IX	58.6	16.0	20.0	5.3	75
(b) counting each implement as one					No. of implements
I	48.2	12.2	33.6	6.1	164
II	54.0	17.7	21.2	7.1	226
III	53.0	14.2	28.2	4.6	351
IV	55.1	15.8	24.9	4.2	285
V	49.7	20.1	24.7	5.6	324
VI	60.4	12.0	22.4	5.2	192
VII	55.1	9.7	29.7	5.5	165
VIII	57.4	8.4	26.8	7.4	202
IX	53.3	17.8	24.4	4.4	45

Table 136   Kaflavana: percentage distribution of implement weights, counting each edge as a separate implement

Horizon	Weight in gm														No. of edges
	0-9	10-9	20-9	30-9	40-9	50-9	60-9	70-9	80-9	90-9	100-9	110-9	120-9	>129	
(a) whole implements															
I	50.0	38.8	11.2	–	–	–	–	–	–	–	–	–	–	–	18
II	39.1	13.1	17.4	13.1	4.3	–	4.3	–	–	–	–	–	–	8.7	23
III	54.1	8.1	21.6	2.7	–	2.7	–	–	–	2.7	–	–	–	8.1	37
IV	50.0	50.0	–	–	–	–	–	–	–	–	–	–	–	–	8
V	46.1	46.1	–	–	–	7.7	–	–	–	–	–	–	–	–	13
VI	39.1	34.8	–	17.4	–	–	–	8.7	–	–	–	–	–	–	23
VII	37.5	50.0	–	–	12.5	–	–	–	–	–	–	–	–	–	8
VIII	22.2	44.4	33.3	–	–	–	–	–	–	–	–	–	–	–	9
IX	23.1	7.7	7.7	61.5	–	–	–	–	–	–	–	–	–	–	13
(b) probably whole implements															
I	49.4	30.1	12.1	2.4	2.4	–	–	2.4	1.3	–	–	–	–	–	83
II	25.8	31.2	18.3	12.9	2.2	3.2	4.3	–	2.2	–	–	–	–	–	93
III	14.1	36.8	21.1	12.5	3.1	2.3	1.6	6.2	0.8	–	–	–	–	1.6	128
IV	16.7	35.7	7.9	13.5	3.2	7.1	3.2	4.8	–	1.6	–	–	3.2	3.2	126
V	28.7	24.8	17.8	4.7	8.5	–	0.8	0.8	–	3.1	1.6	3.9	–	5.4	129
VI	22.1	23.6	13.2	10.3	8.8	8.8	1.5	–	–	–	2.9	4.4	–	4.4	68
VII	22.8	17.6	22.8	14.0	5.3	8.8	1.8	1.8	3.5	1.8	–	–	–	–	57
VIII	21.8	3.5	14.9	21.8	4.6	3.5	–	2.3	–	–	1.1	–	11.5	14.9	87
IX	–	–	16.7	–	33.3	33.3	–	–	–	–	–	–	–	16.7	6
(c) not whole implements															
I	39.4	36.4	15.2	9.1	–	–	–	–	–	–	–	–	–	–	33
II	38.9	16.7	30.5	8.3	2.8	–	2.8	–	–	–	–	–	–	–	36
III	39.7	27.0	22.2	9.5	1.6	–	–	–	–	–	–	–	–	–	63
IV	41.6	25.0	12.5	8.3	4.2	2.1	–	6.3	–	–	–	–	–	–	48
V	27.6	41.4	15.5	8.6	6.9	–	–	–	–	–	–	–	–	–	58
VI	37.2	17.1	20.0	22.8	2.9	–	–	–	–	–	–	–	–	–	35
VII	22.9	39.6	16.7	2.1	10.4	2.1	–	6.3	–	–	–	–	–	–	48
VIII	54.2	20.0	5.7	2.9	8.6	–	–	–	–	–	–	2.9	–	5.7	35
IX	–	–	–	–	–	–	–	100.0	–	–	–	–	–	–	2

Table 137   Kafiavana: percentage distribution of whole implement shapes, counting each edge as a separate implement

Horizon	<0.5	0.5-0.99	1-1.49	1.5-1.99	2-2.49	2.5-2.99	>2.99	No. of edges
(a) length/breadth index								
I	–	–	61.1	33.3	5.6	–	–	18
II	–	–	56.5	39.1	4.4	–	–	23
III	–	–	78.4	18.9	2.7	–	–	37
IV	–	–	71.4	28.6	–	–	–	7
V	–	–	57.1	42.9	–	–	–	14
VI	–	–	65:2	34.8	–	–	–	23
VII	–	–	50.0	25.0	25.0	–	–	8
VIII	–	–	66.7	33.3	–	–	–	9
IX	–	–	15.4	76.9	–	7.7	–	13
(b) breadth/thickness index								
I	–	–	5.6	–	33.3	16.7	44.4	18
II	–	–	17.4	13.0	39.1	21.7	8.7	23
III	–	–	–	13.5	29.7	5.4	51.4	37
IV	–	–	–	14.3	28.6	14.3	42.9	7
V	–	–	7.1	–	50.0	21.4	21.4	14
VI	–	–	4.4	26.1	8.7	26.1	34.8	23
VII	–	–	12.5	–	25.0	25.0	37.5	8
VIII	–	–	–	–	33.3	22.2	44.4	9
IX	–	7.7	–	30.8	–	46.2	15.4	13

Table 138   Kafiavana: percentage distribution of the shape of probably whole implements, counting each edge as a separate implement

Horizon	<0.5	0.5-0.99	1-1.49	1.5-1.99	2-2.49	2.5-2.99	>2.99	No. of edges
(a) length/breadth index								
I	–	–	78.3	13.3	3.6	–	4.8	83
II	–	–	55.9	33.3	9.7	–	1.1	93
III	–	–	83.6	12.5	3.9	–	–	128
IV	–	–	69.0	28.6	1.6	0.8	–	126
V	–	–	65.9	21.7	10.1	0.8	1.6	129
VI	–	–	80.9	13.2	2.9	2.9	–	68
VII	–	–	73.7	14.0	3.5	8.8	–	57
VIII	–	–	74.7	18.4	4.6	–	2.3	87
IX	–	–	100.0	–	–	–	–	6
(b) breadth/thickness index								
I	–	3.6	26.5	18.1	14.5	12.1	25.3	83
II	–	6.5	21.5	23.7	20.4	12.9	15.1	93
III	–	2.3	16.4	21.9	20.3	25.8	13.3	128
IV	–	4.0	23.0	19.1	21.4	19.8	12.7	126
V	1.6	3.9	24.8	29.5	18.6	7.8	14.0	129
VI	–	7.4	19.1	16.2	20.6	16.2	20.6	68
VII	–	–	10.5	26.3	14.0	17.5	31.6	57
VIII	–	6.9	8.1	17.2	27.6	23.0	17.2	87
IX	–	–	16.7	33.3	–	33.3	16.7	6

Table 139   Kafiavana: percentage distribution of core and flake components of the total industry, counting each edge as a separate implement

Horizon	Core or lump	Flake	Trimming flake	Indeterminate	No. of edges
I	17.8	73.4	4.3	4.5	353
II	29.5	62.1	3.8	4.6	478
III	30.1	63.6	2.4	3.9	717
IV	22.1	72.6	2.8	2.6	580
V	32.4	60.4	2.6	4.6	719
VI	29.8	63.4	3.1	3.6	386
VII	21.7	71.1	2.3	4.9	391
VIII	34.9	57.5	1.7	6.0	482
IX	37.3	57.3	–	5.3	75

Table 140   Kafiavana: percentage distribution of the condition of edges

Horizon	Whole	Probably whole	Not whole	Indeterminate	No. of edges
I	9.6	40.5	9.9	39.9	353
II	6.5	37.5	11.1	45.0	478
III	5.6	43.2	10.2	41.0	717
IV	2.9	40.5	11.7	44.8	580
V	6.8	42.3	10.9	40.1	719
VI	7.5	41.2	9.6	41.7	386
VII	4.9	36.8	11.8	46.6	391
VIII	5.0	40.9	8.7	45.4	482
IX	18.7	48.0	-	33.3	75

Table 141   Kafiavana: percentage distribution of base types of all implements

Horizon	Indeterminate	Pebble cortex	Other cortex	Break	Negative bulb	Positive bulb	Not applicable	No. of edges
(a) counting each edge as a separate implement								
I	8.2	4.8	6.0	5.1	18.4	43.9	13.6	353
II	2.5	8.0	8.0	5.0	18.6	48.1	9.8	478
III	2.4	7.5	9.1	3.9	23.2	47.6	6.4	717
IV	2.9	6.9	3.8	2.4	23.8	55.2	5.0	580
V	1.7	7.0	7.2	3.8	23.6	50.1	6.7	719
VI	2.1	7.0	4.7	5.4	26.7	46.6	7.5	386
VII	2.1	3.8	4.9	3.1	19.7	57.8	8.7	391
VIII	2.9	13.3	1.5	4.6	21.4	48.1	8.3	482
IX	5.3	20.0	4.0	4.0	24.0	20.0	22.7	75
(b) counting each implement as one								No. of implements
I	6.7	6.7	6.1	5.5	14.6	43.3	17.1	164
II	4.0	8.4	8.9	5.3	16.8	46.0	10.6	226
III	3.1	7.4	7.7	3.7	21.7	47.3	9.1	351
IV	2.5	6.3	3.5	2.8	20.4	58.8	5.6	284
V	1.5	7.7	7.7	4.3	20.0	49.2	9.5	325
VI	2.6	8.9	4.7	6.8	22.4	44.8	9.9	192
VII	3.6	5.5	4.2	5.5	16.4	56.4	8.5	165
VIII	4.0	14.4	2.0	5.5	17.8	47.5	8.9	202
IX	4.4	13.3	4.4	6.7	28.9	24.4	17.8	45

Table 142   Kafiavana: percentage distribution of preparatory flaking of all implements,
counting each edge as a separate implement

Horizon	Unclear	None	Base struck	Side/end struck	Not applicable	No. of edges
I	13.6	38.0	34.6	0.3	13.6	353
II	15.3	33.7	41.0	-	10.0	478
III	20.6	25.8	46.7	0.4	6.4	717
IV	14.7	28.8	51.2	0.2	5.2	580
V	16.0	31.6	45.3	0.4	6.7	719
VI	13.2	32.4	46.9	-	7.5	386
VII	16.9	22.8	51.4	0.3	8.7	391
VIII	14.5	30.1	46.9	0.2	8.3	482
IX	4.0	37.3	36.0	-	22.7	75

Table 143   Kafiavana: percentage distribution of edge shapes

Horizon	Straight	Concave	Convex	Wavy	No. of edges
(a) whole edges					
I	32.4	41.2	26.5	–	34
II	32.3	51.6	16.1	–	31
III	22.5	65.0	12.5	–	40
IV	29.4	64.7	5.9	–	17
V	30.6	51.0	16.3	2.0	49
VI	24.1	65.5	10.3	–	29
VII	36.8	47.4	15.8	–	19
VIII	20.8	66.7	12.5	–	24
IX	28.6	42.9	21.4	7.1	14
(b) probably whole edges					
I	25.2	65.0	9.8	–	143
II	25.7	63.7	10.6	–	179
III	23.9	70.7	4.5	1.0	310
IV	23.4	69.4	6.8	0.4	235
V	26.3	67.8	5.9	–	304
VI	28.3	66.7	5.0	–	159
VII	20.1	72.9	6.9	–	144
VIII	20.8	70.1	8.6	0.5	197
IX	16.7	77.8	5.6	–	36

Table 144   Kafiavana: percentage distribution of the length of whole and probably whole edges in relation to edge shape

Horizon	0–5	6–10	11–15	16–20	21–25	26–30	31–35	>35	No. of edges
(a) straight									
I	12.8	46.8	27.7	10.6	2.1	–	–	–	47
II	3.6	41.1	35.7	14.3	3.6	–	1.8	–	56
III	3.6	45.7	33.7	10.8	3.6	1.2	1.2	–	83
IV	–	51.6	26.7	15.0	5.0	–	1.7	–	60
V	6.3	44.2	27.4	13.7	3.2	3.2	1.1	1.1	95
VI	13.5	36.6	30.8	15.4	–	3.8	–	–	52
VII	5.6	47.2	25.0	19.5	–	–	2.8	–	36
VIII	10.9	41.3	32.6	10.9	4.3	–	–	–	46
IX	10.0	30.0	30.0	20.0	10.0	–	–	–	10
(b) concave									
I	4.7	44.9	33.6	14.0	0.9	1.9	–	–	107
II	2.3	48.4	33.8	12.3	1.5	1.5	–	–	130
III	3.3	44.5	35.5	14.7	1.6	0.4	–	–	245
IV	1.7	43.1	36.2	13.8	3.4	1.5	–	0.6	174
V	4.3	42.9	34.6	13.4	3.9	0.9	–	–	231
VI	5.6	42.4	33.6	15.2	2.4	0.8	–	–	125
VII	2.6	41.2	36.0	16.7	2.6	0.9	–	–	114
VIII	2.6	44.7	33.8	10.4	4.5	3.2	0.6	–	154
IX	–	50.0	32.4	–	17.6	–	–	–	34
(c) convex									
I	–	17.4	30.4	34.8	8.7	8.7	–	–	23
II	4.2	8.3	29.2	33.3	8.3	8.3	–	8.3	24
III	5.3	15.8	36.8	26.3	10.5	5.3	–	–	19
IV	–	17.6	29.4	29.4	11.8	5.9	–	5.9	17
V	–	15.4	19.2	34.6	15.4	3.8	–	11.5	26
VI	–	18.2	36.4	18.2	18.2	–	9.1	–	11
VII	–	–	7.7	46.2	7.7	7.7	15.4	15.4	13
VIII	–	5.0	35.0	25.0	15.0	15.0	5.0	–	20
IX	–	–	–	–	80.0	20.0	–	–	5

Table 145   Kafiavana: percentage distribution of the degree of indentation of whole and probably whole concave edges, measured by index Lc/D

| Horizon | Lc/D | | | | | No. of edges |
	<3.3	3.3-4.9	5.0-9.9	10.0-19.9	>19.9	
I	0.9	10.3	56.1	32.7	–	107
II	2.3	10.0	63.1	21.5	3.1	130
III	2.5	9.8	63.6	22.5	1.6	245
IV	1.2	8.6	54.6	34.4	1.2	174
V	0.9	11.3	57.6	29.4	0.9	231
VI	0.8	12.0	54.4	30.4	2.4	125
VII	0.9	4.4	69.3	24.6	0.9	114
VIII	0.6	11.0	57.8	25.4	5.2	154
IX	–	17.7	52.9	26.4	2.9	34

Table 146   Kafiavana: percentage distribution of the degree of projection of whole and probably whole convex edges, measured by index Lc/D

| Horizon | Lc/D | | | | | No. of edges |
	<3.3	3.3-4.9	5.0-9.9	10.0-19.9	>19.9	
I	–	13.0	43.5	30.4	13.1	23
II	4.2	–	16.7	62.5	16.7	24
III	–	5.3	47.4	36.8	10.5	19
IV	–	5.9	29.4	52.9	11.8	17
V	–	7.7	34.6	50.0	7.7	26
VI	–	9.1	27.3	45.4	18.2	11
VII	–	–	46.2	23.1	30.8	13
VIII	–	10.0	35.0	40.0	15.0	20
IX	–	–	40.0	–	60.0	5

Table 147   Kafiavana: percentage distribution of retouch types on all edges

| Horizon | None | Step-flaking | | Other unifacial flaking | Bifacial flaking | Other | No. of edges |
		light	heavy				
I	49.9	39.9	8.2	2.0	–	–	353
II	36.0	54.6	7.5	1.7	0.2	–	478
III	34.3	57.5	6.0	2.2	–	–	717
IV	30.0	60.9	6.2	2.9	–	–	580
V	31.4	58.0	8.1	2.4	0.1	–	719
VI	28.0	63.2	5.2	3.4	0.3	–	386
VII	33.5	57.0	7.4	2.1	–	–	391
VIII	35.3	56.9	5.8	1.9	0.2	–	482
IX	52.0	42.7	1.3	2.7	1.3	–	75

Table 148   Kafiavana: percentage distribution of the relationship between retouch type and edge shape on whole and probably whole edges

Horizon	Straight	Concave	Convex	Wavy	No. of edges
(a) no retouch					
I	32.7	45.8	21.5	–	107
II	41.2	38.2	20.6	–	102
III	39.6	48.1	12.6	–	127
IV	39.8	48.9	11.3	–	88
V	40.0	44.5	14.8	0.7	134
VI	39.4	48.5	12.1	–	66
VII	33.3	47.8	18.8	–	69
VIII	28.1	54.2	17.7	–	96
IX	25.0	57.2	17.8	–	28
(b) light step-flaking					
I	20.0	80.0	–	–	60
II	15.1	83.8	1.1	–	93
III	15.9	83.0	1.0	–	195
IV	15.4	79.1	4.7	0.7	149
V	17.9	79.6	2.6	–	191
VI	19.6	77.6	2.8	–	107
VII	16.2	83.7	–	–	80
VIII	15.8	81.5	1.8	0.8	114
IX	14.3	85.7	–	–	21
(c) heavy step-flaking					
I	–	100.0	–	–	10
II	–	100.0	–	–	11
III	5.0	90.0	5.0	–	20
IV	10.0	80.0	10.0	–	10
V	25.0	68.8	6.2	–	16
VI	12.5	87.5	–	–	8
VII	–	92.9	–	7.1	14
VIII	10.0	90.0	–	–	10
IX	–	–	–	–	–

Table 149   Kafiavana: percentage distribution of the relationship between edge angle and retouch type

Horizon	Angle in degrees								Not measured	No. of edges
	20–9	30–9	40–9	50–9	60–9	70–9	80–9	90–9		
(a) light step-flaking										
I	–	–	3.6	9.2	29.1	36.2	14.2	6.4	1.4	141
II	–	–	1.2	13.4	24.9	31.4	18.8	8.1	2.3	261
III	–	0.2	1.9	8.3	29.4	35.0	18.2	4.9	2.2	412
IV	–	–	1.4	6.2	28.3	36.0	20.7	5.4	2.0	353
V	–	–	1.7	6.7	19.4	36.9	22.3	9.6	3.4	417
VI	–	–	0.8	7.8	23.8	34.8	20.5	8.2	4.1	244
VII	–	–	1.8	6.7	22.4	30.0	25.1	9.9	4.0	223
VIII	–	–	0.7	6.9	23.7	31.8	29.9	4.4	2.6	274
IX	–	–	6.3	12.5	53.1	18.8	9.4	–	–	32
(b) heavy step-flaking										
I	–	–	–	3.5	20.7	37.9	31.0	–	6.9	29
II	–	–	–	11.1	22.2	30.6	19.4	5.6	11.1	36
III	–	–	–	–	23.3	32.6	23.3	11.6	9.3	43
IV	–	–	5.6	–	22.2	47.2	19.4	2.8	2.8	36
V	–	–	–	3.5	20.7	43.1	22.4	6.9	3.5	58
VI	–	–	–	–	20.0	10.0	65.0	5.0	–	20
VII	–	–	–	3.5	31.0	37.9	24.1	3.5	–	29
VIII	–	–	–	3.6	32.1	46.4	17.9	–	–	28
IX	–	–	–	–	–	–	100.0	–	–	1
(c) other unifacial flaking										
I	–	14.3	14.3	14.3	28.6	14.3	14.3	–	–	7
II	12.5	12.5	50.0	–	12.5	12.5	–	–	–	8
III	–	6.3	31.3	18.8	12.5	25.0	6.3	–	–	16
IV	–	–	23.5	41.2	35.3	–	–	–	–	17
V	–	23.5	23.5	23.5	17.7	5.9	5.9	–	–	17
VI	–	7.7	23.1	46.2	23.1	–	–	–	–	13
VII	–	–	25.0	37.5	12.5	12.5	12.5	–	–	8
VIII	–	11.1	22.2	44.4	11.1	11.1	–	–	–	9
IX	–	–	50.0	50.0	–	–	–	–	–	2

119

Table 150 Kafiavana: percentage distribution of the occurrence of use-wear on all edges

Horizon	None	'Chattering'	Bifacial	'Utilisation'	No. of edges
I	33.4	46.2	0.6	19.8	353
II	46.0	39.1	-	14.9	478
III	43.9	46.6	-	9.5	717
IV	47.8	43.8	-	8.5	580
V	49.7	40.3	0.1	9.9	719
VI	45.3	46.4	-	8.3	386
VII	43.5	46.3	0.3	10.0	391
VIII	43.0	45.0	0.8	11.2	482
IX	37.3	37.3	-	25.3	75

Table 151 Kafiavana: percentage distribution of the shape of use-wear types, counting whole and probably whole lengths of use-wear only

Horizon	Straight	Concave	Convex	Wavy	No. of occurrences
(a) 'chattering'					
I	29.8	66.7	3.6	-	84
II	41.9	54.8	3.2	-	93
III	39.2	59.7	1.1	-	176
IV	32.3	62.4	5.3	-	133
V	38.1	58.6	3.2	-	155
VI	41.2	55.9	2.9	-	102
VII	40.0	57.8	2.2	-	90
VIII	32.3	64.5	3.2	-	124
IX	14.3	85.7	-	-	21
(b) 'utilisation'					
I	35.8	28.3	35.8	-	53
II	32.1	30.2	37.8	-	53
III	46.9	22.4	28.6	2.0	49
IV	51.6	25.8	22.6	-	31
V	54.4	14.1	29.8	1.8	57
VI	37.1	37.1	25.9	-	27
VII	34.5	31.0	34.5	-	29
VIII	21.6	40.6	37.8	-	37
IX	35.7	21.4	35.7	7.1	14

Table 152 Kafiavana: percentage distribution of the length of use-wear types, counting whole and probably whole lengths of use-wear only

Horizon	Length in mm								No. of occurrences
	1-5	6-10	11-15	16-20	21-25	26-30	31-35	>35	
(a) 'chattering'									
I	16.7	70.2	7.1	3.6	1.2	1.2	-	-	84
II	18.3	58.1	19.4	3.2	-	1.1	-	-	93
III	18.2	56.2	22.2	2.8	0.6	-	-	-	176
IV	11.3	59.4	21.8	6.0	1.5	-	-	-	133
V	20.0	58.7	15.5	4.5	0.6	0.6	-	-	155
VI	22.5	58.8	12.8	4.9	-	1.0	-	-	102
VII	20.0	58.9	16.7	4.4	-	-	-	-	90
VIII	23.4	55.7	16.1	4.0	-	0.8	-	-	124
IX	9.5	61.9	23.8	-	4.8	-	-	-	21
(b) 'utilisation'									
I	-	26.4	37.8	28.3	1.9	5.7	-	-	53
II	1.9	13.2	34.0	32.1	7.5	5.7	1.9	3.8	53
III	2.0	26.5	28.6	26.5	10.2	4.1	2.0	-	49
IV	-	9.7	35.5	29.0	16.1	3.2	3.2	3.2	31
V	1.8	21.1	26.3	21.1	14.1	8.8	1.8	5.3	57
VI	-	11.1	44.4	22.2	14.8	3.7	3.7	-	27
VII	-	17.3	24.2	34.5	3.5	3.5	10.3	6.9	29
VIII	2.7	8.1	37.8	16.2	16.2	16.2	2.7	-	37
IX	-	14.3	28.6	7.1	42.8	7.1	-	-	14

Table 153   Kafiavana: percentage distribution of the degree of indentation, measured by index Lc/D, on whole and probably whole concave lengths of use-wear, in relation to use-wear type

Horizon	0-3.3	3.4-4.9	Lc/D 5.0-9.9	10.0-19.9	>19.9	No. of occurrences
(a) 'chattering'						
I	3.6	10.7	64.3	21.4	–	56
II	4.1	12.2	69.4	14.3	–	49
III	2.9	10.9	71.3	14.9	–	101
IV	3.7	9.8	63.4	23.2	–	82
V	2.2	12.2	63.4	22.2	–	90
VI	–	14.3	67.8	17.9	–	56
VII	4.0	8.0	66.0	22.0	–	50
VIII	–	14.3	67.5	16.9	1.3	77
IX	–	16.7	66.7	16.7	–	18
(b) 'utilisation'						
I	–	6.7	46.7	46.7	–	15
II	6.3	12.5	37.5	31.2	12.5	16
III	9.1	–	36.4	36.4	18.2	11
IV	–	–	12.5	75.0	12.5	8
V	–	12.5	50.0	25.0	12.5	8
VI	–	–	10.0	70.0	20.0	10
VII	–	–	33.3	55.5	11.1	9
VIII	–	6.7	26.6	33.3	33.3	15
IX	–	–	33.3	33.3	33.3	3

Table 154   Kafiavana: percentage distribution of edge angles in relation to use-wear type

Horizon	20-9	30-9	40-9	50-9	60-9	70-9	80-9	90-9	Not measured	No. of occurrences
(a) 'chattering'										
I	–	0.6	8.6	13.5	21.5	27.6	17.2	8.0	3.1	163
II	–	2.1	6.4	12.8	20.3	26.2	19.8	10.2	2.1	187
III	–	1.2	5.1	9.3	24.9	29.6	18.3	6.0	5.7	334
IV	–	–	2.8	5.9	24.4	31.1	24.4	7.5	3.9	254
V	–	1.4	3.8	9.3	22.8	25.2	22.4	11.0	4.1	290
VI	–	0.6	2.2	7.8	17.9	24.6	29.6	10.6	6.7	179
VII	–	–	3.3	12.7	18.8	29.8	26.5	7.7	1.1	181
VIII	0.5	1.4	3.7	8.8	18.0	36.4	20.3	5.1	6.0	217
IX	–	–	7.1	14.3	28.6	25.0	21.4	3.6	–	28
(b) 'utilisation'										
I	12.9	34.3	18.6	15.6	7.1	4.3	4.3	1.4	1.4	70
II	15.5	14.1	21.1	26.8	11.3	5.6	5.6	–	–	71
III	23.5	10.3	33.8	14.7	11.8	2.9	2.9	–	–	68
IV	8.2	16.3	26.5	32.7	14.3	2.0	–	–	–	49
V	11.3	22.5	25.4	11.3	19.7	7.0	2.8	–	–	71
VI	15.6	15.6	37.5	15.6	9.4	3.1	3.1	–	–	32
VII	7.7	25.6	28.2	12.8	12.8	2.6	2.6	5.1	2.6	39
VIII	7.4	22.2	24.1	18.5	18.5	5.6	3.7	–	–	54
IX	5.3	15.8	26.3	10.5	21.1	10.5	10.5	–	–	19

Table 155   Kafiavana: percentage distribution of the relation between use-wear and retouch

| Horizon | Retouch type | | | No. of occurrences |
	None	Step-flaking light	heavy	
(a) 'chattering'				
I	66.7	25.0	8.3	168
II	55.1	39.6	5.3	189
III	55.0	40.1	4.9	347
IV	51.2	46.9	2.0	256
V	54.4	36.1	9.6	291
VI	42.6	53.0	4.4	183
VII	50.5	44.7	4.8	188
VIII	53.4	40.9	5.8	225
IX	69.0	24.1	6.9	29
(b) 'utilisation'				
I	98.6	1.4	–	69
II	100.0	–	–	71
III	97.1	2.9	–	68
IV	100.0	–	–	49
V	98.6	1.4	–	71
VI	100.0	–	–	32
VII	100.0	–	–	39
VIII	98.1	1.9	–	54
IX	100.0	–	–	18

Table 156   Kafiavana: percentage distribution of the relation between retouch and use-wear

Horizon	'Chattering'	Use-wear type Bifacial	'Utilisation'	No. of occurrences
(a) light step-flaking				
I	97.6	–	2.4	42
II	100.0	–	–	75
III	98.6	–	1.4	141
IV	100.0	–	–	120
V	99.1	–	0.9	106
VI	100.0	–	–	97
VII	100.0	–	–	84
VIII	98.9	–	1.1	93
IX	100.0	–	–	7
(b) heavy step-flaking				
I	100.0	–	–	14
II	100.0	–	–	10
III	100.0	–	–	17
IV	100.0	–	–	5
V	100.0	–	–	28
VI	100.0	–	–	8
VII	100.0	–	–	9
VIII	100.0	–	–	13
IX	100.0	–	–	2
(c) no retouch				
I	61.5	1.1	37.4	182
II	59.4	–	41.2	175
II	74.3	–	25.7	257
IV	72.8	–	27.2	180
V	69.0	0.4	30.6	229
VI	70.9	–	29.1	110
VII	70.4	0.7	28.9	135
VIII	67.8	2.3	30.0	177
IX	52.6	–	47.4	38

Table 157　Kafiavana: percentage distribution of implement thickness in relation to retouch type on whole and probably whole implements, counting each edge as a separate implement

| Horizon | Thickness in mm | | | | | | | | | Not measured | No. of edges |
	0-5	6-10	11-15	16-20	21-25	26-30	31-35	36-40	>40		
(a) light step-flaking											
I	8.0	32.0	48.0	4.0	8.0	-	-	-	-	-	25
II	2.6	28.2	23.1	35.9	7.7	-	2.6	-	-	-	39
III	8.3	22.6	38.1	16.7	7.1	7.1	-	-	-	-	84
IV	6.1	21.2	28.8	13.6	22.7	4.5	-	1.5	-	1.5	66
V	3.6	17.9	35.7	19.7	10.7	3.6	5.4	1.8	1.8	-	56
VI	-	19.6	28.3	23.9	17.4	8.7	2.2	-	-	-	46
VII	-	35.7	35.7	21.4	7.1	-	-	-	-	-	28
VIII	-	22.0	17.1	19.5	24.4	-	4.9	7.3	-	4.9	41
IX	-	50.0	-	50.0	-	-	-	-	-	-	2
(b) heavy step-flaking											
I	-	-	-	-	-	100.0	-	-	-	-	1
II	-	50.0	50.0	-	-	-	-	-	-	..	2
III	-	-	50.0	-	-	50.0	-	-	-	-	2
IV	-	-	-	-	100.0	-	-	-	-	-	1
V	-	-	100.0	-	-	-	-	-	-	-	2
VI	-	-	-	100.0	-	-	-	-	-	-	1
VII	-	-	-	66.6	33.3	-	-	-	-	-	3
VIII	-	75.0	25.0	-	-	-	-	-	-	-	4
IX	-	-	-	-	-	-	-	-	-	-	-
(c) no retouch											
I	45.8	19.5	19.5	-	4.2	2.8	2.8	-	-	5.6	72
II	19.7	25.4	22.5	18.3	2.8	-	-	5.6	-	5.6	71
III	26.5	24.1	20.5	19.3	2.4	1.2	-	1.2	-	4.8	83
IV	22.4	20.7	34.4	12.1	5.2	1.7	-	-	-	3.4	58
V	22.8	27.8	25.3	10.1	6.3	1.3	1.3	-	1.3	3.8	79
VI	44.7	26.3	18.4	7.9	2.6	-	-	-	-	-	38
VII	21.2	45.4	21.2	6.1	-	-	-	-	-	6.1	33
VIII	30.8	19.2	11.5	21.2	7.7	7.7	-	-	-	1.9	52
IX	17.7	41.2	17.7	5.9	11.8	-	5.9	-	-	-	17

Table 158　Kafiavana: percentage distribution of the breadth/thickness index in relation to retouch type on whole and probably whole implements, counting each edge as a separate implement

| Horizon | B/Th index | | | | | | | No. of edges |
	<0.5	0.5-0.99	1-1.49	1.5-1.99	2.0-2.49	2.5-2.99	>2.99	
(a) light step-flaking								
I	-	-	20.0	32.0	24.0	16.0	8.0	25
II	-	4.8	26.2	21.4	23.8	19.0	4.8	42
III	-	3.6	17.9	20.2	27.4	19.1	11.9	84
IV	-	3.0	27.3	24.2	19.7	12.1	13.6	66
V	1.8	5.4	35.7	35.7	12.5	7.1	1.8	56
VI	-	6.5	21.7	21.7	23.9	15.2	10.9	46
VII	-	-	7.1	28.6	17.9	25.0	21.4	28
VIII	-	4.9	12.2	17.1	36.5	17.1	12.2	41
IX	-	-	-	-	100.0	-	-	2
(b) no retouch								
I	-	2.8	25.0	6.9	16.7	11.1	37.5	72
II	-	5.6	21.1	19.7	22.5	11.3	19.7	71
III	-	-	6.3	20.0	18.7	24.0	30.7	75
IV	-	5.2	15.5	13.8	22.4	25.8	17.2	58
V	1.3	2.5	15.2	17.7	29.1	10.1	24.0	79
VI	-	5.3	10.5	7.9	10.5	23.7	42.1	38
VII	-	-	9.1	15.2	15.2	15.2	45.4	33
VIII	-	7.8	3.9	15.7	21.6	23.5	27.5	51
IX	-	5.9	5.9	35.3	-	35.3	17.7	17

123

Table 159   Kafiavana: percentage distribution of the relation of retouch angle and implement weight on whole and probably whole implements with light step-flaking, counting each edge as a separate implement

Angle in degrees	Weight in gm 0-9	10-9	20-9	30-9	40-9	50-9	60-9	70-9	80-9	No. of edges
(a) horizon I										
30-9	-	-	-	-	-	-	-	-	-	-
40-9	4.2	-	-	-	-	-	-	-	-	1
50-9	-	20.8	-	-	-	-	-	-	-	5
60-9	-	33.3	-	-	-	-	-	-	-	8
70-9	-	8.3	8.3	12.5	-	-	-	-	-	7
80-9	-	4.2	8.3	-	-	-	-	-	-	3
90-9	-	-	-	-	-	-	-	-	-	-
										24
(b) horizon II										
30-9	-	-	-	-	-	-	.	-	-	-
40-9	-	-	2.4	-	-	-	-	-	-	1
50-9	2.4	4.8	2.4	9.5	-	-	-	-	-	8
60-9	7.1	4.8	7.1	2.4	7.1	-	9.5	-	-	16
70-9	2.4	4.8	2.4	11.9	-	2.4	-	-	-	10
80-9	2.4	2.4	4.8	2.4	-	-	-	-	-	5
90-9	-	-	-	2.4	-	2.4	-	-	-	2
										42
(c) horizon III										
30-9	-	-	1.2	-	-	-	-	-	-	1
40-9	1.2	1.2	-	1.2	-	-	-	-	-	3
50-9	-	8.4	3.6	2.4	-	-	-	-	-	12
60-9	1.2	19.3	15.6	7.2	2.4	1.2	-	2.4	-	41
70-9	2.4	3.6	6.0	2.4	-	-	-	2.4	-	14
80-9	1.2	4.8	2.4	-	-	-	-	1.2	1.2	9
90-9	-	-	1.2	-	1.2	-	-	1.2	-	3
										83
(d) horizon IV										
30-9	-	-	-	-	-	-	-	-	-	-
40-9	-	-	-	-	1.6	-	-	-	-	1
50-9	-	4.7	-	1.6	-	1.6	-	-	-	5
60-9	-	25.0	4.7	6.3	1.6	6.3	4.7	-	-	31
70-9	-	9.4	4.7	9.4	-	3.1	-	3.1	-	19
80-9	-	1.6	1.6	1.6	-	1.6	-	4.7	-	7
90-9	-	1.6	-	-	-	-	-	-	-	1
										64
(e) horizon V										
30-9	-	-	-	-	-	-	-	-	-	-
40-9	5.9	2.0	-	-	2.0	-	-	-	-	5
50-9	9.8	5.9	2.0	-	-	2.0	-	-	-	10
60-9	-	7.8	-	-	5.9	-	-	-	-	7
70-9	5.9	3.9	9.8	3.9	5.9	2.0	-	-	-	16
80-9	7.8	3.9	7.8	-	-	-	-	-	-	10
90-9	-	-	5.9	-	-	-	-	-	-	3
										51
(f) horizon VI										
30-9	-	-	-	-	-	-	-	-	-	-
40-9	2.1	-	-	-	-	-	-	-	-	1
50-9	6.3	4.2	-	4.2	-	4.2	-	-	-	9
60-9	8.3	6.3	6.3	2.1	-	4.2	2.1	2.1	-	15
70-9	6.3	10.4	4.2	-	6.3	6.3	-	-	-	16
80-9	4.2	-	-	2.1	2.1	-	-	-	-	4
90-9	-	-	-	4.2	-	-	-	2.1	-	3
										48

(cont'd)

Table 159 (cont'd)

Angle in degrees	0-9	10-9	20-9	30-9	40-9	50-9	60-9	70-9	80-9	No. of edges
(g) horizon VII										
30-9	–	–	–	–	–	–	–	–	–	–
40-9	–	3.8	3.8	–	–	–	–	–	–	2
50-9	–	3.8	7.7	19.2	–	3.8	–	–	–	9
60-9	3.8	3.8	7.7	3.8	–	–	–	–	–	5
70-9	–	3.8	7.7	–	3.8	–	–	3.8	3.8	6
80-9	–	–	–	–	3.8	3.8	–	–	3.8	3
90-9	–	–	3.8	–	–	–	–	–	–	1
										26
(h) horizon VIII										
30-9	–	–	–	–	–	–	–	–	–	–
40-9	–	–	–	2.6	–	–	–	–	–	1
50-9	2.6	–	10.4	2.6	2.6	2.6	–	–	–	8
60-9	18.4	–	–	13.2	2.6	–	–	–	–	13
70-9	13.2	2.6	7.9	10.5	2.6	–	–	–	–	14
80-9	–	–	–	2.6	–	?.6	–	–	–	2
90-9	–	–	–	–	–	–	–	–	–	–
										38

Table 160   Kafiavana: distribution of trimming flakes

Horizon	F3	F4	F5	F6	F7	G2	Square G3	G4	G5	H2	H3	H4	Total	Implements per trimming flake
I	6	–	–	–	–	16	–	1	–	4	1	–	28	5.9
II	7	–	–	–	–	15	1	2	–	27	10	–	62	3.6
III	8	–	–	1	–	3	13	11	2	31	10	6	85	4.1
IV	5	–	–	1	–	2	4	7	1	20	11	8	59	4.8
V	7	–	3	7	–	1	3	8	8	19	12	16	84	3.9
VI	10	–	1	11	–	5	11	4	1	6	9	8	66	2.9
VII	8	3	1	–	–	–	11	4	1	–	7	2	37	4.5
VIII	4	2	3	–	–	–	5	3	3	1	18	5	44	4.6
IX	–	1	1	–	–	–	–	–	–	–	2	1	5	9.0
Total	55	6	9	20	–	42	48	40	16	108	80	46	470	4.2

Table 161   Kafiavana: distribution of hammers and anvils

	Horizon I	II	III	IV	V	VI	VII	VIII	IX	Total
Hammers	3	–	5	3	4	2	3	6	–	26
Anvils	–	–	–	–	–	2	1	1	–	4

Plate 5   Niobe: A) shelter prior to excavation.   Scale in 20 cm.
                      B) squares A4-5, showing cracked flowstone and concreted
                      soil.   Scale in 20 cm.

VI   EXCAVATIONS AT NIOBE, NEAR CHUAVE

THE SITE

Niobe is a long rock shelter on the eastern backslope of Mt Erimbari, about 3 miles (5.7 km) SSE of Chuave between Kibogu and Leiya villages (6°07'S, 145°10'E) (Salisbury 1962:8).   It is about 2 miles (3.8 km) south of the Kiowa site excavated by Bulmer (1964a, 1966a) and lies at an altitude of about 5400 ft (1660 m) (fig.1).

The shelter is formed by an overhang and is the minor entrance to a major cave system.   The sheltered area is some 18 m long and 4 m wide and is aligned NNW.   The greatest breadth of the shelter is about 6 m where the overhang meets the cave entrance (fig.22a).   A foot-track runs along the outer side of the shelter, under cover (pl.5a).   Human use was indicated by present use as a casual shelter, rock-paintings and the presence of worked stone on the floor.

Discovery and Excavation

The site was recorded by S. Bulmer in 1960 (n.d.:site 73).   A total of 9 m^2 was excavated to a maximum depth of 1.4 m in October 1964 (White 1965a).

Stratigraphy (fig.22b; pl.5b)

Visible layers were scarcely apparent in the whole depth of soil excavated in the front part of the site, though slight changes in colour and texture which appear to be related to the dripline and other natural phenomena rather than to human activity were noted.   The soil was a uniform dark red-brown in colour and became more clayey under and in front of the dripline.   It contained many small blocks of limestone from the roof and these were concentrated above about 75 cm below ground surface.

Towards the back of the shelter large blocks of the deposit were heavily concreted with lime.   Much of this concreted material was capped by slabs (4-10 cm thick) of sterile flowstone, which lay 20-30 cm below ground surface. The slabs sloped downwards towards the dripline and ended abruptly about 50 cm inside the inside edge of the dripline.   Although clearly formed *in situ* as a single block, the upper part of the concreted material had been cracked into several pieces.   Cultural material in a soft dry matrix was found in the fissures between and slightly underneath the edges of the blocks to a depth of about 1 m below ground surface.   The concreted soil contained large amounts of bone, but facilities were not available to remove them.

Division of the Material and Artifact Joins

The material has been divided into two arbitrary horizons, upper and lower, for the purpose of analysis.   This rather coarse division is used because there is evidence for considerable natural disturbance:

1.   The concreted soil, capped by flowstone, is cracked and the interstices
     are filled with cultural material.   This cracking may well have disturbed the surrounding soil and artifact distribution within it.

2.   The scattered position of five fragments of the same ground axe in the
     deposit.   Three fragments were found near the surface: the butt in A3, a large section of body near the A4/A5 boundary, and a small chip in B6. The other two fragments were found 62 and 69 cm below ground surface, both near the same point on the B7/A7 boundary (fig.22b,c).   No signs of a pit were detected.

The upper horizon therefore includes all material above the flowstone,

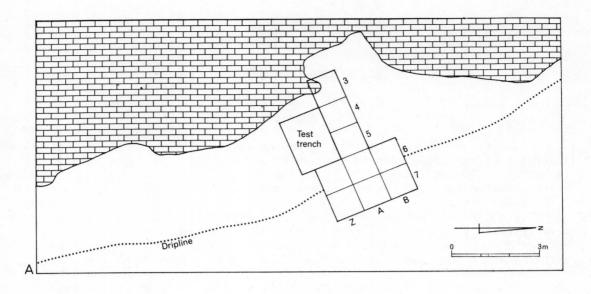

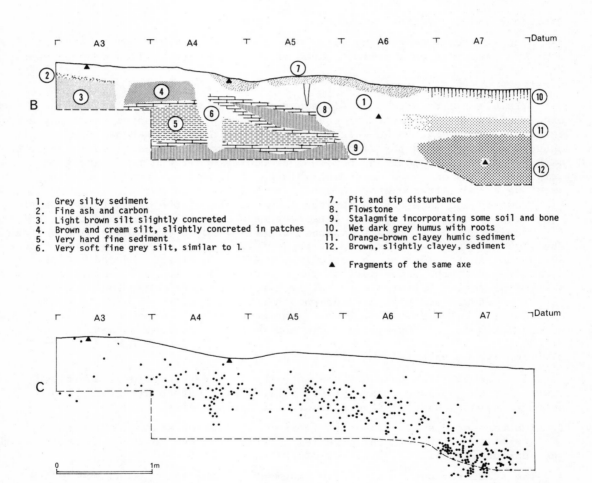

1. Grey silty sediment
2. Fine ash and carbon
3. Light brown silt slightly concreted
4. Brown and cream silt, slightly concreted in patches
5. Very hard fine sediment
6. Very soft fine grey silt, similar to 1.

7. Pit and tip disturbance
8. Flowstone
9. Stalagmite incorporating some soil and bone
10. Wet dark grey humus with roots
11. Orange-brown clayey humic sediment
12. Brown, slightly clayey, sediment

▲   Fragments of the same axe

Fig.22   Niobe: A) plan of shelter; B) stratigraphy of north wall of main trench;
and C) plot of implements from main trench on same wall

128

in the cracks between it, and in the top 70-80 cm in front of it.   Because
of the flowstone and large boulders it was not possible to calculate with any
accuracy the volume of deposit removed.   I estimate that each horizon
contains about 3.5 m^3 of deposit.

For certain analytical purposes square Z7, which appears to be less
disturbed than the others and which is also deep, was divided into four
roughly equal units, each containing approximately 0.35 m^3.   The top two
units and the top third of the next unit are in the top horizon, the rest
being in the lower horizon.

Dating

Carbon samples from this site have not been submitted for dating because
of the problems associated with the disturbed stratigraphy.

FAUNA AND FLORA

A very large amount of fauna was excavated, but a detailed analysis has
not been made.   The mandibles, maxillae and teeth have been extracted and
identified, and basic sorting and counting completed.   All the bone is
rather broken and the teeth have been evulsed from most jaws.

Domestic Animals

Pig (*Sus scrofa*) was found in the top 20 cm only.   All fragments are
likely to represent domestic animals.

Wild Animals

On a within-horizon basis at least 925 animals occur within the excavation.
If each square is considered separately, the number rises to 967.   This is an
approximate figure only and does not take account of the several hundred very
small fragments of mandible found in the site.   Table 162 sets out the data
on animal remains on a within-horizon basis.   It shows that cuscus (*Phalanger*
spp.) and flying fox (family Megachiroptera) make up the majority of the fauna.
The importance of bats no doubt reflects the presence of many nearby caves in
which these creatures roost.   The importance of cuscus probably shows that in
prehistoric times areas of primary or secondary forest persisted in this
topographically broken area.

Table 162   Niobe: minimum numbers of animals

Animals	Adult or Juvenile	Horizon upper	lower	Total
Suidae				
Sus scrofa		2	–	2
Macropodidae	A	82	28	110
	J	27	4	31
Phalangeridae				
Phalanger spp.	A	235	107	342
Dactylopsila or *Dactylonax*		7	4	11
Pseudocheirus (Pseudochirops) spp.		49	17	66
P. (Pseudocheirus) spp.		18	4	22
Peramelidae[1]		23	14	37
Dasyuridae				
Satanellus albopunctatus		1	2	3
cf. *Antechinus*		1	–	1
Megachiroptera[2]		198	94	292
Muridae (large)		7	1	8
Total animals		650	275	925

[1] Calculated by dividing total number of fragments by 4
[2] Calculated by dividing total number of fragments by 5

Table 163, which is based on a finer vertical division within one metre square, suggests that the absolute number of animals and the relative number of species in this square declined in more recent times, but there is no evidence of any environmental change over time. The flying fox bones consist mostly of ulnas, radii and femurs; practically no other bat bones were recognised. In nearly all cases the proximal ends were intact but the distal ends of the bones were missing, which may refer to cooking and eating habits.

It is interesting to note that Kiowa, 2 miles (3.8 km) away, also produced 'an enormous amount' of fauna (Bulmer 1966a:94). At Kiowa dog has been identified only at the surface and pig from levels 2 and 3. Among the wild animals which make up the bulk of the fauna, *Dendrolagus*, *Phalanger*, *Pseudocheirus* and *Dobsonia* are common. This is different from Niobe, where domestic animals are apparently more recent and the common macropodid is *Thylogale bruijni*. However, in the absence of any analysis of the Kiowa faunal material, either by excavated levels or in terms of the number of animals involved, comparisons are difficult to make. Differences may also arise from a disparity in ages between the two sites.

Table 163   Niobe: square Z7, minimum number of animals

Animals	Adult or Juvenile	Spits							
		1-3		4-8		9-13		14-20	
		no.	%	no.	%	no.	%	no.	%
Macropodidae	A	1	9.1	4	16.7	13	12.4	10	10.2
	J	2	18.2	–	–	–	–	–	–
Phalangeridae									
Phalanger spp.		7	63.6	7	29.2	42	40.0	48	49.0
Dactylopsila or *Dactylonax*		–	–	–	–	–	–	2	2.0
Pseudocheirus (Pseudochirops) spp.		–	–	1	4.2	3	2.9	6	6.1
P. (Pseudocheirus) spp.		–	–	1	4.2	2	1.9	–	–
Peramelidae[1]		–	–	1	4.2	7	6.7	4	4.0
Dasyuridae									
Satanellus albopunctatus		–	–	–	–	–	–	1	1.0
Megachiroptera[2]		1	9.1	9	37.5	36	34.3	27	27.6
Muridae									
Hyomys goliath		–	–	1	4.2	2	1.9	–	–
Total animals		11		24		105		98	

[1] Fragments divided by 4
[2] Fragments divided by 5

Fish

A few fragments of fishbone were found. F.H. Talbot considers that they probably come from freshwater species.

Birds

All bones provisionally identified as bird were submitted to J.C. Yaldwyn. He reports (pers. comm.) that only 12 fragments were bird remains, none of them being domestic fowl. In addition, all bones from eight spits spread vertically through the site were carefully scanned for bird remains by R.J. Scarlett. Only four bird bones were found, one of which may be a cassowary claw.

The virtual absence of cassowary in these samples is surprising when Kiowa contains 'large quantities of Cassowary' (Bulmer 1966a:94). If there is in fact a difference, which cannot yet be proven, it is difficult to point to a reason for it. It might be that Niobe postdates Kiowa and cassowaries were rarer then, or it might be that the sites were put to different uses.

Small pieces of cassowary eggshell occurred throughout the site. In the upper horizon there were 191.0 gm, while there were 50.9 gm in the lower horizon. This means that at least four eggs are represented, and probably many more were in fact present.   Other eggshell was àlso present (total 18.6 gm) throughout the site.   It has not been identified.

Reptiles

Two fragments of agamid lizard dentary were identified by R.E. Barwick. In addition, one tip of a dentary or maxilla comes from a member of the sub-family Pythoninae, but the other four fragments are not further identifiable.

Mollusca

Three fragments of marine shell from the upper horizon were identified by McMichael.   Two are yellow olive shells (*Oliva carneola*) and one is a cowry, probably the ringed money cowry (*Cypraea annulus*).   All other shells are unidentifiable freshwater mussels or unidentifiable bivalves and nearly all occurred in the upper horizon.   There were also very large numbers of snail shells.   Most are broken and none shows signs of use as a tool.   Many if not all of them probably occurred naturally in the site.

Human Remains

Nine pieces of human bone were found scattered throughout the site, mostly towards the back of the site and in the top horizon.   They have been identified by N.W.G. Macintosh who points out (pers. comm.) that it is difficult to identify single teeth and, therefore, some of the identifications could be challenged.   A minimum of two people are represented by these bones. They are described by square/(spit).

A3/(2)   Three specimens:

1. Permanent maxillary left central incisor.   The incomplete root suggests that this tooth is from a young person.

2. Maxillary left second premolar.   The crown is chipped off and the dentine worn.   An old person.

3. Maxillary left first premolar.

A3/(3)   Permanent maxillary right central incisor, very worn.   An extremely thick tooth, rather unusual in this respect.

A4/(2)   Right mandible with some unusual features.   Clearly not a juvenile, but may have suffered some periodontal disease.   Evulsion of a tooth occurred premortem and there are perhaps traces of an abscess.

A4/(9)   Two specimens:

1. Incisor, probably lateral.

2. Mandibular first premolar.   The tooth had not erupted, suggesting that it came from a child about 8 years old.

A5/(7)   Mandibular left lateral incisor.   Some traces of periodontal disease.

B7/(1)   Proximal and middle phalanges of the second metatarsal of the left foot.

Z7/(6)   Deciduous mandibular left first molar.

Floral Remains

Most of the vegetable matter was heavily carbonised and unidentifiable. R.W.R. Muncey identified a Palmaceae from the upper horizon and R. Pullen identified the stone of a Sapotaceae, probably *Planchonella*, from the lower part of the same horizon.   *Planchonella* is a member of the gutta-percha family; fruits of other members of this family are eaten elsewhere in the Pacific, while the seeds are regarded as having medicinal properties in the Philippine Islands (Pullen, pers. comm.).

EXOTIC ARTIFACTS

Several post-contact artifacts were found. They include a blue bead (diameter 2 mm) which was found 20-30 cm below the surface. Although this very small bead probably moved easily in the deposit, its presence at this depth is perhaps a further indication of some disturbance.

GROUND-STONE TOOLS

Axe-adzes

All axe-adzes and fragments were found in the upper horizon of the site, mostly within the top half of this unit. A total of 44 pieces was found. These comprise four whole axes and 40 fragments. Of 14 determinable cross-sections at least 12 are lenticular, while one has definite sides and might be called planilateral (fig.23c).

Some of the stone from which axes are made has been examined by J.M.A. Chappell. He reports that axes are made of hornfels, of the type known locally as *gaima*, from the Kafetu quarry on the Daulo Pass, some nine miles (17 km) northeast of Niobe. One butt fragment is *besaiya* hornfels from the same quarry. Chappell calls one small chip of bright green stone amphibolitic ?actinolite. This is known to occur in the Schrader Ranges, but there are possibly outcrops near Bundi and in the upper Chimbu valley between Gogme and Gembogl. Other stones are amphibolitic schist, hornblende-hornfels and slatey hornfels, all probably of local origin.

Rectangular Blades

There are five pieces of very thin rectangular blades which are unlike other axe-adzes. The most complete of these is 10.4 cm long, 5.8 cm wide and a maximum of 1 cm thick (fig.23a). It is ground all over, the sides are parallel and the straight cutting edge is set at right angles to them. The cross-section is very flat and lenticular with very sharp sides. Two other fragments, one of which appears in fig.23b, also have the same curious cross-section which distinguishes these blades from other very flat, thin quadrangular-sectioned blades commonly made for Western Highlands ceremonial use (Bulmer 1964a; Vial 1940). Chappell (pers. comm.) says that the slatey material of which these implements are made would tend to split flat and that this may account for their thinness. I suggested earlier (1965b:52) that in view of their shape and the fact that all these blades were found within 50 cm of the surface, they might be skeuomorphs (Childe 1956:13) of European artifacts. However, it is perhaps more useful to think of them as some kind of local variant of ceremonial axes. I have been unable to locate similar specimens in the literature or museum collections.

Waisted Blades

Two waisted blades were found in the lower horizon. One (fig.23d) is shouldered rather than waisted, with the shoulder flaked and the blade ground more on one side than the other. The other blade is clearly waisted but is broken just above the waist. It has been very heavily water-rolled subsequent to its manufacture. The implements seem to be comparable in size to those found by Bulmer at Kiowa (1964a:262).

Axe-grinding Stones

Three pieces of abrasive rock with smoothly ground, slightly concave faces were found in the top 20 cm. In many respects they resemble unbroken axe-grinding stones excavated by Lampert (1966:7) near Mt Hagen. Their presence at Niobe suggests that axes were re-sharpened at the site.

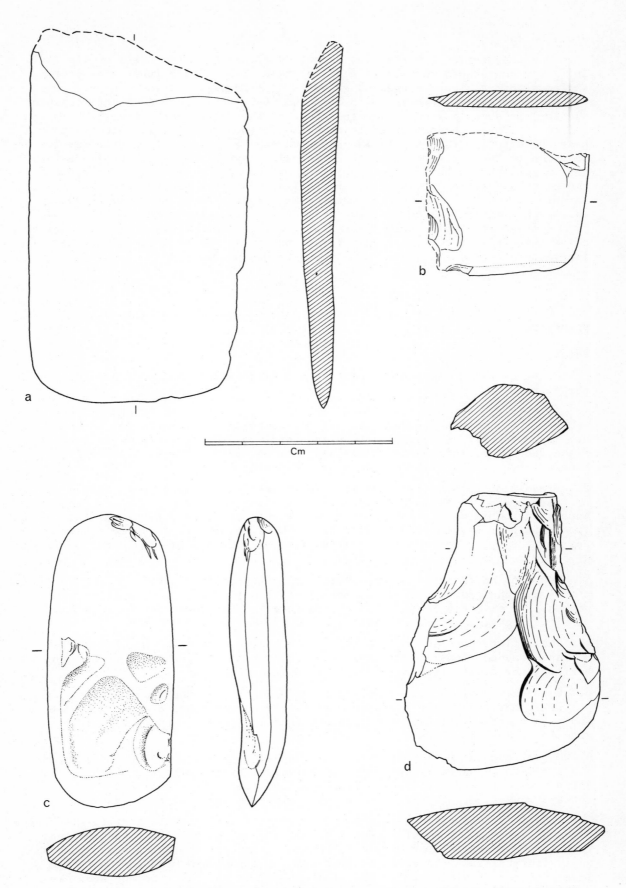

Fig.23   Niobe: ground-stone artifacts: a,b) fragments of rectangular blades
(164.A6/(3) and No.(2), test trench); c) axe-adze (D4.A3/(1));
d) waisted blade (224.A6/(9))

Stone Mortar

One fragment of a mortar was excavated 37 cm below the surface (fig.24a). It is a wedge-shaped section of a plain stone dish. Both inner and outer surfaces form a smooth curve and there is no sign of a flattened base. The rim was apparently circular, with a radius of 9.1 cm, and the height (measured outside) is about 5.2 cm. The thickness of the stone ranges from 1.25 to 1.5 cm. J.M.A. Chappell, who thin-sectioned the specimen, says (pers. comm.) that the material is a hornblende andesite and he tentatively attributes its location to Banz or further west. Chappell reports that the hornblende is not in equilibrium but is decomposing to ore and ore + diopside. A certain amount of diopsidic pyroxene has crystallised (at some depth) with the hornblende. There has been no metamorphism in the rock, the only secondary metamorphic mineral being analcite zeolite. Catalogue number is D5.A3/(4).

A fragment of stone rim apparently from the same artifact was found 31 cm below the surface. These fragments are the first mortar fragments to be excavated under controlled circumstances in New Guinea.

BONE ARTIFACTS

Forty-six pieces of worked bone were recovered, the majority of them being points of various kinds.

Points

Five distinct classes of points and a sixth miscellaneous group are recognised.

1. Awls (6). Two are illustrated in fig.24b,c. All are from the upper horizon, towards the surface. Three complete specimens 63-83 mm long are made from bird or bat long-bone and retain a proximal epiphysis. Local Siane and Chimbu informants recognised them as tools for making armlets of orchid fibre. The figured pieces are 98.A4/(4) and A3/(3).

2. Broad flat points (11) made from split sections of long-bone, probably macropodid or cassowary (fig.24f). All specimens are broken. They are much larger than most points from sites further east; only the large bipoint from Aibura is within their size range. Four points are from the lower part of the upper horizon, the remaining seven points from the lower horizon. The illustrated example is 453.Z6/(9).

3. One bipoint from the upper horizon, illustrated in fig.24d. Length is 54 mm, the cross-section is oval (5 x 3.3 mm) and one tip is slightly broken. A slightly longer bipoint, rectangular in cross-section, was found at Kiowa, level 4 (Bulmer 1966a:100). The Niobe piece is 117.A4/(5).

4. Small flat spatulate points (4). All have a cross-section of 3 x 1 mm and rounded tips. Three specimens come from the upper part of the lower horizon, the fourth from the lower part of the upper horizon.

5. Heavy semi-cylindrical chunky points (3), all from the upper part of the lower horizon. The tips are made fairly abruptly but are not very sharp. The points are heavy, made from rounded sections of solid bone, bird being used in at least one case.

6. Miscellaneous small points (8). These are all short tips only (length 10-20 mm), too heavy for awls but not classifiable with the other types. All are pointed and polished. Cross-sections range from oval to concavo-convex. Four are from the upper horizon and four from the lower.

The locations of some bone points from this site allow a tentative sequence to be suggested. The awls seem to be recent, being found near the surface; they have no parallels at Kiowa. The broad flat points, which are probably equivalent to Kiowa 'jabbers' (Bulmer 1966a:102,106) are more common in the lower horizon of Niobe, below the single bipoint: this is also the sequence at Kiowa. If this pattern is compared with the Kiowa sequence, it might be argued that the lower horizons of Niobe are roughly comparable with Kiowa

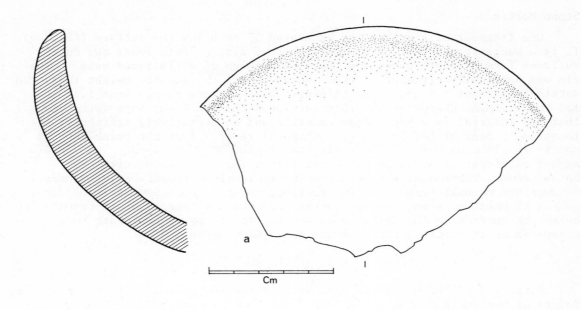

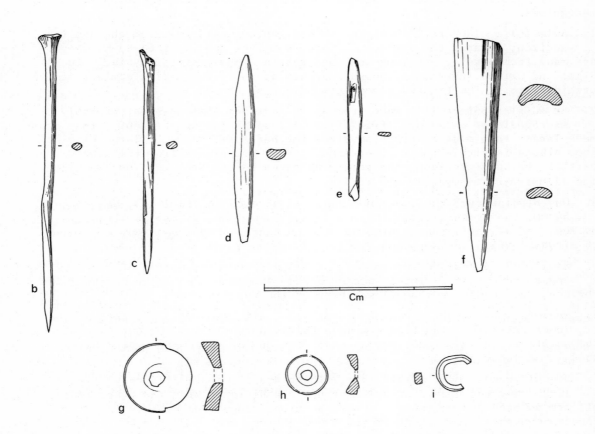

Fig.24 Niobe: stone mortar (a), bone artifacts (b-f,i) and fossil shark vertebrae (g,h)

levels 4-8, while the tools in the upper part of Niobe are similar to those of Kiowa 1-2 (older than about 5000 BP).   Such a suggestion is speculative, especially when the time range of particular bone artifacts is unknown, but it is clearly worth considering along with other evidence.

Miscellaneous

1.   Broken pieces of worked bone (9).

2.   A chisel-bevelled chunk of solid bone, with a high degree of use-polish on the bevel, from the lower horizon.   Measurements are 24 x 7.5 x 6.5 mm, length of bevel 10 mm.

3.   A flat-sectioned rectangular splinter of highly polished long bone which has a very small hole bored through one end (fig.24e).   The boring has been done from one side only.   This is presumably a decorative piece and should be compared with a similar artifact from the lower levels of Aibura. It was found near the surface.   Catalogue number is D2.A3/(1).

4.   Three-quarters of a bone ring from the upper horizon, 2 mm thick, with an outer circumference of 10 mm (fig.24i).   The outer edges are bevelled.   Provenance is square A4/spit (3).

5.   A piece of bird bone with one end rounded off, found in the lower horizon.

OCHRE AND OCHRE-KNIVES

Three hundred and fifty pieces of ochre were found, mostly in the lower part of the upper horizon.   About 6% of the pieces showed grinding or rubbing marks and may have been used for painting rocks, bodies or artifacts.
Four stone flakes, two of them trimming flakes, show smears of ochre along one edge.   All are from the upper horizon.   Three have ochre on one side of the edge only and these edges are unworn.   The fourth edge is heavily worn and has ochre on both sides of it.   There are more smears on one side and the ochre can be seen streaked at an angle of about 45° to the edge. This suggests that it was used to shave off ochre powder.

FOSSIL SHARK VERTEBRAE

Scattered vertically through the lower horizon in one square (Z7) were four large and at least ten small annuli (fig.24g,h).   They were originally identified as fossilized bone, and then sent to J.A.F. Garrick (Department of Zoology, Victoria University of Wellington), who states (pers. comm.) 'I would find it not unreasonable to accept them as parts of shark vertebra'. Their clustering in the site suggests that they originally came from the same source, possibly a necklace or other decoration, since the central hole would make them ideal for stringing.   These specimens are heavily mineralised and dissolve entirely in HCl.   In view of the unmineralised condition of other bones from the site, it seems that they must have been collected as fossils. M.D. Plane suggests that they would be more easily collected from tertiary mudstones a few miles west of Chuave than from the local hard limestone which is not easily dissolved.   All these marine formations might be expected to contain fossils of this type.   The figured pieces are 681.Z7/(15) and Z7/(15). The use of fossils of various kinds, usually in magical contexts, is not uncommon in the Highlands (Berndt 1954; R. and S. Bulmer 1962), although these are usually ammonites or mollusca.   This appears to be the first record of the use of shark vertebrae in the area, but whether they were regarded as 'stones of power' or even stones cannot now be determined.

USE-POLISHED TOOLS

Thirteen pieces of stone with use-polish were found.   Six are apparently whole or nearly-whole tools, the others are broken.   Only two are made of the non-greasy black chert normally used for flaked artifacts.   In many cases the use-polish is fairly faint and not easy to classify, and many of the tools also have step-flaked edges.   Three pieces have polish which is not further identifiable.   Four classes of polish may be identified among the other tools.

1.   Five pieces have bifacial use-polish similar to Kafiavana class (1). The striations are all at right angles to the edge.

2.   One piece, a large chunky flake, has wear like class (1) above but unifacial.   This is similar to Kafiavana class (4).

3.   Three pieces have polish on the edge only and not on either face.

4.   One small chip has use-polish similar to type (1), but about 10% of the striations are angled some 15-20° away from the vertical.

PEBBLE TOOLS
(fig.25)

Thirty pebble tools were found, 12 in the upper horizon.   Nearly all are made on light non-greasy chert, which feels slightly chalky.   None is made on the dark chert commonly used for smaller implements.   All the pebble tools weigh between 134 and 1017 gm.   Six of the tools are unretouched but otherwise appear to be 'pebble tools': they have been used as cores. The pebble tools show no obvious changes between upper and lower groups, but the numbers are too small to make useful statements.

Upper horizon   Three are worked all round a base.   One of these is nearly circular and looks a little like a 'horsehoof' (McCarthy 1967:18), but the central keel is missing.   Four are smooth oval river pebbles retouched on one side or end and one is worked round three sides.   Several have clearly been used as cores prior to retouching.

Lower horizon   There is one classic, if small, 'horsehoof' (fig.25b).   Two tools are retouched on two planes and four are somewhat irregular chunks. Seven tools are smooth pebbles with retouch along a side or end.

WASTE MATERIAL

Nearly 10,000 pieces of unretouched and apparently unused stone were recovered.   This material is in an overall ratio to flaked implements of 11:1, which is rather less than would be normally expected if all implements were knapped at the site.   The ratio may be partly explained by the fact that the site is not very close to raw material sources, so that some roughing out was probably done away from the site and more stones taken to the site were used as tools.   A wide variety of material was used.   Black, non-greasy chert was the most common stone, but other cherts and some indurated shales were also used.

FLAKED-STONE TOOLS
(fig.26)

The implements from Niobe have been classified according to the standard typology (table 164), but an attribute analysis has not been made.   The flaked implements from this site are very similar to those from other sites described here.

Scrapers

The numbers in each class of 'scraper' in the two horizons appear in table 164.   The implements are more heavily worked than at other sites, there are more chunky tools, both large and small, and multi-platform tools are more common.   Most tools are made of dark chert, with the common black non-greasy chert of the area being preferred.   It is noticeable that more heavily retouched tools are made in these cherts, while less retouched tools are found in a wider range of materials and include some flakes which could have come from pebble tools.

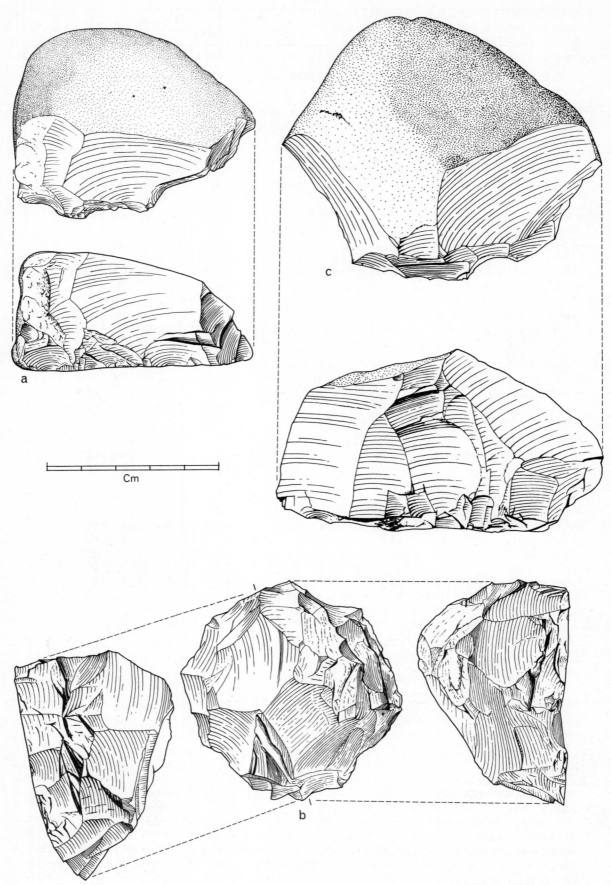

Fig.25   Niobe: pebble tools: a) No.(7), test trench; b) No.(7)14, test trench;
          c) No.(8), test trench

138

Table 164   Niobe: distribution of flaked-stone tool types

	Horizon	
	upper	lower
Total tools (add 1-4)	484	452
1. Whole retouched tools	193	203
(a) Scrapers (total)	174	184
(i) side	38	48
(ii) end	12	19
(iii) double side	11	10
(iv) side and end	15	16
(v) double side and end	-	2
(vi) double end	1	-
(vii) discoid	11	12
(viii) double-concave	-	2
(ix) miscellaneous	7	4
(x) multi-platform	79	71
(b) Bifacial retouch/use	2	1
(c) Scalar retouch	5	-
(d) Pebble tools	12	18
2. Broken retouched tools	211	189
3. Utilised pieces	73	52
4. Cores	7	8
1 as % of total	39.9	44.9
2 as % of total	43.6	41.8
3 as % of total	15.1	11.5
(x) as % of (a)	45.4	38.6

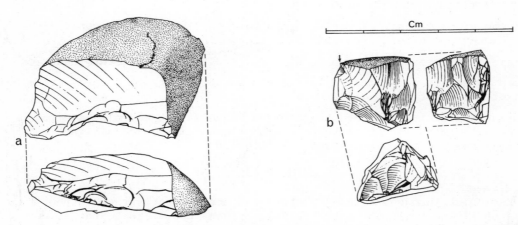

Fig.26   Niobe: flaked-stone artifacts: a) side scraper, Z7/(8)3; b) multiplane
scraper, 361.A7/(6)

Among the less retouched tools, side scrapers predominate (fig.26a).
Neither these nor the end, double-side, or side and end tools provide examples
of the thick, very heavily retouched tools which occur further east.   Another
interesting feature is that at least 15 of these tools would be called 'pebble
tools' except for their small size.

Tools with more retouch tend to be smaller and many are heavily as well
as extensively retouched.   In the upper horizon the discoid scrapers are
mostly retouched all around the base.   A group of seven are almost circular,
about 3 cm in diameter, and made on thick flakes.   This type does not occur

in the lower horizon, where the tools which are retouched all around the base are flatter and more rectangular in shape.   In the lower horizon there are two tools with deep concavities on either side of a ridge which recall similar tools at Batari.

The multi-platform tools are very chunky and often heavily worked and more of them have been used as cores than occurs at other sites.   These tools also are rather smaller than similar ones found further east (e.g. fig.26b); there are more light implements (<15 gm) at Niobe than in all but Horizons I-II at Kafiavana.   There are also many more multi-platform tools at Niobe than in Horizons III-IX at Kafiavana.

Other Tools

There are a few tools with scalar retouch on flat thin edges, and three thin flat pieces with bifacial retouch or use-wear at one or both ends.   This may be the result of a particular kind of use or it may be purely fortuitous. Utilised flakes form only about 10% of the industry.   They are mostly small and thin, but a few larger ones occur.

Comparisons with other Sites

Comparisons with Kiowa site, which is closest to Niobe, are difficult, for not only is the typology used here very different from S. Bulmer's, but her sample is small - 288 retouched tools, 91 cores and 47 pebble tools - from a deposit ranging over more than 5500 years: at Kiowa there were 14 tools per m^3; at Niobe 116 tools per m^3.   In general Kiowa seems to have rather more pebble tools (9.5% of the total number of retouched and utilised pieces), though this may be because of differing definitions.   Utilised pieces also seem much more common at Kiowa, where they consistently form 30% or more of the total flaked tool assemblage (Bulmer 1966a:108a).   However, it is impossible to compare the flaked tools from Niobe and Kiowa satisfactorily without similar classifications being employed.

Comparisons with Kafiavana suggest that, assuming some technological equivalence between the two areas:

1.   All the Niobe deposit is earlier than Horizons I-II at Kafiavana, since the percentage of utilised flakes is always low at Niobe.

2.   Pebble tools are more common at Niobe, suggesting a different tradition.

3.   The presence of more small multi-platform tools suggests a more economical use of raw material at Niobe.

On the basis of the flaked tools alone Niobe may be correlated with the main upper concentration of flaked tools (Horizons III-V) at Kafiavana and, very tentatively, with phases B and C at Kiowa.

TRIMMING FLAKES

These occur throughout the industry and there is an average of four for every seven flaked implements (table 165).   There appear to be rather more implements per trimming flake in the lower part of the site, which suggests that implements were re-trimmed rather more frequently later in the site's history.   The high number of trimming flakes is consistent with the economic use of raw material referred to earlier.

Table 165   Niobe: distribution of trimming flakes

Horizon	Number	Implements per trimming flake
Upper	301	1.60
Lower	207	2.18
Both	508	1.84

HAMMERS

Eight river-pebble hammerstones were found, made of a variety of materials from feldspar-porphyry to hornblende-diorite and ranging from 63 to 1000 gm. All types of stone used bruise rather than shatter when struck and they are plentiful in the local streams half a mile (0.9 km) or more away.

CONCLUSION

Niobe was clearly intensively used. Large numbers of animals were eaten there and a good deal of stone was knapped. The range of artifactual material suggests that a wide range of activities was carried out.

Occupation - though whether human or animal is not clear - appears to have begun in the old cave mouth and a deposit was built up. Some of the deposit was then concreted and further, definitely human, occupation occurred in front and on top of the flowstone. The absence of hearths and other features may be related to the intensity of occupation as well as exposure to the weather. At a later stage in the accumulation of the deposit considerable disturbance seems to have occurred, so that the original relationship between particular artifacts may now be destroyed.

In very broad terms the sequence seems to parallel that found at Kiowa, with pebble tools, flake tools and some bone tools in the lower levels and the same material, together with polished axe-adzes and domestic fauna, above. There are some additional items of material culture not found at Kiowa: the use of fossil shark vertebrae in the lower level, the strange, thin, axe-like blades and the mortar fragments in the upper. Waisted blades seem to appear before axes and this has been noted at Yuku site much further west. Tentatively, then, the site seems to span all three of the stages recorded by S. and R. Bulmer at Kiowa (1964). Further, the low percentage of utilised flakes throughout suggests that intensive use of the excavated part of the site ceased before at least 1000 BP, while the large numbers of axes in the upper level, together with the presence of bone awls still recognised as such by local people, seem to point to rather more use of Niobe compared to Kiowa in the more recent period.

S. Bulmer's and my typologies are so different that a comparative study of the flaked stone tools is very difficult. Unfortunately, it was impossible to analyse both Niobe and Kiowa collections according to the same typology.

An interesting feature at Niobe is the presence of pebble tools in all levels; this was also found at Kiowa. In spite of difficulties in defining these tools and theorising about their use, it does appear that this feature differentiates both Niobe and Kiowa from sites further east. I do not know whether this is simply due to traditionally different techniques or arises from some different way of exploiting the environment; the first appears to be more likely but remains a problem for future study.

Further information about the site will come from excavations carried out there by M.J. Mountain in 1971.

VII   TOWARDS A PREHISTORY

The two sites in the Lamari valley, Batari (fig.27) and Aibura (fig.27), provide an overlapping record from about 8000 BP to the present. Flaked stone and bone tools were made from the start of occupation. The stone tools show some degree of regional similarity and continuity throughout the whole period. Lenticular and planilateral ground-stone axe-adzes may have occurred from about 3000 BP, but small grooved and ground stone and shell artifacts, marine shell and pigs are definitely dated only to about 2000 years ago. Ceramics and perhaps fowls were introduced some 800 years ago, while dogs were found only in the most recent level. Waisted blades, pebble tools and tools with use-polish are absent from the deposits at both sites. This absence may be due simply to sampling error but since both sites present a similar picture, it probably reflects the general cultural pattern of the area.

The faunal evidence suggests that much of the conversion from forest to grassland, at least around Aibura, occurred during the last 1000 years. At Aibura it is within this period also that fewer implements were retouched and more were simply used; this change is not found at Batari, where use of the site probably decreases around 800 years ago.

Kafiavana, the Asaro valley site with its 4 m of deposit (fig.28), was first occupied at least 11,000 years ago by people who ground stone axe-adzes, flaked pebble tools and 'scrapers' and produced use-polish on a few tools. They very soon began to receive marine shells. They appear never to have had waisted blades, and before very long they stopped making more than the occasional pebble tool. Small retouched tools were made in some quantity for about 5500 years and they show only slight and gradual changes over this time.

The first pig bones appear at Kafiavana at least 6500 years ago and axe-stone was obtained from Kafetu quarry slightly later. From about 4500 BP Kafiavana was apparently less used or abandoned, but we do not know for how long. It was possibly reoccupied only around 1000 BP, for retouched tools were rarer and flaked tools were generally smaller after the re-occupation and this is similar to the change which occurred at Aibura at this date. Occasional pieces of obsidian were used in this recent period. Pigs became commoner too, but no dog remains were ever left around the site. It is likely that the topmost levels of Kafiavana were deposited during the immediate pre-contact period.

The sequence at Niobe, adjacent to Kiowa, shows some similarities with S. Bulmer's site, and differs in several ways from sites to the east. Many pebble tools occurred throughout the deposit, along with flaked stone and bone tools. Two waisted blades were found in the lower level and fossil shark vertebrae were used, possibly for decoration. Ground stone axe-adzes, thin axe-like blades, bone awls and a mortar fragment occurred in the upper level. Pigs were found in the top of the site only, while dog remains were not found.

If it is assumed that the distribution of artifacts in the excavation represents the real picture reasonably accurately, then comparison with the Kiowa sequence suggests that Niobe was occupied from at least 6-7000 BP. It was probably used until quite recently, although the absence of large numbers of utilised pieces may suggest that it was not used for activities requiring flaked stone tools after about 1000 BP. Such an argument assumes, of course, that a partial abandonment of retouched tools occurs west of the Asaro-Chimbu divide as well as east of it.

Any attempt to use this material to construct a prehistory for the Central Highlands must take account of two general problems.

1. It has been generally assumed that the first occupants of the Highlands

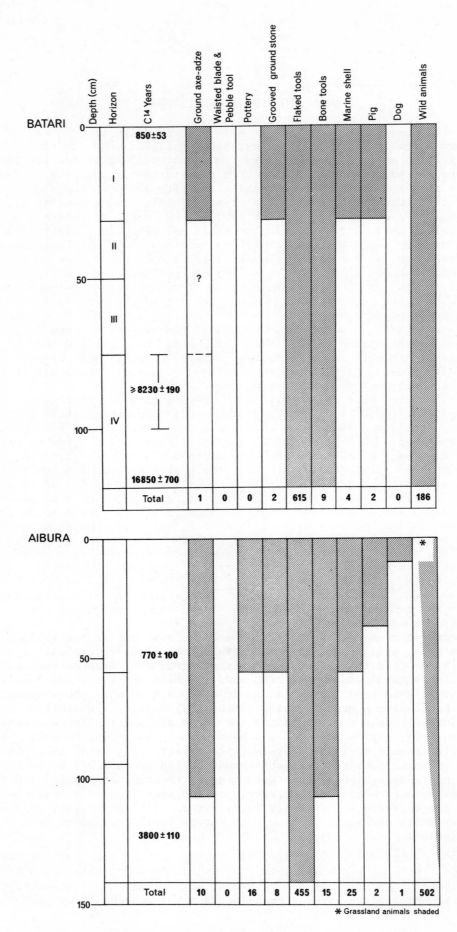

Fig.27   Batari and Aibura: summary of evidence

143

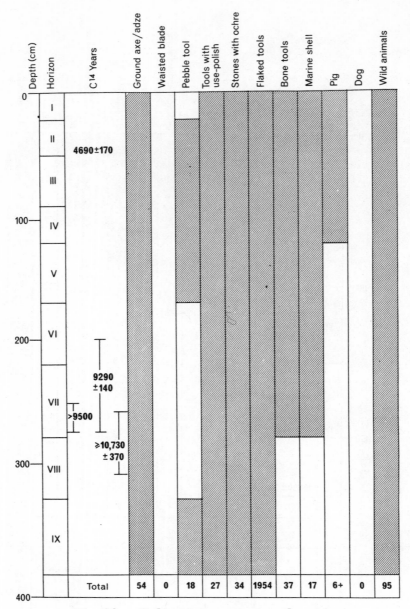

Fig.28   Kafiavana: summary of evidence

were hunter-gatherers and that at some later time either horticulturalists migrated into the area and hunter-gatherers became horticulturalists by acculturation or else the original inhabitants gradually adopted horticulture under influences from outside the Highlands.   While these are reasonable theories, it must be remembered that we do not yet know what the artifactual markers of horticulture are.   Bulmer (1966a:152) considers that the polished stone axe-adze 'is only a pre-condition of large scale gardening and forest clearing and could easily be used in a hunting and collecting context' and agrees that there are no absolutely definite markers.   It has also been argued that the presence of pigs, which must be fed if they are to be kept tame, is a good indication of some gardening by their owners (Bulmer 1966a:152; 1966b).   As Bulmer recognises, however, the earliest Highlands pigs could be feral, and there is nothing directly to link them with agriculture at any stage.   Any construct which is made must recognise this problem, even if only as the background to a theory.

2.   The kinds of indestructible material which remain in rock shelters after different sorts of occupation, and the degree to which this material represents both the particular activity and, more generally, the material culture of the people concerned, constitute a major problem in its own right

(e.g. L.R. and S.R. Binford 1966:268-70; Piggott 1959:8; Thomson 1939:209-10).
On theoretical grounds it seems likely that in the Highlands, for instance,
the archaeological evidence now available should provide qualitatively
different data from different periods if a 'neolithic revolution' occurred
during the period of occupation.

In this area only three open sites, Kosipe (White 1965a; White *et al.*
1970), the Manton site (Golson *et al.* 1967) and Kuk (Allen 1970) have
been reported, although work on others is proceeding.   None of these three
is definitely a living site, while present-day peoples use rock shelters
mostly during gardening, hunting, travelling or as refuges in times of
conflict and actually live elsewhere nearly all of the time.   It could be
argued from this that remains resulting from the activities of horticulturalists
using shelters are likely only to reflect limited aspects of material culture
and that it is only in unusual circumstances that they will represent the
full range.

By contrast, it might be expected that earlier occupation levels, if
deposited by hunter-gatherers, would present a wider picture of man's
artifacts and activities.   This is because hunter-gatherers often actually
live in rock shelters and caves, whereas horticulturalists rarely do
(C.G. and B.Z. Seligmann 1911:80-7; Spencer 1928:II, 823-4; Spencer 1914:31-2;
Stow 1905:33).   Furthermore, hunter-gatherers generally seem to carry a
larger range of their possessions with them as they move around their
territory, so that the chances of a wide range of objects being left in
shelters are higher with these people than they are with horticulturalists.

Any attempt to apply this theoretical contrast in the use of rock
shelters to the Highlands, however, is currently vitiated by two problems
arising out of the available archaeological data.   These are:

1. We do not yet know which (if any) levels of the shelters relate to
    hunter-gatherers' occupations, so that the economic contrast in this
area cannot be put into concrete terms.

2. The degree of contrast between early and late levels in the sites is not
    great, and indeed a somewhat greater range of material comes from the
later levels.   This presumably indicates better preservation of more recent
material; but it may also suggest that the activities which leave the
majority of preserved remains were in fact carried on in rock shelters
throughout the entire period.   These activities presumably included the
preparation of hunting gear and the processing of some plant and animal
food.   A closer study of the uses of different prehistoric tools is,
however, needed before detailed interpretations of this kind can be made.

In 1964, before radiocarbon dates were available, S. and R. Bulmer
suggested that Highlands prehistory should be divided into three phases.

1. Phase I (Kiowa A) saw the region occupied by 'pre-neolithic' people
    lacking edge-ground implements, who probably lived by hunting and
gathering.

2. In Phase II (Kiowa B, Yuku A-B) a number of new implements was introduced,
    namely the lenticular-sectioned axe-adze, flaked waisted blades (possibly
hoes or digging tools) and the pestle-and-mortar complex of artifacts; these
introductions were probably associated with that of agriculture, or at least
of new crops.   The detailed similarities between Highlands and north coast
examples of stone mortars and figurines possibly indicate an immigration of
people to the Highlands, but the other excavated artifacts showed little
evidence of technological discontinuity with Phase I.

3. Phase III (Kiowa C, Yuku C) was marked by the planilateral-sectioned
    axe-adze and, in the Eastern Highlands, pottery-making.   The evidence
of the flaked tools does not suggest any major break with the preceding phase.
Intensive sweet potato cultivation probably occurred within Phase III; before
this crop was available, the altitudinal limit of settlement may have been
lower.

S. and R. Bulmer concluded (1964:74) that although Eastern and Western Highlands may have had slightly different histories 'there is no archaeological evidence for or against a single main migration into and through the Highlands either by preagricultural or agricultural peoples'.

By 1966 it was· known that the Highlands had been settled for at least 10,000 years and that very little of the excavated evidence referred to the later part of the settlement period (Bulmer 1964b). In this situation Bulmer (1966a:156-8) modified her earlier system.

1. Phase I remained the same.

2. In Phase II, which dated from about 6000 BP, horticulture was adopted
    although hunting and food gathering continued to be very important.
Pigs may have been domestic if enough food was being grown to feed them. She stressed the development of local economic variations in this period. Axe-adzes and waisted blades were introduced, as were pestles and mortars at about 4000 BP or later.

3. Phase III was restricted to the sweet potato gardeners and pig-raisers who
    occupied the Highlands when the Europeans arrived. This phase, which was
not yet documented archaeologically, included only the period of 'socio-economic "revolution" which the adoption of the sweet potato implies' (1966a:158) and may therefore be no more than several hundred years old (cf. Watson 1965a, 1965b).

Any attempt at 'culture-historical integration' on the basis of only two stratified sites is, as S. and R. Bulmer recognised, liable to be premature, although at the time their construct was extremely insightful. However, these phases now need to be considerably modified in the light of further evidence. It is apparent, for instance, that polished axes are not a phase-marker in the Highlands, so that the basis of Phase II (1964) is doubtful, while Phase III (1966) must be reconsidered in the light of recent evidence for agriculture at 2300 BP (Golson et al. 1967), as well as objections to any theory of socio-economic revolution following the introduction of the sweet potato into Highlands agricultural systems (Brookfield and White 1968).

Any reconsideration also needs to remember the following:

1. The number of artifacts on which parts of the Bulmers' constructs are
    based is exceptionally small. The primacy of the lenticular over the
planilateral axe-adze is argued on one definite but undated, and one dated but only probable, example in a total of 11 pieces, while only three waisted blades have been found in dated contexts. It seems quite likely that the chances of excavation may account for part of the pattern and the same may well account for the absence of ground axe-adzes prior to about 5000 BP at Kiowa.

2. S. Bulmer (1966a:143) considers that the proportion of waste flakes is
    sufficiently high·at both Kiowa and Yuku to show that tools were normally
made on the site and that Kiowa, at least, was used for the same purposes throughout its history. The figures are given in table 166 (Bulmer 1966a: 96-129).

Table 166   Kiowa and Yuku: distribution of artifact classes

	Retouched tools	Utilised flakes	Waste flakes	Waste flakes per tool
Kiowa C	115	35	226	1.5
Kiowa B	70	25	136	1.4
Kiowa A	202	106	849	2.8
Yuku C	14	2	51	3.2
Yuku B (incl. crevice)	92	60	666	4.4
Yuku A^2	2	–	30	15.0
Yuku A^1	8	8	17	1.1

The tool/waste ratios are quite unusual for workshop sites and therefore the claim that they are such must be doubted. In addition, one must also consider that the waste flakes are very large; at Kiowa they range in size from 1.0 to 7.5 cm (median lengths 2.0-3.0 cm) and for Yuku the range is 0.75 to 6.75 cm (medians 1.75-3.75 cm). The fact that no waste material smaller than 1 cm long was recovered from either site is highly unusual and it may be suggested that the excavation procedures were insufficiently precise to recover the smaller material. There is no evidence for or against this suggestion at present, but it seems that the evidence of the stone artifacts should not be used to argue that Kiowa site was continuously inhabited for the same purposes throughout its history.

The general sequence of Highlands prehistory derived from the available evidence and with the qualifications discussed above, may now be reviewed.

By about 26,000 BP the Papuan Highlands at least were being seasonally exploited, as shown by the site of Kosipe (White *et al.* 1970). This is the only evidence for the Pleistocene occupation of New Guinea to date, but we may expect intermittent occupation of much of the Highlands by this time (cf. White 1971:46-7).

By 11,000 BP small groups of people, probably hunters and gatherers, became semi-permanent occupants of the Highlands. It seems likely that they lived mostly in the main valleys where it was warmer, though they would hunt in the higher altitude forests. They were equipped with pebble tools and flaked tools and bone artifacts. They presumably made wooden artifacts, including bows and arrows, with their stone tools and processed vegetable matter in various ways. Trade for the valuable marine shells probably went on from the beginning and these, together with red ochre, were used for decoration.

The absence of now-extinct forms among the animals hunted, except for *Thylacine* (Van Deusen 1963), may suggest that settlement of this area occurred considerably earlier (Martin 1967) but there is no direct evidence from the Central Highlands to support this theory.

There is some suggestion that two technological regions have been present throughout the post-Pleistocene period. Waisted blades and 'bifaces' seem to be restricted to Chuave and further west, while east of this the early abandonment of pebble tools as a major tool type has been noted. In more recent periods, of course, the restriction of quadrangular-sectioned axe-adze blades to the western area is well known.

The first economic change seen in the archaeological record is the presence of pig around 6500 BP. On available evidence its arrival had no technological correlates and until the economic status of the animal is known, the economic and social changes its arrival may have caused cannot be assessed.

After the initial settlement of the Highlands no major artifactual change can be seen for some considerable time. Unless waisted blades came into use well after 10,000 BP (as the evidence from Kiowa suggests), there is only a slight and gradual change in the retouched tools until at least 4000 BP. There were few additions to the tool-kit, although the planilateral axe-adze may have developed before 5000 BP.

It is at and after this date that some major changes in the use of rock shelters occurred. In the light of traditional dates for horticulture in Southeast Asia (Chang and Stuiver 1966), it is at this time that one might begin to look for the beginnings of horticulture in the Highlands. Whether the changes in shelter-use do in fact relate to horticulture is unknown, for there is no definite archaeological referent for horticulture in the Highlands yet. Recent pollen evidence however shows that extensive forest clearance occurred at two sites in the Wahgi valley more than 5000 years ago (Powell 1970) and this, together with the presence of pigs around 6500 BP, provides strong support for the suggestion that horticulture was in fact being practised (cf. White 1971:49-50). The similarities with data from Portuguese Timor may also be noted (Glover 1971).

Horticulture, using complex methods, was definitely established in at least one main valley by 2500 BP or earlier (Golson *et al.* 1967). It is likely that both horticultural methods and implements such as paddle-shaped wooden spades were introduced from outside the Highlands (cf. Barrau 1958:9), but there is no evidence as to how these were adopted. It may have been a long slow process with people continuing to rely on hunting and gathering for a number of generations, or it may have been a fairly swift economic change associated with the arrival of some new artifacts, something which one could call a 'neolithic revolution'. The current archaeological evidence supports neither case, nor is the evidence from other disciplines which bears on this question as definite as has sometimes been assumed. The change probably occurred in different ways and at different times throughout the Highlands. The adoption of horticulture presumably allowed a general increase in population density, with increasing pressure on the forests leading to the formation of grasslands in environmentally less favourable areas. In the Eastern Highlands, at least, the faunal evidence suggests that this process had not greatly advanced by about 900 BP.

At both Aibura and Kafiavana fewer retouched tools and more unretouched pieces were found in the period starting at least 1000 years ago. It is possible that this change is gradual rather than sudden and that the process may have been accelerated by the arrival of European tools. The archaeological evidence is not precise enough to allow this to be determined and the meaning of the change is also elusive. Some pottery began to reach the Eastern Highlands within the last 1000 years.

The most recent prehistoric changes probably occurred less than 400 years ago with the arrival of the sweet potato. This new addition to the crops would have been easily adopted into a horticultural system already based on root crops, especially as it allowed occupation to extend higher up the valley slopes. The social and demographic effects of this adoption are much less clear but were probably not very marked in most areas.

Perhaps the most surprising absence from the archaeological record is that of dog, which has been found only in the most recent levels at any site. This absence may not be a real one, of course, and it might be suggested that the important part played by dogs in some Highlands cultures has something to do with their absence from rock shelters sites (R. Bulmer 1967:19). Nevertheless dog was on the south Papuan coast by 1500 years ago (F.J. Allen, University of Papua and New Guinea, pers. comm.) and has been found in the earliest settlement levels of islands in the Central Pacific (Golson 1972). It is present in Australia from about 7000 BP (R. Edwards, pers. comm.). There seems no reason, then, not to expect dogs in the Highlands for at least the last thousand years, or perhaps for as long as pigs.

SUMMARY

The dominating impression produced by a collection of prehistoric stone and bone implements from the Central Highlands is one of sameness and continuity. In spite of slight changes, the bulk of the tool-kit is the same from Aibura to Baiyer River and, apparently, Nipa in the Southern Highlands (Bartlett 1964). It is also very similar from 9000 BC to the present. This perhaps indicates only that some basic aspects of life in the Highlands continued unaltered by other economic or technological changes. However, it may point also to a stability and continuity in Highlands technology not often found in post-Pleistocene prehistory. Even within Australia, presumably as isolated from other cultural influences as the Highlands, there were far greater technological changes (e.g. Mulvaney 1966, 1969). This continuity in the Highlands suggests, most importantly, that it may be legitimate to apply some ethnographic, especially technological, information to the analysis of the archaeological materials. If this is indeed so, then an analytical tool of some power is available for the area. This will help to create a complex and integrated prehistory of 'the land that time forgot'.

VIII ACKNOWLEDGEMENTS

In the course of the work reported here I was assisted by many people, both while in the field and during the analysis of the material. I would like to thank the following and apologise to any who feel they too contributed but whose names are not recorded: no slight is intended.

In Papua New Guinea, many Niuginians helped me find and excavate sites on their land. The research would not have been possible without their help, and I would like to mention in particular the people of Legaiyu and Barabuna villages, where we worked for some time.

Many members of the Administration helped me both formally and informally, as did a number of friends. My thanks to Dr D. Bettison, J. Campbell, J.D. Cole, K. Connolly, Dr J. Dean, M. Dudley, Dr E. Giles, J. Higginbotham, G. Hogbin, C. Julius, Mr and Mrs W. Larner, E. Lazaron, M. Lishmond, F. Parker, N. Stagg, Mr and Mrs P. Thomas, V. Tolley, W.E. Tomasetti, L. Tomasetti, M. Tyler, Mr and Mrs A. Vincent, Professor J.B. Watson, Dr. V. Watson, S. Whiting.

The analysis of excavated materials is a complex process and I was greatly helped by specialists in various fields. My understanding of matters geological was improved by Mr J.N. Jennings and Mr R.M. Frank (both Department of Geography, Research School of Pacific Studies, ANU), Dr K.A.W. Crook (Department of Geology, School of General Studies, ANU), Mr B. Butler and Dr R. Brewer (Division of Soils, CSIRO, Canberra), and Mr B.P. Ruxton (Division of Land Research, CSIRO, Canberra). Soil analyses were carried out by Professor E. Schmid and Dr I. Grüninger (both Universität Basel). Petrographic studies of the pottery were kindly made by Mr C.A. Key (Department of Anthropology and Sociology, Research School of Pacific Studies, ANU), while Mr J.M.A. Chappell (Department of Geography, School of General Studies, ANU) placed his wide knowledge of Highlands axe-stone quarries at my disposal.

Specific faunal determinations were made by Dr D.F. McMichael (Curator of Molluscs, The Australian Museum, Sydney) on shellfish; Dr F.H. Talbot and Dr J.C. Yaldwyn (respectively Curators of Fishes and of Crustacea, The Australian Museum) and Professor J.A. Garrick (Department of Zoology, Victoria University of Wellington) on fishes, including the enigmatic fossil shark vertebrae; Dr R.E. Barwick (Department of Zoology, School of General Studies, ANU) on reptiles; Mr J.A. Mahoney (Department of Geology, University of Sydney) on rats; Mr C.L. Cram (Department of Anthropology and Sociology, ANU) on dogs and pigs; Dr M.D. Plane (Bureau of Mineral Resources, Geology and Geophysics, Canberra) on fossil mammals and Mr R.J. Scarlett (Canterbury Museum, Christchurch) on birds. Mr J.H. Calaby (Division of Wildlife, CSIRO, Canberra) and Mr B.J. Marlow (Curator of Mammals, The Australian Museum) helped me with both identifications and nomenclature, while Drs L.J. Brass and H.M. Van Deusen (both American Museum of Natural History) gave me advice on the sizes and ranges of Highlands animals. Mrs D. Gregory (Department of Anthropology and Sociology, ANU) sorted and initially classified all the material from Niobe.

Analyses of plant materials were made by Drs H.D. Ingle and R.W.R. Muncey (both Division of Forest Products, CSIRO, Melbourne), Mr R. Pullen (Plant Herbarium, CSIRO, Canberra) and Mr W.H. Litchfield (Department of Geography, Research School of Pacific Studies, ANU), while more general assistance was given by my fellow students Mr J.R. Flenley and Miss J.M. Wheeler (both Department of Geography, Research School of Pacific Studies, ANU).

The analysis of human skeletal remains was expertly carried out by Dr L. Freedman (Department of Anatomy, University of Sydney) and problems were also discussed with Professor N.W.G. Macintosh and Mr A.G. Thorne, both of that Department.

For assistance with numerical and statistical matters, I am indebted to Dr W.J. Ewens (Department of Statistics, School of General Studies, ANU),

Miss M. Rose (Computer Programmer, Research Schools of Social Sciences and Pacific Studies, ANU), Mr A. Minson and Mrs E. Minson (both Department of Genetics, John Curtin School of Medical Research, ANU) and Dr W.T. (Bill) Williams (Division of Computing Research, CSIRO, Canberra).   Mrs Susan Bulmer (Department of Anthropology, University of Auckland) generously shared her comprehensive knowledge of Highlands archaeology with me.   Mr H.A. Polach (ANU Radiocarbon Dating Laboratory) extracted useful results from poor samples.   Dr S.A. Wurm, Dr D.C. Laycock and Mr D.J. Prentice (all Department of Anthropology and Sociology, ANU) listened to tapes and reassured me that I had not grossly misinterpreted information.

   In some ways, the drawings of artifacts are the most elegant part of this report and I am deeply indebted to Miss Winifred Mumford (Department of Anthropology and Sociology, ANU) for them.   Some specimens were also drawn by Mrs J. Dornstreich.   Mr T.S. McMahon (Visual Aids Unit, ANU) printed many photographs clearly and rapidly, while bureaucratic paths within ANU were smoothed by Mrs E. Ballestrin, Mrs E. Lynch, Miss E. Vincent, Mrs L. White and Mrs N. Young.

   For sharing their knowledge of the country and its people with me I am grateful to Dr R.N.H. Bulmer (Department of Anthropology, University of Auckland), Dr M.A. Chowning (Department of Anthropology and Sociology, ANU) and especially Dr H.C. Brookfield (Department of Geography, Research School of Pacific Studies, ANU).   Some others I remember with gratitude for their discussions and friendship: my colleagues in the Department of Anthropology and Sociology, F.J. Allen, W.R. Ambrose, R.J. Lampert and J.R. Specht; B. Hiatt and R. Jones in the Department of Anthropology, University of Sydney; L. Ryan and M.F. Little for this and considerable editorial assistance.

   For the production of this volume I am particularly indebted to three people: to Mrs Beverley Fox who has typed the entire script, text and tables, to Mr Dragi Markovic for his photography of all tables, plates and line drawings and again to Miss Winifred Mumford who has been completely responsible for the revision of the illustrations and the layout of the volume.

   Two people must be thanked especially for their constant help, encouragement, guidance and assistance.   My wife Carmel's contribution in the field and laboratory is immeasurable; Jack Golson supervised the research with an acumen which I did not always appreciate at the time and has edited this memoir similarly: he bears no responsibility for any errors but must take much of the credit if any is forthcoming.

APPENDIX 1

SOME COMMENTS ON THE ECOLOGY OF SOME HIGHLANDS MAMMALS

Macropodidae

1. *Thylogale* is the true grass wallaby of the Highlands.   It is the maker
    of the 'pads' so frequently seen in the alpine and subalpine grasslands.
It will evidently go as high as there is grass to eat.   Greater weights may
be reached than indicated in table 167 but there are no data.

2. *Dorcopsulus* is primarily a mid-mountain forest wallaby.   It will feed
    out in grassland regularly, but never far from the forest.   *Dorcopsis*,
as Tate (1948:285-90) states, is normally a rainforest, low-elevation animal.

3. *Dendrolagus* at higher elevations (e.g. Mt Kubor) may feed a good part of
    the time on the ground.   This refers to *D. matschiei* and subspecies
goodfellowi.   The former may venture into grassland borders, but there is no
proof of this.   *D. dorianus* and probably *ursinus* are closely restricted to
the forest.   In good forest *Dendrolagus* may spend a lot less time on the
ground.

Phalangeridae

4. *Phalanger orientalis* is strictly arboreal and usually rainforest though
    it may also be found in the lower oak forest.   *Phalanger gymnotis* is
probably a ground forager.   Both may occur in the excavated collections, as
may *Phalanger vestitus*.

5. *Dactylopsila* is primarily a rainforest animal.   *Dactylonax* tends to
    replace *Dactylopsila* in the mid-mountain rainforests and many animals in
Highlands sites may be expected to be *Dactylonax*.

6. *Petaurus breviceps*   The mountain species is a small dark forest animal.

7. *Eudromicia*   Present from about 4000 ft (1225 m) to the peaks and as one
    goes higher it becomes more common.   Aboreal, forest only.   Common in
the subalpine forest.

8. *Pseudocheirus*   There is altitudinal zonation in this genus, but much
    more work remains to be done.   Generally *forbesi* (sub-genus *Pseudocheirus*)
is lowest, then *corinnae* and finally *cupreus* (both sub-genus *Pseudochirops*),
but there is a great deal of overlap.   The first two are strictly forest but
cupreus often seems to venture out of the forest to forage in the tussock grass
at higher elevations.   All these species occur in the Eastern Highlands.

Peramelidae

9. *Peroryctes longicauda* or *Echymipera kalubu* or *E. clara* may be present.
    The former is present from 3500 ft (1075 m) to the highest peaks, so that
in the upper parts its habitat is grassland.   This species becomes commoner
at the higher altitudes.   *P. raffrayanus* may take over the *longicauda*
habitat in some areas (e.g. Huon Peninsula).

Dasyuridae

10. *Satanellus* is more often found in forest, but it will wander out into
     the grassland also.

11. *Antechinus* is strictly a forest dweller.

Muridae

12. *Hyomys* is primarily a forest animal though it may go into grassland. It does not therefore compete much with *Mallomys*.

13. *Mallomys* seems to be primarily a grassland animal though it may also forage in the forest.

14. *Uromys* is primarily a ground-dwelling rainforest rodent, but it climbs very readily. When *U. anak* is present in the oak forest, it is doubtful if *U. caudimaculatus* ranges above 2000-3000 ft.

Tachyglossidae

15. *Zaglossus* appears to be quite strictly a forest dweller and probably grows to a larger size than is given in the table.

H.M. Van Deusen,
Curator of the Archbold Collections,
American Museum of Natural History,
New York, 1966.

Table 167   Habitat, altitudinal range and maximum weight of some Highlands mammals

Name	Habitat	Altitudinal range in feet	metres	Maximum weight in kg
Macropodidae				
1 *Thylogale*	forest and grass	0-14,000	0-4250	6.58
2a *Dorcopsulus*	forest and grass	2500-9500	750-3000	2.95
b *Dorcopsis*	forest	0-1300	0-500	2.89
3 *Dendrolagus*	forest and grass (?)	3000-11,000	1000-3250	8.39
Phalangeridae				
4a *Phalanger orientalis*	forest	0-4000	0-1200	2.83
b *Phalanger gymnotis*	forest	0-8000	0-2500	3.43
c *Phalanger vestitus*	forest	5000-10,000	1500-3000	0.97
5a *Dactylopsila*	forest	0-5000/6000	0-1500/1800	0.51
b *Dactylonax*	forest	4000-8000	1200-2500	0.45
6a *Petaurus breviceps* (lowland)	forest	0-3000	0-1000	0.13
b *Petaurus breviceps* (mountain)	forest	3000-8000	1000-2500	0.07
7 *Eudromicia*	forest	4500-13,000	1250-4000	0.03
8a *Pseudocheirus forbesi*	forest	2000-9000	500-2750	1.05
b *Pseudocheirus corinnae*	forest	4000-9000	1200-2750	1.13
c *Pseudocheirus cupreus*	forest and grass	5000-13,000	1500-4000	2.44
Peramelidae				
9a *Peroryctes longicauda*	forest and grass	4000-15,000	1200-4500	0.45
b *Echymipera kalubu*	forest and secondary grassland	0-5000/6000	0-1500/1800	1.36
c *Peroryctes raffrayanus*	forest	1500-12,000	500-3750	1.53
Dasyuridae				
10 *Satanellus*	forest and grass	0-10,000	0-3000	0.93
11a *Antechinus* (sp.1)	forest	0-5000	0-1500	0.05
b *Antechinus* (sp.2)	forest	6000-10,000	1800-7000	0.05
c *Antechinus* (sp.3)	forest	5000-8000	1500-2500	0.05
Muridae				
12 *Hyomys*	forest and grass (?)	4000-10,000	1200-3000	1.31
13 *Mallomys*	forest and grass	5000-12,500	1500-3750	1.81
14 *Uromys*	forest	0-6000	0-1750	0.71
Tachyglossidae				
15 *Zaglossus*	forest	4000-9500	1200-3000	7.26
Pteropodidae				
16 *Dobsonia*	forest	0-6500	0-2000	0.57
			(average	0.45)

APPENDIX 2

HUMAN SKELETAL REMAINS FROM AIBURA CAVE, NEW GUINEA

A total of 86 fragments of human skeletal remains was excavated from Aibura. Most of the material is badly damaged, eroded and very fragmentary, but there are two fairly large calvarial fragments, the right half of a palate, four loose teeth, most of two tibiae and several reasonably intact hand, foot and digital bones. Examination of the whole assemblage clearly indicates that the remains are from a number of individuals, but because of the nature and fragmentary condition of the specimens, the exact number, as also sex and race, is difficult to determine. Some of the fragments show signs of gnawing, probably by rodents, and a few may have been in or near fire.

Description of the Individual Specimens

The excavated material includes:

1. 35 fragments of skull bones including four teeth;

2. 15 mostly very small pieces of bones from the axial skeleton (sternum, vertebrae and sacrum) plus two small uncertain fragments;

3. 13 upper limb bone fragments of varying size and condition;

4. 21 lower limb bone fragments, again of varying size and condition.

All specimens are referred to by site number/individual number where applicable:square/(level)e.g. A64/N25.IV/(7).

Skull

The skull fragments from Aibura include a number of specimens which show interesting features and more than one individual is clearly represented.

1-8. Eight calvaria fragments, A64/XV/(4). These are all yellowish in colour and come from various parts of the calvaria roof, probably of a single individual. Two fragments join together, but the edges of the other fragments do not appear to articulate. Two fragments show small portions of cranial sutures; one shows a small blackened area consistent with charring. One fragment is about 3.5 mm thick, the rest range from 6-8 mm.

9-16. Eight calvaria fragments, A64/IV/(7). Six of these are very thick fragments, mostly from the midline region of an occipital bone, plus a small portion of the adjacent parietal bone in one specimen. These six fragments are all blackish in colour (possibly the result of slight charring) and almost certainly are from a single individual, although they cannot be joined together. One fragment includes an articular edge, probably for the adjacent parietal bone. The parieto-occipital (lambdoid) suture on one specimen is completely synostosed endocranially and almost obliterated ectocranially.
The remaining two fragments are 5.7 mm thick, i.e. rather thinner than the other six, and blackish-yellow in colour. These two fragments are articulating fragments of a parietal and an occipital bone and quite likely come from a different individual from the above six fragments.

17. Calvaria roof fragment, A64/VIII/(5). This is a small fragment with the inner table of bone missing and the outer showing signs of gnawing.

18. ?Parietal fragment, A64/VII/(5). This small fragment shows an articular edge and some grooving on the ectocranial surface. This fragment is probably a small portion of a parietal bone, from the region of

153

articulation with the temporal bone, just above the mastoid process.

19. Left temporal fragment, A64/IV/(5). This blackish-yellow specimen is considerably damaged and eroded. The mastoid process is partially broken but would not have been very large; the mastoid notch medial to it is very deep. The external acoustic meatus has lost its anterior wall. The small remaining postero-inferior portion of the squamous part of the bone is thick (± 6 mm) and a small blackened area present is possible evidence of charring.

20. Right temporal squama, A64/IV/(5). This whitish specimen consists of the anterior part of the squama, plus a small portion of the root of the zygomatic process. The bone is flat and thin and only a small sloping, central part of the articular surface for the articulation with the parietal remains.

21. Right frontal fragment, A64/VII/(6). This small brownish fragment is from the supero-lateral corner of the orbit. The articulation for the zygomatic is present. Signs of rodent gnawing can be seen in two places.

22. Right frontal fragment, A64/VIII/(5). A brown-coloured fragment of supero-lateral corner of orbit. The frontal surface is damaged but the articulation for the zygomatic bone is present.

23. Calvaria roof fragment, A64/VIII/(5). A small fragment (parietal or frontal), showing extensive gnawing internally and externally.

24. Right half of palate, A64/VII/(4). The specimen consists of the alveolar and palatine processes of the maxilla, plus the small portion of the palatine bone enclosing the greater palatine foramen. The basal part of a large maxillary sinus can be seen from above. No teeth are present, but the alveoli, all of which are present, suggest that all of the teeth had fully erupted and were lost post-mortem. The first molar had three roots, the third a single root and the second a fused root. The palate is deep and ridged, but generally rather small in its dimensions (maxillo-alveolar length 57 mm and breadth 62 mm; palatal depth 13.5 mm). The palate slopes down steeply anteriorly and there is no alveolar (or dental, it would seem) prognathism. There is no palatine torus and the incisive foramen is small. The anterior surface of the maxilla is corrugated by the incisor root alveoli. The inferior margin of the anterior nasal aperture takes the form of a simian groove, the floor of the nasal cavity being very indistinctly demarcated from the anterior surface of the maxilla.

25. Right ramus and posterior part of body of mandible, A64/IV/(7). This yellowish fragment consists of the lower part of the ramus and a short posterior portion of the body of a mandible, all showing very extensive gnawing. The alveolus of the third molar (M_3) is present and the tooth appears to have been lost post-mortem. The alveolus shows that the tooth was double-rooted. The height of the body at the level of M_3 is about 32 mm and the ramus is antero-posteriorly broad, being about 39 mm. The mandibular foramen lies about 2 cm posterior to, and at about the level of, M_3 and there is no development of a lingula; the mylohyoid groove is short. Most of the gonial angle region has been lost, but, from what remains, the region appears to have been well developed. The submandibular groove is fairly deep; the alveolar prominence and the mylohyoid line are prominent. The trigonum postmolare is clearly delimited.

26. Upper posterior part of left body of mandible, A64/N174.IV/(5). In this yellow-brown specimen the alveoli of the posterior molars (M_3 and M_2) and possibly of the first molar (M_1) are filled by alveolar bone. The mandibular fossa is very deep and the mylohyoid line very prominent. The bone shows signs of crushing and gnawing.

27. Mandibular symphyseal region, A64/IV/(5). This is a small fragment of the symphyseal region in which the upper and lower portions are missing.

The only features of note are the well-developed genial tubercles on the inner surface.

28. Left mandibular condyle, A64/IV/(5). A small yellowish condyle, 20 mm in breadth.

29. Right mandibular condyle, A64/VII/(4). A large yellowish specimen, badly damaged (breadth ± 27 mm).

30. Right frontal bone, A64/N174.IV/(5). A brown-coloured fragment including most of the frontal part of the bone. The specimen shows little development of the supercilliary ridges; the zygomatic trigone and glabella are mostly missing but would appear to have been only weakly developed. There is no trace of an ophryonic groove. The fragment is difficult to orient correctly, but it would seem that the forehead region must have receded markedly. There are no traces of frontal bosses; the temporal lines show moderate development. Most of the coronal suture region is present and was fused endocranially. At bregma the frontal bone projected posteriorly as seen in the Cohuna cranium.

31. Left parietal bone, A64/N255.XV/(6). This large yellow fragment includes most of the central part of a left parietal, the portions adjacent to the coronal and lambdoid sutures having been lost; the posterior third of the region of articulation with the left temporal bone can be seen. A small central fragment of the right parietal is also present. The sagittal suture between the left and right parietal bones is synostosed endo- and ecto-cranially, and ectocranially there is heaping of bone in two places. Parietal foramina are present bilaterally for emmissary veins; the temporal line on the left parietal is well developed. This specimen is noteworthy because of its considerable thickness: maximum 14 mm, average between temporal and mid-lines about 10 mm. Endocranially numerous small foramina can be seen piercing the inner table of bone. They are situated in the vascular grooves on the endocranial surface.

32. Permanent mandibular left lateral incisor (I_2, left), A64/IX/(5). This tooth is considerably damaged, the mesial quarter of the labial half of the crown and the whole labial half and distal quarter of the apical two-thirds of the residual part of the root have been lost. The portions of the root which are present have a thin mineral encrustation and the apical half is blackened throughout its substance; the crown shows slight ante-mortem spotted staining. The tooth has the typical characters of an I_2 and arch form indicates that it comes from the left side. Wear on the incisal edge is even (one facet) and quite considerable (dentine is exposed). The dimensions of the crown are: mesio-distal length 6.9 mm; labio-lingual breadth 7.0 mm. These dimensions match closely the only New Guinea specimen available for comparison, but they are larger than the mean values, although within the ranges, of the Aboriginal equivalents described by Campbell (1925).

The mesio-distal dimensions of this tooth and the three which follow are, of course, not the eruptive maximum dimensions, because of the varying degrees of occlusal and interstitial wear to which they have all been subjected. Further, the small numbers and varying degrees of wear of the New Guinea teeth with which comparison is made render those comparisons of limited value.

33. Maxillary right second premolar (P^2, right), A64/IX/(5). This tooth is undamaged, except for a small chip missing from the mesio-buccal part of the crown. The tooth shows very slight ante-mortem staining of the crown and there is slight mineral encrustation of the root, mainly on the mesial side. The overall contours of the crown and single root make the tooth clearly a P^2; the slightly more mesial position of the lingual cusp and the distal inclination of the root place it on the right side. Wear on the occlusal surface is considerable and dentine is exposed; interstitial facets are present mesially and distally. There are slight signs of erosion in the region of the distal cemento-enamel junction. This tooth has a mesio-distal length of 6.0 mm and a bucco-lingual breadth of 9.6 mm. The length dimension

is short compared to those of two New Guinea equivalents to which it was compared and also to the mean figures and range for Aborigines given by Campbell (1925); the breadth dimension is similar to that of the available New Guinea P^2 teeth and slightly narrower than the Aboriginal equivalents.

34. Mandibular right second premolar (P_2, right), A64/I/(7). This is an undamaged tooth showing slight mineral encrustation and colouring of the root and very slight staining of the crown. The cylindrical root and large crown, with markedly inrolled buccal surface, clearly indicate the tooth to be a P_2. The tooth shows large mesial and distal interstitial facets and the occlusal surface is worn flat, exposing the dentine. The distal inclination of the considerably worn occlusal surface implies that the tooth comes from the right side of the mandible. The measured dimensions of the tooth are: mesio-distal length 7.6 mm; bucco-lingual breadth 9.8 mm. The length is similar to that of the three available New Guinea specimens and also to the Aboriginal series described by Campbell (1925); the breadth is greater than that in the New Guinea specimens and just within the range of the Aboriginal equivalents.

35. Permanent maxillary left second molar (M^2, left), A64/XII/(4). The buccal roots and apical tip of the lingual root have been lost and there is slight damage to the distal part of the occlusal surface of the crown. The roots have a black encrustation and the crown has only very slight staining. The tooth shows a fair degree of wear, particularly on the lingual third of the crown, but dentine has not been exposed. There is a very large mesial and smaller distal interstitial wear-facet. The tooth is four-cusped and the mesio-buccal cusp is well developed, whilst the disto-lingual cusp shows slight reduction. The tooth is large, with a mesio-distal length of 11.8 mm and bucco-lingual breadth of 13.6 mm, which would tend to suggest its being a first molar (M^1), but the lack of divergence of the lingual root and the relative sizes of the cusps indicate more strongly that the tooth is almost certainly an M^2 of the left side. The tooth is slightly larger than the ranges for the dimensions of the equivalent tooth in 12 New Guinea specimens and slightly larger than the means, but within the ranges, of the Aboriginal equivalents in Campbell's (1925) series.

Axial skeleton

The fifteen fragments recovered from Aibura which come from various parts of the axial skeleton are mostly too fragmentary to be of much value and will only be briefly listed. There are also two uncertain specimens. There is no clear indication of the number of individuals represented, but it could be only one.

36-41. Six small fragments of thoracic vertebrae, A64/X/(4). One shows signs of charring.

42. Lower thoracic vertebral body fragment, A64/VII/(5).

43. Thoracic vertebral body fragment, A64/XI/(4).

44. A fairly complete lumbar vertebral body (L5), A64/85.X/(4).

45. Lumbar vertebral body fragment, A64/XI/(4). Slight blackening possibly due to charring.

46. Small fragment of a lumbar vertebral body, A64/X/(4).

47. Fragment of ala of sacrum, A64/X/(4).

48. Sacral fragment from right superolateral side, A64/XI/(4).

49. Sacral fragment, probably superolateral part, A64/IX/(6). Shows signs of gnawing.

50. Left superolateral part of manubrium sterni, A64/VII/(6).

51-2. Two specimens too small for identification, A64/VII/(5). One at least is possibly from a vertebral body.

Most of the above specimens have a basically brown colour, but three (48-50) are slightly lighter, no. 44 is much lighter and four specimens (39,40,45,47) are darker.

Upper limb

The upper limb fragments from Aibura are few in number and either small fragments or bones which are not especially informative.

53. Right clavicle, lateral half, A64/XV/(4). This is a yellowish-coloured specimen and the portion preserved is in reasonably good condition. The lateral supero-inferiorly flattened part of the specimen is slightly damaged but was clearly relatively small; the oval-shaped more medial part is slightly more substantial. Overall, the specimen would seem to have come from a small, lightly built individual, possibly young, female or both.

54. Head of left humerus, A64/35.XI/(3). This specimen comprises the major portion of the articular surface of the head of a left humerus. Two small parts of the adjacent shaft of the bone have been forced into the cancellous under-surface of the fragment. The articular surface of the specimen is coated with a thin, mostly black, mineral encrustation.

55. Small fragment, probably of head of humerus, A64/IV/(5).

56. Small fragment of long-bone shaft, possibly radius, A64/35.XI/(3).

57. Right scaphoid, A64/IV/(5). Yellowish, well preserved.

58. Right fourth metacarpal, A64/IV/(5). Brownish-yellow, proximal end slightly weathered.

59. Distal half of right first metacarpal, A64/IV/(5). Blackish, damaged fragment.

60. Proximal phalanx, first digit, right hand, A64/X/(4). Blackish mineral encrustation.

61. Proximal phalanx, probably third digit, A64/X/(4). Brownish, with blackish mineral encrustation.

62. Proximal phalanx, fourth or fifth digit, A64/VIII/(5). Dark brown in colour.

63. Proximal phalanx (proximal end lost), A64/XIV/(4). Yellow in colour.

64. Intermediate phalanx, epiphysis lost and distal end damaged, A64/XI/(4). Note that epiphysis fuses to shaft at about 17-19 years of age.

65. Proximal half of intermediate phalanx, A64/XIII/(1). Brownish.

Lower limb

The lower limb material recovered seems from more than one individual and although two long bones are present in most of their extent, one end is missing in each case and accurate stature determination is not possible.

66-9. Right tibia minus head, A64/85.X/(4). The four fragments comprising this specimen are well preserved and brownish-coloured. A few areas are covered with a blackish mineral encrustation. The bone shows no unusual features and clearly comes from an adult individual of substantial size: maximum length ± 35.5 cm; mid-shaft antero-posterior diameter ± 31.5 mm; mid-shaft medio-lateral diameter ± 20.5 mm; stature, based on adult European estimates, would be about 1625-1650 cm (Comas 1960). There are no squatting facets on the anterior lip of the inferior articular surface, but the inferior end of the medial malleolus is rather blunt.

70. Left tibia, proximal two-thirds, A64/38.XI/(3). A well preserved yellow specimen with a fairly thick, black mineral encrustation, particularly distally. This specimen probably comes from the same individual as fragments 66-9. The specimen agrees with these in many small anatomical

details and likewise suggests a substantial adult individual.   Platycnemic index 63.9, which is mesocnemic.   There is a 4 cm-long gnawed area on the postero-lateral part of the shaft.

71.   Left tibia, distal third but lacking distal end, A64/37.XI/(3).   A small
      fragment, with a thick, black, mineral encrustation, probably of the
distal part of 70.

72.   Left femur, proximal third, but no head, A64/229.I/(8).   A robust yellow
      fragment, in which the whole posterior surface shows extensive signs of
gnawing and of which the distal end is blackened, possibly as a result of
charring.

73.   Right talus, A64/IV/(7).   A brownish-coloured specimen of which the
      posterior part has been lost.

74.   Right talus, A64/85.X/(4).   A complete specimen with blackish
      encrustation.   Slightly larger than specimen 73 and showing no unusual
features.

75.   Right cuboid, A64/IX/(4).   Yellowish with some blackish encrustation.

76.   Left medial cuneiform, A64/XIII/(4).   Lateral half of the bone is missing,
      but the bone was clearly small.   Lower surface yellow, upper surface
blackened, possibly due to charring.

77.   Left lateral cuneiform, A64/IV/(5).   Badly damaged fragment.

78.   Tarsal bone, possibly cuboid fragment, A64/IV/(7).   Yellow.

79.   Tarsal fragment, probably calcaneum, A64/VII/(5).   Brown.

80.   Right second metatarsal, A64/X/(4).   Specimen completely covered by
      greyish encrustation.

81.   Left fifth metatarsal, A64/IV/(7).   Well preserved, brownish specimen.

82.   Proximal phalanx of right foot, A64/X/(4).   Small fragment of bone only,
      blackened, probably by fire.

83.   Proximal phalanx, left foot, second, possibly third digit, A64/VII/(7).
      Well preserved, brown-coloured bone.

84.   Proximal phalanx, first digit (hallux), left foot, A64/XI/(4).   Yellow
      with black encrustation.   Large specimen.

85.   Proximal part of second metatarsal, left foot, A64/IV/(5).   Yellowish
      fragment, considerably damaged.

86.   Left tibial fragment midshaft, A64/IV/(5).   Pale yellowish fragment with
      evidence of rodent gnawing.

Summary

     The 86 human bone fragments recovered from the Aibura cave are mostly small and few are well preserved.   Some show signs of weathering and others have a blackish mineral encrustation.   There are signs of probable rodent gnawing on about nine fragments (mostly of the skull) and about 11 fragments (eight from the skull) show blackening, which appears to be charring due to fire.   No obvious signs of pathology were found in any of the specimens, but the very thick parietal bone, no. 31, did suggest the possibility of Paget's Disease, until study of its measurements (and structure) indicated that the thickness was within the range of variation displayed by comparative New Guinea and Australian material.
     It is difficult to assess how many individuals are represented by the material.   From the upper limb, teeth and axial skeleton remains, it could be a single individual, but from the lower limb and skull fragments it is clear that the bones of at least two individuals are present.   Overall consideration of the material indicates a minimum of two individuals, but the individual age differences indicated by epiphyses at the one extreme and

158

fusing of the parietal bones at the other, suggest that one or more additional individuals could be present. Archaeological association does not assist greatly in assessing the number of individuals represented.

With regard to the sex of the individuals represented, the temporal fragment with the small mastoid process (no. 19), the small palate (no. 24) and the small mandibular condyle (no. 28), each point to a female (or young) individual, whilst the large tibiae (nos. 66-9,70,71), the thick parietal (no. 31) and the large mandibular ramus (no. 25) and condyle (no. 29) each suggest a male, probably large.

The most significant fragments with regard to race determination are the heavy thick parietal bone (no. 31) and the receding forehead of specimen no. 30. Insufficient comparative material is available from New Guinea to make any accurate assessment, but New Guinea skulls with similar morphology are present in the collection of the Department of Anatomy, University of Sydney. Further, it is of interest to note that these two Aibura specimens can be matched almost exactly in the Aboriginal Australian material in that same collection.

Acknowledgements

It is my pleasure to thank A.B. Bailey, Department of Anatomy, University of Sydney, for assistance with comparative material and identifications of the above specimens.

L. Freedman
Department of Anatomy,
University of Sydney, 1966

Archaeological Comment (J.P.W.)

During excavation, the following associations suggested themselves; the bones comprising them are referred to by their number in the listing above: 1-8, 31, 53; 54, 56, 70, 71; 9-16, 25, 34, 73, 78 and questionably 26, 30 and 72; 44, 66-9, 74 and questionably 26, 30 and 72. Unfortunately a large proportion of the material (54 of the 86 specimens) was not detected in the field and it is only located to a specific square metre and to a specific level within this.

Later assessment, made in the light of the stratigraphy, overall distribution of remains and Dr Freedman's identifications suggest that remains of at least three individuals are present. There seem to be three clusters of fragments in the site; they are set out by square/(level) and the numbered bones within these units.

1. X/(4), nos 36-41, 44, 46-7, 60-1, 66-9, 74, 80, 82
    XI/(3)-(4), nos 43, 45, 48, 54, 56, 64, 70-1, 84
    XII/(4), no. 35
    XIII/(4), no. 76
    XIV/(4), no. 63
    XV/(4), nos 1-8, 53

2. IV/(5), nos 19-20, 26-8, 30, 55, 57-9, 77, 81, 85-6
    VII/(4)-(6), nos 18, 21, 24, 29, 42, 50-2, 79
    ?VIII/(5), nos 17, 22-3, 62

3. I/(7)-(8), nos 34, 72
    IV/(7), nos 9-16, 25, 73, 78

In addition there are a few fragments which are not definitely associated with any one cluster. These associations seem to be in line with the identifications, which suggest a few individuals. So much of the bone is fragmentary that most human remains were probably deposited in a fragmentary or at least dis-articulated state, i.e. as a secondary burial.

APPENDIX 3

THE MINERALOGY OF THE POTTERY FINDS AT AIBURA

The 16 sherds of pottery found in the excavation at Aibura included only two undiagnostic rims. Because of the absence of diagnostic morphological characteristics, it was decided to investigate the mineral inclusions in the sherds. These inclusions can under favourable circumstances suggest a place or a general area of origin.

Six sherds from the Aibura site and a further six from pots of known origin were chosen for examination. All the sherds are coarse, more or less oxidised earthenware of varying thickness. Thin sections were prepared for examination under the petrological microscope. The minerals were then identified and their proportions determined with a point-counter on five of the thin sections.

Thin sections from sherds nos XV/3, VI/3, 22.IX/3 and VIII/3 and from a modern pot collected in the Kainantu area by Coutts (1967:482) show that all are made from clay which was lean by nature. The natural inclusions are badly sorted and range in size from 0.1-1.5 mm. They consist of granite and quartzite rock fragments and fragments of weathered K-Na feldspar, quartz and occasional green hornblende. They do not contain mica or other heavy minerals. This pottery must therefore originate in a fairly specific locality which has a residual deposit of clay away from schists, phyllites and basic rocks. The only area where these conditions may possibly be satisfied is that mapped by McMillan and Malone (1960:pl.1) as the Bena Bena formation to the west and north of Kainantu. This is essentially the same region which Watson (1955:121) describes as the Agarabi language area. However, the pottery described by her is very much thicker, up to 1.5 cm, than the excavated sherds, which ranged from 3 to 6 mm.

Thin sections from sherds XIV/3 and 239.XIII/3 are of an entirely different type. These show a matrix of clay with an added, well sorted filler consisting of fresh angular pyroxene, feldspar and rounded basalt rock fragments. Sherd no. XIV/3 contains, in addition to these, occasional calcite shell fragments and one test of a foram, indicating that a beach sand was used. Beach sand which answers this description is and was used by the potters along the Madang coast (Smith 1967:11), which is backed by a large area of Upper Tertiary basic volcanics. Sherds from the island of Yabob which were examined showed the same mixture of clay and mineral fragments.

Three Aibura thin sections, one from a Madang (Yabob) pot and one from a modern Kainantu pot had the percentage of their constituents determined.

Table 168   Comparison of constituents of selected pottery

(a) Aibura and Madang

Origin	Clay	Feldspar and quartz	Pyroxene	Basalt fragments	Shell
AIB XIV/3	64.3	12.1	13.6	7.9	2.2
AIB XIII/3	61.0	17.3	12.6	9.2	-
YABOB 5	68.4	17.6	5.8	2.9	5.4

(b) Aibura and Kainantu

Origin	Clay	Quartz	Feldspar	Rock	Hornblende
AIB VIII/3	54.8	23.3	12.7	9.4	-
KAINANTU 2	58.8	25.0	10.4	5.2	0.8

In each of the above two classes the similarity of sherd to modern pot is obvious. Furthermore, the well-sorted mineral inclusions in the Madang-type pots would seem to have been added by a potter using the proportions of one handful of beach sand to two of clay.

Sherds with similar feldspar-pyroxene-basalt inclusions, but unsorted and without.shell, may be expected from pots made on the southern flanks of the Finisterre Ranges, north of the Ramu River. However, the sherds would be thicker and they would not contain such a constant proportion of mineral to clay. Pots are known to be made in the Mari area (H. Holzknecht, pers. comm.) and in the Nahu and Rawa areas (Schmitz 1960:81). These pots are very similar in shape to those found in the Eastern Highlands but no pots were available for thin-section work.

One other modern pot-type was thin-sectioned. The pot was from the Azera area in the Markham valley and is of the type described by Holzknecht (1957:104). The clay matrix in this case contains a large amount of very weathered material, which seems to consist of rounded rock fragments completely altered to cohesive books of clay. These pellets seem to be a natural part of the clay and not an added filler. The source of this clay may be either serpentinized basic rocks found along the upper stretches of the Wanton River or basic rocks of the Saruwaged Ranges, north of the Markham River. No excavated sherds were seen to have been made of this material however.

The evidence provided by the mineralogy of the sherds points to at least two different origins for the pottery found at Aibura. One is possibly a local product, while the other is almost certainly traded over very rugged terrain from the Madang coast, 80 miles away (130 km).

C.A. Key,
Department of Anthropology and Sociology,
Research School of Pacific Studies, ANU, 1967
Revised 1969

APPENDIX 4

THE FORMATION OF THE DEPOSITS AT
KAFIAVANA : THE RESULTS OF A SEDIMENTARY ANALYSIS

The soil samples were examined according to the various methods described by E. Schmid (1958, 1963). First the samples were washed (elutriated) to show the grain size of material finer than 2 mm in diameter. This material was divided into six size fractions. The coarser elements (>2 mm) were analysed by sieving into four size fractions. The elutriated and sieved material was inspected microscopically to look for the different elements which composed the soil. Chemical tests were used to define the proportions of $CaCO_3$ (lime), phosphate and humus (Schmid 1958:34-6).

The results obtained are given in table 169. The fourth and fifth columns show the percentage occurrence of the different grain-size groups in the elutriating (<2 mm) and sieving tests (>2 mm). The sixth column gives the percentage of $CaCO_3$. The seventh and eighth columns indicate the phosphate and humus contents by reference to colour-values (Schmid 1958:35-6). The third column sets out the Munsell soil colours of dry samples inspected in the laboratory.

All these results have been compared and discussed in the light of experience gained in interpreting similar material from Western and Central Europe and Northern America including Alaska. In the evaluation of these soils special emphasis was laid on the granulometric analysis of the soil material.

General Principles

1. As a general rule it may be said that a high percentage of clay (fraction I, <0.02 mm) may result from intense chemical destruction of rock or loose sediments or from sedimentation in still water.

   The presence or absence of $CaCO_3$ and the nature and type of coarse elements will allow a choice between these alternatives to be made.

2. Aeolian sedimentation has occurred where there is a very high percentage of fraction II (0.02-0.05 mm) and where fraction I is between 50 and 100% of fraction II. The relative quantities of coarser fractions allow a distinction to be made between material of a loessic character and drift sand.

3. If there are similar percentages of fractions I (<0.02 mm), II (0.02-0.05 mm), III (0.05-0.1 mm) and IV+V+VI (0.1-2.0 mm), sedimentation of very fine grains in a quiet bay of a river valley or by flooding is indicated. In German this is called *Auelehm* ('ewe-clay').

4. The carbonate content of a soil may be the same now as at the time of soil deposition, or it may have been lessened by secondary dissolution or increased by infiltration. Traces of the different processes are visible microscopically.

5. The phosphate content of a soil is generally increased by human or animal activity, due to the decomposition of faeces and wasted meat in the soil. The humus content, however, may be due to the autochthonous formation of soil or to man or animals bringing plants into the shelter and allowing the rotting remains to accumulate there.

   In a humid climate both phosphate and humates may be increased due to infiltration of the lower strata from those above, though the amount of material infiltrated depends on the force of the washing-in process. The humus content may at times be reduced by the burning out of organic material by strong fires made in a pit.

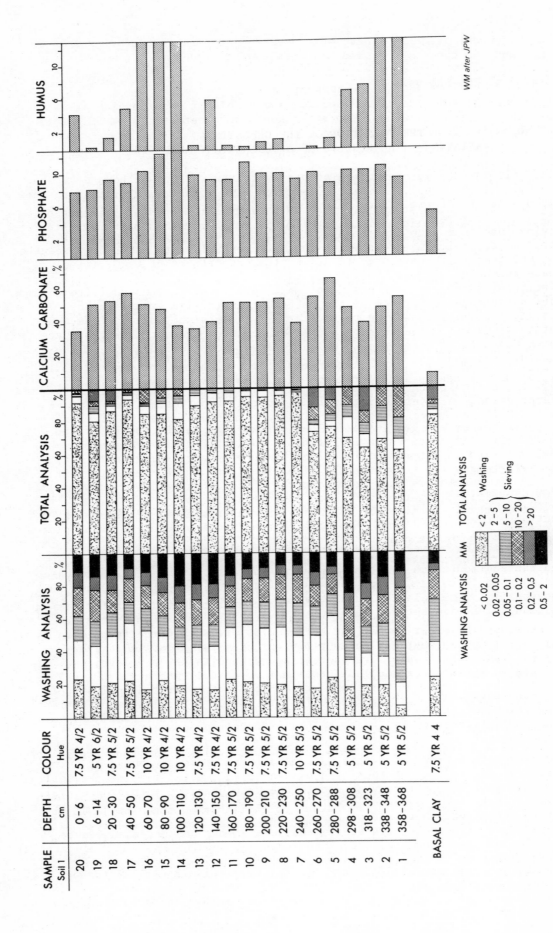

Table 169   Kafíavana: results of sedimentary analysis

163

These general principles have been used in determining the origins of the sediments and the processes of sedimentation at Kafiavana.

The Results of the Analysis

There are 21 soil samples. No. 21 is a sample of sterile clay at the base of the section, while nos 1-20 are taken from alternate 10 cm of a soil column, numbering from the bottom up.

Basal clay This material was also found between the cultural layers and the rock wall at the rear of the site. The elutriation analysis shows that there are almost equal percentages of fractions I, II and III (<0.02, 0.02-0.05, 0.05-0.1 mm); this percentage distribution is similar to that found in the *Auelehm* (ewe-clay) in Western Europe. In addition, the unusual presence of manganese and probably limonite concretions in most fractions also suggests that this soil was sedimented in water, combined with occasional drying.

Some grains, including some smaller pebbles, are covered in places with manganese but are normally clean. This, the presence of many quartz crystals in the fine-grained fractions, the fact that many small pieces of limestone are slightly corroded and the low content of $CaCO_3$ (9%) confirm that this sediment was deposited in a special way. It was probably formed by non-autochthonous material, which might even be of volcanic origin, carried in by water with a low lime content. The deposit being close to the rock wall, some other materials, such as pieces of limestone, pieces of naturally broken siliceous minerals, small fragments of animal bones and egg and snail shells, were also easily incorporated. It seems very likely that this sediment was formed by repeated floodings and we think it probable that it is a remainder of pluvial times.

Zone A Comprising samples 1-4 and 75 cm thick, this is the lowest of the five different soil zones we have distinguished in the cultural layers.

Sample 1 shows no trace of immediate human presence. Its small clay grains are strongly stuck together by lime sinter and the humus content is high. The impression is that decayed parts of the rock wall were deposited under wet conditions together with lots of rotted plants.

In samples 2-4 fraction VI (0.5-2 mm) increases steadily. The high percentage of burnt clay lumps shows that the site was used as a living place. In samples 3-4 the humus content decreases.

Zone B Comprising samples 5-11 and 1.4 m thick, this is remarkable for the high proportion of fraction II (0.02-0.05 mm) throughout. In this the sediment is very similar to loess. However, microscopic examination does not reveal the large amounts of quartz which characterises loess. Rather, it is very similar to the clayish sediment which is called 'parna' in Australia. Woldstedt (1965:122 after Butler and Hutton 1956) says of parna formations that in the main they must have been blown out of existing soils during periods of dryness. We are sure that this sediment is not a volcanic aeolian sediment since these do not contain lime at all, whereas $CaCO_3$ values for the aeolian sediment at Kafiavana are 40-66%. Compare the analysis of pumice sediments at Jaguar Cave, Idaho (Schmid 1966). The low humus content makes it probable that sedimentation was rather rapid and there were only a few plants rotting on the site.

Zone C This comprises samples 12-14 and is 60 cm thick. In the material of <2 mm the coarser fractions are mainly made up of burnt clay. A high intensity of human occupation in sample 14 is indicated by the coarser fraction in the sieving test and an extraordinarily high phosphate content. The high quantity of humus in sample 14 may be due to infiltration from sample 15, but at least part could have been brought in by man, e.g. for a fireplace. It is remarkable that the small pebble grains present in the upper part of zone B and in zones D and E are absent here.

Zone D Comprising samples 15-17 and 60 cm thick, this is similar to Zone B in its high percentage of fraction II (0.02-0.05 mm), although sample 15 is transitional. Apparently a sort of parna formation was again in progress, though for a shorter time and with the deposit being more intensely affected by human activity. The high humus content of levels 14-16 may indicate that the surface during sedimentation was seasonally open to the growth of plants for a longer time, the rotting of these plants producing humus. The high quantity of phosphate in samples 14-16 does not contradict this as the phosphate is of primary origin, i.e. is the product of human occupation during the formation of these sediments.

The section photographs show several big (up to 20 cm) angular stones at this level. Like the small pieces of limestone in the samples, they originated most probably from the rock wall. If they were not deposited by man, they confirm the climatic peculiarities of this time.

Zone E Comprising samples 18-20 and 35 cm thick, this is not a unit on the basis of either the mechanical or chemical analysis. It seems likely that sedimentation has been effected by human influences and the decomposition of the parent rock.

Observations on Different Ingredients in the Samples

The microscopic inspection of residues from the elutriation and sieving tests showed the sediments had the following peculiarities:

1. Roots of recent age are present down to sample 3; they are enclosed by rootlet tubes which occur alone in samples 1 and 2.

2. There is a high proportion of elements with a diameter of >10 mm or even >20 mm in Zone A. They consist of clayish lumps of sinter and superficially corroded pieces of limestone, some of which are covered on the lower side with a grey lime sinter.

3. Biggish flakes of siliceous minerals (>10 mm) are numerous in the two lowest samples of Zone B. Very small flakes which can be identified even in fraction IV (0.1-0.2 mm) are present in all samples from 3 onwards. These very fine flakes indicate that retouching work was done on the site. Quartzite, rock crystals and agates are the most prominent varieties of siliceous minerals present.

4. The small clay lumps present in all zones from sample 2 upward mostly have a rough surface. Their cohesiveness comes partly from burning and partly from the lime sinter. The clay was apparently frequently intermingled with short chopped plants, the impressions of which are preserved in the lumps.

5. Fragments of bones and teeth are found in all layers and partly burnt fragments in all samples except 1 and 19. The species of animals cannot be determined but the teeth in the basal clay resemble those of rodents (Appendix 5).

6. Other remains of animals include small pieces of egg shell and fragments of snail shell. The egg shells may have fallen naturally from nests above. They are present as single and small plates in all samples (including the basal clay) except 1, 17, 18 and 20. Thin fragments of small snail shells clearly record an autochthonous fauna. They occur in the basal clay, Zone A, samples 5, 6 and 10 of Zone B, samples 15 and 17 of D and 18 and 20 of Zone E. This suggests that an analysis of snails could reveal the local climate and its fluctuations. For example a snail from level 1 resembles the Western European *Goniodiscus*, which is a forest dweller.

7. Sixteen small fish vertebrae were found in samples 4, 13, 15 and 16; the specimens in 15 and 16 were partly burnt.

8. Charcoal occurs only in very small pieces and is not found in all samples. It is present only in sample 1 (Zone A) and is completely missing from Zone B. Above this it occurs only in samples 12, 14, 16, 17, 19 and 20.

Summary

The samples were too small to give a numerical expression of the intensity of human occupation. The presence of man is, however, confirmed by the small flakes of siliceous materials in sample 3 upwards and the small burnt lumps of clay which were partly interspersed with plant impressions in sample 2 upwards.

The basal clay was probably settled as *Auelehm* during the last pluvial period. Some volcanic material may have been included in it.

During the formation of Zone A human influence became more important. These layers were deposited under a humid climate and include disintegrated parts of the rock wall. Perhaps this documents the last oscillation at the end of the pluvial period.

The sediments of Zone B can be defined as a sort of parna, i.e. an aeolian sedimentation of soil particles. There must have been a dry period, we think during the period of deglaciation at the end of the Pleistocene. Only in a dry climate could enough ice be melted in the New Guinea Highlands to make the glaciers retreat. Further, we know that in the northern hemisphere the pluvial period ended at about 10,000 BP (Behre 1966:76). As a hypothesis, we suggest that this immediately post-glacial time, after 10,000 BP, would have been the best period for the deposition of the aeolian sediments in Zone B. The sedimentary analysis therefore confirms the range of the typological and radiocarbon dating and suggests the environment which prevailed at that time. It should be possible to find further proofs of the dryness of the Zone B period in the pollen and animal remains. The snails could be used as an indicator of local climate.

The wet phase of Zone C can be compared with the Atlantic period of the northern hemisphere. It is followed by a short and temporarily dry period with the formation of parna, our Zone D. It is not yet possible to give an absolute date for this. Our knowledge of post-pluvial climatic change in New Guinea is too limited yet to comment on the radiocarbon date of about 4500 BP. However, it must be remembered that the site may have been abandoned for a while at the end of this dry period. We consider that Zone E was formed during a more humid climatic phase.

Table 170 summarises the relevant results of our analysis.

Table 170   Kafiavana: interpretation of sedimentary analysis

Depth in m	Zone	Sediment	Climate	Time before present geological	radiocarbon
0.35	E sediments		humid		
0.95	D with	parna-like aeolian	temporarily dry		c4500
1.55	C cultural		humid	7500	
2.95	B remains	parna-like aeolian	dry	10,000	9000->9500
3.70	A		humid		
	Basal clay	semi-fluviatile: *Auelehm*	pluvial		

E. Schmid and I Grüninger,
Laboratorium für Urgeschichte,
Universität Basel, 1966
Translated by C. Kaufmann,
Museum für Völkerkunde, Basel.

Comments

We consider that while the report gives a sound and useful picture of the soils in the shelter, we do not think that it provides adequate evidence for the inferences which are made about either the climate or the local environmental conditions under which deposition occurred. We do not believe that principles derived from the study of soils in temperate Europe and America should be used, without consideration of local conditions, in tropical New Guinea. We agree with the authors that climatic inferences may be better drawn when more evidence from several disciplines is available but consider the present attempt is premature. We consider that the proferred interpretation is simply one among a number of possible explanations of the data.

We point specifically to the following:

1. While the precipitation of manganese and limonite concretions does imply oscillations in the quantity of locally available water, they are not necessarily deposited in water. Even if water were present, this need only reflect very local conditions.

2. Although the report refers only to 'parna-like' soils, it would perhaps be better simply to use the term 'aeolian'.

'Parna' in Australia is not a uniform sediment. Several rather different materials have been called parna: it is defined not only by its particle size but also by such features as its stratigraphic relations with sand dunes, fluviatile deposits etc. Several parnas are superimposed in some areas and were formed in different periods.

A careful and accurate description of the 'parna' referred to in the report is clearly necessary. For example, in Widgelli parna the clay fraction (<0.002 mm) ranges from 29% to 69% (mean 59%) of the material <2 mm in size (Butler and Hutton 1956). This is considerably more clay than in *any* Kafiavana sediment. One might also wonder where, in the Highlands, possible sources of parna occur.

3. The report refers to the large angular rocks in Zone D as supporting an interpretation of dry conditions. Other conditions such as crystal wedging (hydration, salt sprengung, etc.) leading to erosion and disintegration of the rock wall would be equally likely to bring down geometrically *shaped* rocks. Further, since the authors have not handled these boulders, their judgement as to the angularity and sharpness of their *edges* must be tentative.

4. It is not clear that glaciers in the Highlands would only melt in a dry climate. Studies in some other parts of the world show that ablation by warm rain is at times a more important cause of glacial retreat than melting by the sun. We know too little about local conditions in the Highlands to make a generalisation about this.

5. From the table it appears that a high percentage of fine silty sediment (<0.05 mm) tends to be correlated with a high percentage of $CaCO_3$ (see especially samples 5, 17). If the finer sediment is in fact aeolian, it is difficult to explain the presence of more $CaCO_3$. The correlation of these two things tends to suggest that local seepage within the shelter has brought down both fine sediment and lime; the variation would therefore be due to local and not large-scale effects.

J.N. Jennings and R.M. Frank,
Department of Geography,
Research School of Pacific Studies, ANU, 1967

APPENDIX 5

FAUNA FROM THE BASAL CLAY AT KAFIAVANA

The only families represented in this sample are Macropodidae, Phalangeridae and Muridae.   Both modern and extinct forms occur.

Murid material is most abundant, being represented by more than 20 incisors, a cheek tooth and post-cranial elements.   Both large ('giant') and small rodents are found in the fauna.   The cheek tooth can be assigned to *Rattus*. Little is known of the antiquity of the murids in New Guinea.   A small murid is known from the Pliocene, and Simpson (1961) has speculated that the murids must have been in or passed through the island since the Miocene.

A phalangerid mandible assignable to *Petaurus'* is the sole representative of this family.   *Petaurus* is the sugar glider extant today along the Australian eastern seaboard, Cape York, Arnhem Land and in the forests of New Guinea.

The Macropodidae are represented by a single broken upper molar, probably M^2 or M^3.   No definite assignment can be made for this tooth which has similarities to the genera *Protemnodon* and *Sthenurus*.   The stage of evolution of this macropod is difficult to assess on this fragmentary tooth.   It is low crowned, has a narrow steep median valley and weakly developed mid-link and the labial end of the median valley is blocked by anterior and posterior spurs from the metacone and paracone.   The posterior cingulum is small and confined to the back of the tooth.

Both *Protemnodon* and *Sthenurus* are extinct today.   *Protemnodon* is the predominant macropod in the Pliocene of New Guinea (Plane 1967), while *Sthenurus* has not been reported from the island.   In Australia *Protemnodon* is the predominant macropod in Pleistocene deposits (Stirton 1963) and is abundant in the Pliocene; it has a questionable record back in the late Miocene (Woodburne 1967).   *Sthenurus* occurs only south of a line from Chinchilla (Queensland) to Lake Eyre: it occurs in deposits of possible Pliocene age and is abundant in the Pleistocene (Tedford 1966).   Both *Sthenurus* and *Protemnodon* are grazing rather than browsing animals and the presence of either can be taken to indicate the existence of open grassland.

It is difficult to imagine how the macropod tooth may have been introduced into the deposit.   A carnivore's den seems to be unlikely since we know of no carnivore large enough to have preyed on a macropod which was probably as large as the living red kangaroo.   Human activity is ruled out since the basal clay predates human occupation.

It should be noted that this specimen may possibly be derived from older material since the type of permineralization seems to differ from that of the other specimens.   Were it not for this, a Pleistocene age would be appropriate for the fauna and still seems most likely.

M.D. Plane,
Vertebrate Palaeontologist,
Bureau of Mineral Resources, Geology and Geophysics,
Canberra, 1966

APPENDIX 6

POLLEN ANALYSIS OF SOME SAMPLES FROM KAFIAVANA

Four samples were submitted.   Their soil column reference numbers and depths below the surface are:

20 :   0-10   cm
18 :   22-32   cm
17 :   42-52   cm
 9 : 200-210 cm

Analysis of Coarser Material

All samples were made up of clay and rock fragments of various sizes. Charcoal was present in all, abundant in 20.   Plant fibres and rootlets were common in 9 and 17, few in 18 and absent from 20.

Pollen Extraction

Two main methods, and some modifications of these, were used for extraction (Faegri and Iversen 1964).

1. HF method: material treated with KOH (potassium hydroxide), HF (hydrofluoric acid), followed by acetolysis.

2. Gravity separation method: material dispersed in sodium polyphosphate, frothed with polyvinyl alcohol followed by ultrasonic agitation and ZnBr (zinc bromide) flotation; followed by acetolysis.

The latter method was the only one which gave results.   In this case a 10 gm sample of 20 gave a recovery of 100+ grains, showing that while pollen was present it was in very low concentrations.   About seven pollen types were present, together with a few spores.   Some Myrtaceae and Gramineae were identified along with one grain each of *Casuarina* and *Wahlenbergia*.   No *Ipomoea batatas* was seen.

For better results modification of the gravity separation method is required, plus some method of reducing the carbon content.

One possible explanation for the low concentration of pollen is the amount of burning which has obviously taken place.   An oxidizing atmosphere must be present at these times and destroy most of the pollen.

J.M. Wheeler and W.H. Litchfield,
Department of Geography,
Research School of Pacific Studies, ANU, 1966

BIBLIOGRAPHY

Adam, L. 1953 The discovery of the Vierkantbeil or quadrangular adze head in the Eastern Central Highlands of New Guinea. *Mankind* 4(10):411-23

Allen, J. 1970 Prehistoric agricultural systems in the Wahgi valley: a further note. *Mankind* 7(3):177-83

Barrau, J. 1958 *Subsistence agriculture in Melanesia*. Honolulu: Bernice P. Bishop Museum, Bulletin 219

Bartlett, H.K. 1964 Note on flint implements found near Nipa, central Papuan highlands. *Records of the South Australian Museum* 14:669-73

Behre, K.E. 1966 Untersuchungen zur spätglazialen und frühpostglazialen Vegetationsgeschichte Ostfrieslands. *Eiszeitalter und Gegenwart* 17:66-84

Berndt, R.M. 1954 Contemporary significance of prehistoric stone objects in the eastern Central Highlands of New Guinea. *Anthropos* 49:553-87

Binford, L.R. and S.R. Binford 1966 A preliminary analysis of functional variability in the Mousterian of Levallois facies. Pp 238-95 of Clark, J.D. and F.C. Howell (eds) *Recent studies in palaeoanthropology*. *American Anthropologist* 68(2) part 2, Special Publication

Blackwood, B. 1950 *The technology of a modern stone age people in New Guinea*. Oxford: Pitt Rivers Museum, Occasional Papers in Technology 3

Bordes, F. 1961 *Typologie du Paléolithique Ancien et Moyen*. Bordeaux: Université de Bordeaux, Institut de Préhistoire, Mémoire 1

Brookfield, H.C. 1964 The ecology of Highland settlement: some suggestions. Pp 20-38 of Watson, J.B. (ed) *New Guinea: the Central Highlands*. *American Anthropologist* 66(4), part 2, Special Publication

────   and D. Hart 1966 *Rainfall in the tropical southwest Pacific*. Canberra: Australian National University, Research School of Pacific Studies, Department of Geography, Publication G/3 (1966).

────   and J.P. White 1968 Revolution or evolution in the prehistory of the New Guinea Highlands: a seminar report. *Ethnology* 7:43-52

Bulmer, R. 1967 Why is the cassowary not a bird? A problem of zoological taxonomy among the Karam·of the New Guinea Highlands. *Man* (n.s.)2:5-25

────   and S. 1962 Figurines and other stones of power among the Kyaka of central New Guinea. *Journal of the Polynesian Society* 71:192-208

Bulmer, S. n.d. *Report on archaeological fieldwork in the New Guinea Highlands, October 1959 to May 1960*. Auckland: University of Auckland, Department of Anthropology, mimeo

—— 1964a Prehistoric stone implements from the New Guinea Highlands. *Oceania* 34(4):246-68

—— 1964b Radiocarbon dates from New Guinea. *Journal of the Polynesian Society* 73:327-8

—— 1966a *The prehistory of the Australian New Guinea Highlands*. Auckland: University of Auckland, MA thesis (unpublished)

—— 1966b Pig bone from two archaeological sites in the New Guinea Highlands. *Journal of the Polynesian Society* 75:504-5

—— and R. 1964 The prehistory of the Australian New Guinea Highlands. Pp 39-76 of Watson, J.B. (ed) *New Guinea: the Central Highlands. American Anthropologist* 66(4), part 2, Special Publication

Butler, B.E. and J.T. Hutton 1956 Parna in the Riverine Plain of south-eastern Australia and the soils thereon. *Australian Journal of Agricultural Research* 7:536-53

Campbell, T.D. 1925 *The dentition and palate of the Australian Aboriginal*. Adelaide: University of Adelaide, Publication under the Keith Sheridan Foundation no. 1

Chang Kwang-chih and M. Stuiver 1966 Recent advances in the prehistoric archaeology of Formosa. *Proceedings of the National Academy of Sciences* (Washington) 55:539-43

Chappell, J. 1966 Stone axe factories in the Highlands of East New Guinea. *Proceedings of the Prehistoric Society* (n.s.) 32:96-121

Childe, V.G. 1956 *Piecing together the past*. London: Routledge and Kegan Paul

Clark, J.D.G. 1954 *Excavations at Star Carr*. Cambridge: Cambridge University Press

Cole, S. 1964 *The prehistory of East Africa*. London: Weidenfeld and Nicolson

Comas, J. 1960 *Manual of physical anthropology* (rev.edn). Springfield (Illinois): Charles C. Thomas

Coon, C.S. 1951 *Cave explorations in Iran, 1949*. Philadelphia: University of Pennsylvania, University Museum, Museum monographs

Cornwall, I.W. 1958 *Soils for the archaeologist*. London: Phoenix House

Coutts, P.J.F. 1967 Pottery of Eastern New Guinea and Papua. *Mankind* 6(10):482-8

Davidson, J. (ed) 1961 A guide to the description of adzes: by members of a study group of the Auckland University Archaeological Society. *New Zealand Archaeological Association Newsletter* 4(3):6-10 (117-21 of reprint of vol.4)

Dow, D.B. and M.D. Plane 1965 *The geology of the Kainantu goldfields*. Canberra: Department of National Development, Bureau of Mineral Resources, Geology and Geophysics, Report 79

Faegri, K. and J. Iversen 1964 *Testbook of pollen analysis*. Copenhagen: Munksgaard

Gardner, R. and K.G. Heider 1968 *Gardens of war*. New York: Random House

Glover, I.C. 1971 Prehistoric research in Timor. Pp 158-81 of Mulvaney, D.J. and J. Golson (eds) *Aboriginal man and environment in Australia*. Canberra: Australian National University Press

Golson, J. 1972 The Pacific Islands and their prehistoric inhabitants. Pp 5-33 of Ward, R.G. (ed) *Man in the Pacific Islands: essays on geographical change in the Pacific Islands*. Oxford: Clarendon Press

——— R.J. Lampert, J.M. Wheeler and W.R. Ambrose 1967 A note on carbon dates for horticulture in the New Guinea Highlands. *Journal of the Polynesian Society* 76:369-71

Grove, D.S. 1947 *Patrol Report KI, Kainantu, 14 August*. Kainantu: Department of District Administration, Sub-District Office, MS

Haantjens, H.A. (ed) 1970 *Lands of the Goroka - Mount Hagen area, Territory of Papua and New Guinea*. Canberra: Commonwealth Scientific and Industrial Research Organisation, Land Research Series no. 27

Heizer, R.F. 1960 Physical analysis of habitation residues. Pp 93-157 of Heizer, R.F. and S.F. Cook (eds) *The application of quantitative methods in archaeology*. New York: Wenner-Gren Foundation for Anthropological Research, Viking Fund Publication in Anthropology no. 28

Higgs, E.S. 1962 Fauna. Pp 271-4 of Rodden, R.J. Excavations at the Early Neolithic site at Nea Nikomedeia, Greek Macedonia (1961 season). *Proceedings of the Prehistoric Society* (n.s.) 28:267-88

——— and J.P. White 1963 Autumn killing. *Antiquity* 37:282-9

Holzknecht, K. 1957 Über Töpferei und Tontrommeln der Azera in Ost-Neuguinea. *Zeitschrift für Ethnologie* 82:97-111

Inskeep, R.R. 1959 A Late Stone Age camping-site in the upper Zambezi valley. *South African Archaeological Bulletin* 14:91-6

Jones, R. 1966 A speculative archaeological sequence for north-west Tasmania. *Records of the Queen Victoria Museum, Launceston* 25:1-12

Kigoshi, K. and H. Kobayashi 1966 Gakushuin natural radiocarbon measurements V. *Radiocarbon* 8:54-73

King, J.E. 1962 Report on animal bones. Pp 355-60 of Wymer, J.J. Excavations at the Maglemosian sites at Thatcham, Berkshire, England. *Proceedings of the Prehistoric Society* (n.s.) 28:329-61

Lampert, R.J. 1966 *Archaeological reconnaissance in Papua and New Guinea: 1966*. Canberra: Australian National University, Department of Anthropology and Sociology, mimeo

——— 1967 Horticulture in the New Guinea Highlands: C14 dating. *Antiquity* 41:307-8

Laurie, E.M.O. and J.R. Hill 1954 *List of land mammals of New Guinea, Celebes and adjacent islands.* London: British Museum (Natural History)

McCarthy, F.D. 1964 The archaeology of the Capertee valley, New South Wales. *Records of the Australian Museum* 26(6):197-246

———   1967 *Australian Aboriginal stone implements.* Sydney: Australian Museum

Macintosh, N.W.G., R.J. Walsh and O. Kooptzoff 1958 The blood groups of the native inhabitants of the Western Highlands, New Guinea. *Oceania* 28(3):173-98

McMillan, N.J. and E.J. Malone 1960 *The geology of the eastern Central Highlands of New Guinea.* Canberra: Department of National Development, Bureau of Mineral Resources, Geology and Geophysics, Report 48

Martin, P.S. 1967 Pleistocene overkill. Pp 75-120 of Martin, P.S. and H.E. Wright Jr (eds) *Pleistocene Extinctions.* New Haven and London: Yale University Press

Mason, R. 1962 *Prehistory of the Transvaal.* Johannesburg: Witwatersrand University Press

Matthews, J.M. 1964 *The Hoabinhian in South East Asia and elsewhere.* Canberra: Australian National University, PhD thesis (unpublished)

———   1965 Stratigraphic disturbance: the human element. *Antiquity* 39:295-8

Movius, H.L. Jr 1954-5 Palaeolithic archaeology in southern and eastern Asia, exclusive of India. *Journal of World History* 2:257-82, 520-53

Mulvaney, D.J. 1966 The prehistory of the Australian Aborigine. *Scientific American* 214(3):84-93

———   1969 *The prehistory of Australia.* London: Thames and Hudson

———   and E.B. Joyce 1965 Archaeological and geomorphological investigations on Mt Moffatt station, Queensland, Australia. *Proceedings of the Prehistoric Society* (n.s.) 31:147-212

Piggott, S. 1959 *Approach to archaeology.* London: A. and C. Black

Plane, M.D. 1967 *Stratigraphy and vertebrate fauna of the Otibanda formation, New Guinea.* Canberra: Department of National Development, Bureau of Mineral Resources, Geology and Geophysics, Bulletin 86

Polach, H.A. and J. Golson 1966 *Collection of specimens for radiocarbon dating and interpretation of results.* Canberra: Australian Institute of Aboriginal Studies, Manual no. 2

———   J. Golson, J.F. Lovering and J.J. Stipp 1968 ANU radiocarbon date list II. *Radiocarbon* 10:179-99

———   J.J. Stipp, J. Golson and J.F. Lovering 1967 ANU radiocarbon date list I. *Radiocarbon* 9:15-27

Powell, J.M. 1970 The history of agriculture in the New Guinea Highlands. *Search: Journal of the Australian and New Zealand Association for the Advancement of Science* 1(5):199-200

Read, K.E. 1954 Cultures of the Central Highlands, New Guinea. *Southwestern Journal of Anthropology* 10:1-43

Reed, C.A. 1963 Osteo-archaeology. Pp 204-16 of Brothwell, D.R. and E.S. Higgs (eds) *Science in Archaeology*. London: Thames and Hudson

Riesenfeld, A. 1950 *The megalithic culture of Melanesia*. Leiden: E.J. Brill

Roe, D.A. 1964 The British Lower and Middle Palaeolithic: some problems, methods of study and preliminary results. *Proceedings of the Prehistoric Society* (n.s.) 30:245-67

Salisbury, R.F. 1962 *From stone to steel*. Melbourne: Melbourne University Press

Schmid, E. 1958 *Höhlenforschung und Sedimentanalyse*. Basel: Institut für Ur- und Frühgeschichte der Schweiz, Schriften Nr 13

——   1963 Cave sediments and prehistory. Pp 123-38 of Brothwell, D.R. and E.S. Higgs (eds) *Science in Archaeology*. London: Thames and Hudson

——   1966 Jaguar Cave, Idaho: Ergebnisse der Sedimentanalysen. Translated into English in H. Kooros-Sadek, *Excavations in the Jaguar Cave*. Cambridge:Harvard University, Peabody Museum, PhD thesis (unpublished)

Schmitz, C.A. 1960 *Historische Probleme in Nordost-Neuguinea: Huon Halbinsel*. Veröffentlichung des Frobenius-Instituts an der Johann Wolfgang Goethe-Universität zu Frankfurt-am-Main, Studien zur Kulturkunde 16. Wiesbaden, Franz Steiner Verlag.

Seligmann, C.G. and B.Z. 1911 *The Veddas*. Cambridge: Cambridge University Press

Semenov, S.A. 1964 *Prehistoric technology*. London: Cory, Adams and Mackay

Simpson, G.G. 1961 Historical zoogeography of Australian mammals. *Evolution* 15:431-46

Smith, J. 1967 The potter of Yabob. *Australian Territories* 7(1-3):9-13

Spencer, B. 1914 *Native tribes of the Northern Territory of Australia*. London: Macmillan

——   1928 *Wanderings in wild Australia* (2 vols). London: Macmillan

Stirton, R.A. 1963 A review of the macropodid genus *Protemnodon*. *University of California Publications in Geological Sciences* 44(2)

Stow, G.W. 1905 *The native races of South Africa*. London: Swan Sonnenschein & Co.

Strathern, M. 1965 Axe types and quarries: a note on the classification of stone axe blades from the Hagen area, New Guinea. *Journal of the Polynesian Society* 74:182-91

——   1969 Stone axes and flake tools: evaluations from two New Guinea Highlands societies. *Proceedings of the Prehistoric Society* (n.s.) 25:311-29

Tate, G.H.H. 1948 Results of the Archbold Expeditions no. 59: studies on the anatomy and phylogeny of the Macropodidae (Marsupialia). *Bulletin of the American Museum of Natural History* 91(2)

Tedford, R.H. 1966 A review of the macropodid genus *Sthenurus*. *University of California Publications in Geological Sciences* 57

Thomson, D.F. 1939 The seasonal factor in human culture, illustrated from the life of a contemporary nomadic group. *Proceedings of the Prehistoric Society* (n.s.) 5:209-21

Van Deusen, H.M. 1963 First New Guinea record of *Thylacinus*. *Journal of Mammalogy* 44:279-80

———— and K. Keith 1966 Range and habitat of the bandicoot, *Echymipera clara*, in New Guinea. *Journal of Mammalogy* 47:721-3

Vial, L.G. 1940 Stone axes of Mt Hagen, New Guinea. *Oceania* 11(2):158-63

Wakefield, N.A. 1964 Mammal remains. Pp 494-8 of Mulvaney, D.J., G.H. Lawton and C.R. Twidale Archaeological excavation of rock shelter no. 6, Fromm's Landing, South Australia. *Proceedings of the Royal Society of Victoria* 77:479-516

Walker, D. and A. de G. Sieveking 1962 The Palaeolithic industry of Kota Tampan, Perak, Malaya. *Proceedings of the Prehistoric Society* (n.s.) 28:103-39

Watson, J.B. 1963 A micro-evolution study in New Guinea. *Journal of the Polynesian Society* 72:188-92

———— 1964 Anthropology in the New Guinea Highlands. Pp 1-19 of Watson J.B. (ed) *New Guinea: the Central Highlands*. *American Anthropologist* 66(4), part 2, Special Publication

———— 1965a From hunting to horticulture in the New Guinea Highlands. *Ethnology* 4:295-309

———— 1965b The significance of a recent ecological change in the Central Highlands of New Guinea. *Journal of the Polynesian Society* 74:438-50

Watson, V. 1955 Pottery in the Eastern Highlands of New Guinea. *Southwestern Journal of Anthropology* 11:121-8

White, J.P. 1965a Archaeological excavations in New Guinea: an interim report. *Journal of the Polynesian Society* 74:40-56

———— 1965b An archaeological survey in Papua-New Guinea. *Current Anthropology* 6:334-5

———— 1967 Ethno-archaeology in New Guinea: two examples. *Mankind* 6(9):409-14

———— 1968a Ston naip bilong tumbuna: the living stone age in New Guinea. Pp 511-16 of de Sonneville-Bordes, D. (ed) *La préhistoire: problèmes et tendances*. Paris: Centre National de la Recherche Scientifique

———— 1968b Fabricators, outils écaillés or scalar cores? *Mankind* 6(12):658-66

———— 1969 Typologies for some prehistoric flaked stone artefacts of the Australian New Guinea Highlands. *Archaeology and Physical Anthropology in Oceania* 4:18-46

—— 1971 New Guinea: the first phase in Oceanic
settlement. Pp 45-52 of Green, R.C. and M. Kelly (eds)
Studies in Oceanic culture history (vol. 2). Honolulu:
Bernice P. Bishop Museum, Department of Anthropology,
Pacific Anthropological Records no. 12

—— and C. 1964 A new frontier in archaeology: rock art
in Papua-New Guinea. *Illustrated London News* 245:775-7

—— K.A.W. Crook and B.P. Buxton 1970 Kosipe: a late
Pleistocene site in the Papuan highlands. *Proceedings
of the Prehistoric Society* (n.s.) 36:152-70

Williams, F.E. 1940 Natives of Lake Kutubu, Papua. *Oceania*
11(2):121-57

Woldstedt, P. 1965 *Das Eiszeitalter* (3 vols). Stuttgart: Enke

Woodburne, M.O. 1967 *The Alcoota fauna, Central Australia.*
Canberra: Department of National Development, Bureau of
Mineral Resources, Geology and Geophysics, Bulletin 87

Wurm, S.A. 1961 New Guinea languages. *Current Anthropology*
2:114-16

Zeigler, A.C. and W.Z. Lidicker, Jr 1968 Keys to the genera of
New Guinea Recent land mammals. *Proceedings of the
California Academy of Sciences* (fourth series) 36(2)